VETERAN'S GUIDE TO BENEFITS

Veteran's Guide to Benefits

5th Edition

P. J. Budahn

STACKPOLE
BOOKS

Copyright © 2011 by Stackpole Books

Published by
STACKPOLE BOOKS
5067 Ritter Road
Mechanicsburg, PA 17055
www.stackpolebooks.com

This book is not an official publication of the Department of Veterans Affairs or the Department of Defense, nor does its publication in any way imply its endorsement by these agencies.

Cover design by Tessa J. Sweigert

Printed in the United States of America

10 9 8 7 6 5 4 3 2 1

Library of Congress Cataloging-in-Publication Data

Budahn, P. J. (Phillip J.), 1949–
  Veteran's guide to benefits / P.J. Budahn. — 5th ed.
    p. cm.
  Includes index.
  ISBN 978-0-8117-3645-9
  1. Veterans—Services for—United States. 2. Military pensions—United States. 3. Consumer education—United States. I. Title.
  UB357.B83 2011
  362.860973—dc22
                            2010053887

CONTENTS

INTRODUCTION

A unique band of people is scattered throughout the United States. They can be found in every major city, each suburb, and the smallest towns. They are on the farm and in the shopping mall, occupying every imaginable rung on the social ladder—and a few that are unthinkable—from the boardroom to the soup kitchen.

And though there are twenty-three million people in this group, they're considered a special band of people by the general public, by the government, and most especially, by themselves.

Of course, I'm talking about the men and women who have served their country in the military.

They have shared the mixture of excitement and dread during those long nights before reporting for their first day of training. They have experienced the indignities of boot camp designed to change them from civilians into members of the armed forces. And together they have known the hardships of moves and separations from loved ones, the bafflement of fitting into strange new environments, and the fear of realizing that if troops must take to the field anywhere in the world to protect the security or interests of the United States, they're the ones who will go.

When the day came to take off their uniforms, they assumed a new, special status, one that set them apart from the rest of the citizenry, one so special that it will probably be written in their obituaries even if they live for many decades after their discharge.

They are called "veterans."

For their sacrifices to the nation, the veterans of military service are entitled to a vast array of programs and benefits. A nationwide network of hospitals and clinics, a competitive edge when it comes to getting government jobs, financial help in paying for education or buying a home, special business loans, regular monthly pensions for disabilities—these are among the programs that have been put in place for people who have served in the military.

It is while confronting this wide selection of programs and benefits, however, that veterans realize they have another bond with each other: They're all confused.

There are so many programs to choose from, and each is different. Programs for veterans are a mishmash, and each has its own eligibility criteria.

This confusion helps explain why most veterans never take advantage of the benefits they've earned by serving in the military. Only one veteran in three ever steps into a VA hospital, according to official estimates, and many never claim any sort of veterans benefit.

Veteran's Guide to Benefits was designed to take the guesswork out of being a veteran. In simple English and clearly organized chapters, it spells out the basic facts about each major program—who's eligible, what's available, and how to get benefits. This book also highlights common misunderstandings about the various programs.

Not everyone interested in veterans benefits is a veteran. Spouses have their own needs, and some are married to veterans who are too ill to fight their own way through the legalistic jumble around many benefits. It helps to know what to expect—or not to expect—from veterans benefits when doing long-range family planning. Although most veterans benefits go directly to the veteran, widows and widowers of some veterans have a legal right to their own government pensions.

For them, this book proudly carries the stamp "spouse-friendly." This also means that others who are interested in veterans benefits but unacquainted with the special language of the military or the jargon of the Department of Veterans Affairs can use this book to gain a practical understanding of programs available to the men and women who served their country.

Whether you hung up your uniform decades ago, are a member of the reserves or National Guard, or are still on active duty and planning your transition back to the civilian world, you should know what you are entitled to receive as a veteran.

Several obstacles make it tough to learn about any federal benefit or government program. The initial problem involves language. Rule books are written by lawyers and experts, not by ordinary people. Even after you've figured out what a sentence means in simple English, you can't be sure if a legal detail has any practical consequences.

And once you've ascertained what a rule book is really saying and whether a given detail has importance in the real world, often it's another struggle to figure out how each detail applies to people in your specific circumstances.

Veteran's Guide will help you overcome those obstacles to understanding your veterans benefits. The language here is straightforward, and practical advice is found throughout. Few readers will want to study every page, so, like any user's guide, this book is designed to give you quick access to the information you need.

Early portions of this guide summarize the veterans benefits for six categories of veterans and for spouses: just-plain-veteran veterans, disabled veterans, low-income veterans, "bad paper" veterans, military retirees, special veterans, and spouses and survivors. You're in the "just-plain-veteran" category unless one of the other categories applies to you.

Later chapters contain detailed information about each benefit and program. Each chapter is organized around a major topic, including health care programs, disability pay, home loans, educational programs, and resolving problems with the military.

At the back of the book is a collection of specialized information. It includes a state-by-state summary of facilities operated by the Department of Veterans Affairs, plus a state-by-state listing of state-run veterans homes.

Veteran's Guide is a road map to your veterans benefits, but even the best map can't predict what roads will close, which bridges will be built, or where a new street will run. Changes in veterans benefits are made every year by Congress, the Department of Veterans Affairs, and other government agencies.

The information in *Veteran's Guide* came from many sources, including federal law, publications of the Department of Veterans Affairs, the VA staff in Washington, veterans organizations, veterans advocacy groups, and countless veterans, active-duty servicemembers, and spouses. The author is grateful for their help, but they are not responsible for any errors.

So before making a major decision based upon the information in this book, verify it through official sources. Generally, changes tend to broaden programs, so the information here can usually be viewed as a conservative, bare-minimum description of programs and benefits.

When it comes to VA medical benefits, it may be useful to consider this edition of *Veteran's Guide* as a snapshot of the rules as they were in the year 2010. Later editions will update the picture and fill in more details.

A grateful nation has created a host of benefits for the men and women who devoted a portion of their lives to military service. Now, it's your job to figure out what you can get and how you get it.

Veteran's Guide to Benefits is here to help you.

ONE

BASICS ON VETERANS BENEFITS

For many people, an understanding of veterans benefits is often confused by family folklore, by their own philosophy about the role of government, and by memorable "horror stories."

> About one out of every five adult males in the United States is a veteran.

If Uncle Fred's financial future seemed secure for the rest of his days after he was wounded during the Vietnam War, you may approach your own discharge with unreasonable confidence, certain that your new status as a veteran will smooth out the bumpy spots in life.

Or you may remember that Uncle Fred was bitter for the rest of his life because he felt betrayed and abandoned by his government after he took off his uniform.

For most people leaving active duty, the truth is somewhere in between. Being a veteran won't open every door, solve every problem, or provide a lifelong income simply because you had a rough time in the military. Neither is it true that the American people have turned their collective back on the men and women who once served in uniform, canceling benefits in the name of austerity and walking away from obligations through simple indifference.

> The federal government spends more than $110 billion yearly on veterans.

Either stereotype can be dangerous to someone approaching the issue of veterans benefits for the first time. You're not likely to persevere if you think all the benefits have been sacrificed to hold down federal spending. Nor are you likely to stick it out if you believe veterans should be wards of the government for the rest of their lives (which happens only to those with the severest service-related disabilities).

The "good old days" weren't as generous as they seem, and the present era isn't as miserly as the headlines sometimes indicate.

Veterans benefits weren't established to solve every financial problem faced by everyone who ever served in the armed forces. They were created, at specific times, by lawmakers intent on solving specific problems. Some benefits linger on the books long after those problems disappear.

Whatever the origin, the rules underlying all veterans benefits were written to make important legal distinctions. Those rules aren't always clear to laypeople. It takes time, effort, and patience to figure out where you—or a loved one—fit into the bureaucratic categories.

For many veterans benefits, the important factor is the type of discharge you received. For others, the key question is when you were on active duty. A few even depend on where you served. Income is the major determinant of eligibility for other veterans benefits.

It may soothe some frustration to understand why this happened. A certain amount of the confusion about the rules for veterans benefits stems, ironically, from too much zeal on the part of Congress and the executive branch in trying to help the men and women who served their country in uniform.

Lawmakers have always been eager to improve existing programs or to create new ones. With each improvement, the fine print in the eligibility rules changes to correct some oversight or to address a problem that is beginning to emerge.

Because many veterans programs have been around since the end of World War II, it's inevitable that the rule books should become the legal equivalent of a patchwork quilt. To follow the thread linking most programs, it's helpful to keep in mind the five basic rules for veterans benefits:

1. Your discharge papers are your ticket to most benefits. Simply saying that you're a veteran may get you a free beer in a bar, but it won't open the door to any meaningful veterans benefits. You must prove that you're a veteran. The basic proof required for most veterans benefits is your official discharge papers. They've had many names over the decades, but in recent years they've been technically called "DD Form 214."

You get your discharge papers (which are actually just one document) on your last day on active duty. Be sure to keep them in a safe place. Many veterans rent a safety-deposit box at a neighborhood bank just to store this valuable document. Others take it to the clerk of courts in their hometown, who will preserve a copy among the court's official records, making it easier to get copies later.

Whatever you decide, make sure that other family members know where your discharge papers are. You might not be able to help them when they need to find them. And if you don't know where your discharge papers are, decide today to get a copy. Don't put it off. For details about getting copies of your discharge papers, see chapter 13, "Tying Up Loose Ends with the Military."

2. The burden is on you to show that you're eligible for a benefit. The most important benefits—free medical care, VA pensions, home loans, and educational benefits—cost the government money, and money wrongly spent on benefits for ineligible people means there's a little less money left to pay for benefits for eligible, deserving veterans.

The same scrutiny applies to the spouses of veterans who attempt to qualify for certain benefits. They will be expected to produce marriage certificates before receiving any benefits offered to the spouses of former servicemembers.

Remember that paperwork "gatekeepers" guard the entrance to every major veterans program. Ultimately, those gatekeepers help you by ensuring that scarce federal resources aren't being wasted on ineligible people. Still, that knowledge won't always make it easier to deal with frustration and delay. But remembering that at least makes some of the "paperwork exercises" a little less crazy.

3. Getting approved for some benefits takes time. Qualifying for VA disability compensation or a VA pension can take months. Fortunately, however, for some of the major veterans benefits, it takes only a few minutes to pass through all the gatekeepers. So long as you have your DD Form 214 or other discharge papers, you should be able to get rapid approval to buy a home using a GI Bill home loan or to draw on your GI Bill educational benefits at school.

VA medical care falls somewhere between the extremes. Most patients at VA hospitals and clinics are there because they've already qualified for VA disability compensation or VA pensions. In recent years, VA health care facilities have reached out to all veterans, although many may get a bill from the VA hospital for services. VA hospitals give the highest priority to the neediest veterans and to those with medical problems that have been officially rated as service connected.

Don't wait until you're ill before figuring out whether you might qualify for free treatment in a VA medical facility. Take the time, while you have the time, to find out how the rules apply to you.

4. Everything changes. Officials in Congress, the White House, the Department of Veterans Affairs, and even the Pentagon are constantly refining the rules that affect veterans benefits. Solving problems, resolving inequities, and meeting the limitations of budgets are among the factors that keep veterans benefits in constant—though largely minor—flux.

> Change is a certainty for VA programs. Make sure you have the latest details.

As the United States ended the first decade of the twenty-first century, however, a sentiment for change touched the nation's medical system and veterans benefits in general. These movements held the potential for sweeping changes in the programs available to veterans. Whatever does, or doesn't, happen will have an impact on the VA medical system.

Former servicemembers and their families should remember that all explanations of veterans benefits will eventually become outdated. Even *Veteran's Guide.*

As the title of this volume states, this is a "guide," not a bible. Even the best road map changes, but that's no reason to keep your car in your driveway forever.

5. There are plenty of experts to help you. In every department store, some salespeople are better than others. Their skills and personalities cover the human spectrum. Some of them will appeal to you, some will turn you off, and to most you'll be indifferent. Despite their diversity, those salespeople will share a common trait: They're all interested in selling you something.

Keep that in mind when you're dealing with the employees of the Department of Veterans Affairs. They're as diverse as any group of people, but they also share a common trait: They have their jobs because they want to work with veterans. For the latest in information and for personalized help in obtaining veterans benefits, there's no substitute for a VA employee.

At most VA medical centers, the folks with the most comprehensive information are called "veterans benefits counselors." VA regional offices and benefits offices are also good places to go for help and information.

A list of all these VA facilities is found in the back of this book. Also in the back is a listing of major veterans groups that offer free, professional assistance to any veteran who requests it. That work is done by full-time staffers known as "service officers." Frequently, VA offices will refer veterans to a service officer for help in filing a claim for benefits.

You don't have to belong to a particular veterans group to consult its service officer. They exist to help all veterans, not just members.

And let's not forget the internet. The VA's official website—www.va.gov—opens the doors to a mountain of information.

TWO

KINDS OF VETERANS (AND SPOUSES, TOO)

In This Chapter:

- *Just-Plain-Veteran Veterans*
- *Disabled Veterans*
- *Low-Income Veterans*

- *"Bad-Paper" Veterans*
- *Military Retirees*
- *Special Veterans*
- *Spouses and Survivors*

Unique programs, valuable benefits, and important services are available to meet the needs of those who have served our country in the military, but getting them requires that would-be recipients take an active role. You must be your own advocate. You must know what's reasonable to ask for, and which fights you can never win.

That's where *Veteran's Guide* comes in. It will help you to familiarize yourself with the benefits available to you, or to your veteran. To make that self-instruction a little easier, this chapter divides veterans into six major categories.

JUST-PLAIN-VETERAN VETERANS

Most benefits for most veterans are, mostly, straightforward. There is an established array of programs. Eligibility rules have been constant. And it doesn't take a legal wizard to figure out who gets what.

Complications begin to arise when veterans have specific problems—a disability or an adverse discharge—that put them into a legally distinct category for qualifying for veterans benefits.

The benefits for those special cases are outlined later in this chapter. Here we'll look at a summary of the major programs and benefits available to what we'll call the "just-plain-veteran" veteran. And since no discussion of a government program would be authentic without an acronym, let's call them the JPV vets.

What's a JPV vet? It's the typical man or woman who joins the military, serves a tour or two in uniform, and then returns to the old hometown, without any complications or problems connected with his or her military service. Most veterans are JPV vets.

Specifically, the JPV vet meets all of the following conditions:

- Not eligible for retirement.
- Not receiving exit bonus.
- Not disabled.
- Received an honorable or general discharge.

The JPV vet qualifies for the basic package of veterans benefits offered by the federal government. And if you qualify as a JPV vet, you've passed through the first set of rules on the road to some of the most important veterans programs—especially health care in a facility run by the Department of Veterans Affairs.

The benefits for all veterans are built on the basic benefits package of the JPV vets. Here's a summary:

Transition Benefits
- *Exit bonus:* No.
- *Final physical:* Yes.
- *Final dental checkup:* Yes.
- *Time off for job and house hunting:* Yes, but determined by the individual services.
- *Job-hunting classes, counseling, data banks:* Yes.
- *Payment for unused annual leave:* Yes.
- *Government-paid move back home:* Yes, but military may limit to original home or home of record.
- *Government-paid storage of household goods:* Yes, for 180 days.

Back in Civilian Community
- *Unemployment compensation:* Yes, at least twenty-six weeks.
- *Reemployment rights:* Yes, but with many legal subtleties.
- *Obligation toward reserves:* Not unless part of original enlistment or commissioning contract.
- *GI Bill education benefits:* Yes, if served 90 days on active duty since September 11, 2001. Other rules apply for reservists, National Guardsmen, or earlier service.
- *GI Bill home loans:* Yes, but must meet financial qualifications for loan.
- *Life insurance:* Yes, but must sign up within 120 days after discharge, must pay regular premiums.
- *Preference for government jobs:* Yes, highest preference for disabled vets.
- *On-base military medical care:* No.
- *VA medical care:* Low priority, may have to pay fee.
- *Transition health insurance:* Yes, for most vets. Limited duration, out-of-pocket costs.
- *VA dental care:* Yes, for all vets within 180 days after discharge. Later, restricted eligibility.

- *Visit military commissary, exchange:* No, must qualify as retiree, reservist, or exit bonus veteran.
- *Continuing job-hunting help:* Yes.
- *Small-business loans:* Yes, but limited program with restricted eligibility.
- *VA disability compensation:* Only for medical problems officially recognized as related to military service.
- *VA pension:* Only for low-income veterans in poor health.

Other Veterans Issues
- *Wear military uniform:* At appropriate events.
- *Wear medals:* As appropriate, usually lapel pin.
- *Replace medals:* Can request at any time.
- *Improve discharge:* Can apply at any time.
- *Correct military records:* Can apply at any time.
- *Homes for veterans:* Must meet local eligibility rules.
- *Burial in national cemetery:* Yes, for most vets, plus spouses and dependent children.
- *Burial payments:* Yes, for most vets.
- *Burial flags:* Yes, for most vets.
- *Last honor guard:* Yes, but may face scheduling problems.

Spouse's and Children's Benefits
- *VA pension for widows, widowers:* Not for JPV vet. Must qualify in some other category.
- *Pension for children:* Not for JPV vet. Must qualify in some other category.
- *Educational benefits:* Not for JPV vet. Must qualify in some other category.
- *Appointment to military academy:* Not for JPV vet. Must qualify in some other category.

DISABLED VETERANS
Even during peacetime, the military is a dangerous place to be. The federal government recognizes that, and traditionally

has offered special benefits to the men and women who have wounds, illnesses, or medical problems linked to their military service.

The major benefits involve free treatment in VA medical facilities and a monthly payment called "disability compensation."

Many veterans discover that the eligibility rules have been written generously. A medical problem doesn't have to be *caused* by military service: It's enough if a problem was *aggravated* during your time in uniform.

And there's no distinction between combat-related and non-combat-related problems. Veterans advocates like to point to the case of two veterans with the same chronic knee disorder. One was caused by a bullet in a firefight during combat, the other by a cleat in a softball game during leave. Both knee injuries officially qualify as "service connected," and that's the only distinction important under VA rules.

Once medical problems are rated as service connected, the veteran is then assigned a percentage figure ranging from 10 percent to 100 percent that reflects the severity of the problem.

Disabled veterans qualify for the full range of benefits offered to JPV vets. They also get more. Here are some special benefits for disabled veterans who already have rulings for service-connection status and percentage of disability:

Transition Benefits
- *Exit bonus:* Can't receive this if being discharged with disability.

Back in Civilian Community
- *Unemployment compensation:* Varies. If disability affects job performance, might not qualify.
- *Obligation toward reserves:* Only if disability is 20 percent or less.
- *Home grants:* In addition to GI Bill loans, may receive money to adapt home to accommodate disability.

- *Life insurance:* Special program for veterans with VA disabilities.
- *Lump-sum disability payment:* Only for severest, combat-related injuries.
- *Vehicle allowance:* Grant for veterans with impaired mobility.
- *Clothing allowance:* $716 annually in 2010 if using prosthetics or orthopedics.
- *Preference for government jobs:* High priority.
- *On-base military medical care:* Unlikely. Space-available for 100-percent-disabled.
- *VA medical care:* Free, high priority.
- *Transition health insurance:* No coverage for service-connected disabilities. May be covered for other medical problems.
- *VA dental care:* Yes, if 100 percent disabled or service-connected disabilities related to dental problems.
- *VA vocational rehabilitation:* Yes.
- *Visit military commissary, exchange:* If 100 percent disabled; privilege extends to spouse and dependent children.
- *VA disability compensation:* Yes.
- *VA pension:* No, cannot receive pension and disability compensation at same time.

Other Veterans Issues

- *Burial in national cemetery:* Yes.
- *Burial payments:* Yes.

Spouse's and Children's Benefits

- *VA pension for widows, widowers:* Yes, called "Dependency and Indemnity Compensation."
- *Pension for children:* Yes, if (1) unmarried and under eighteen, (2) in school and under twenty-three, or (3) older but medically incapable of self support.

- *Educational benefits:* Special program for survivors, spouses, and children of disabled vets.
- *Home loans:* One-time benefit for spouses of disabled vets who die from a service-connected disability.
- *Appointment to military academy:* Small number of appointments set aside for children of disabled veterans.

LOW-INCOME VETERANS

Veterans were the beneficiaries of the country's original social safety nets. Going back to the time of the American Revolution, communities did special things to help the people who responded when the call to arms went out.

Then and now, not all of the things done for veterans relate directly to the hardships and health problems of serving in the military. The system of VA pensions provides an economic lifeline for thousands of veterans. The pensions don't have anything to do with what you did in the military or what happened to you on active duty. Rather, VA pensions are given to veterans with low incomes. With the pensions goes eligibility for a range of other benefits.

Two pieces of fine print deserve special attention. First, VA pensions aren't welfare. Recipients must be unable to work because of age or a medical problem that doesn't qualify for VA disability compensation. Among the additional benefits that go with VA pensions are educational and vocational programs to get veterans back into the workforce.

Second, VA pensions are the one major veterans benefit that's linked to service during wartime: They are available only to veterans who served on active duty during officially declared periods of hostilities.

As with all veterans, recipients of VA pensions qualify for the basic package of benefits offered to JPV vets. Additionally, they're subject to these changes in that package:

Back in Civilian Community

- *Obligation toward reserves:* Can't serve while drawing a VA pension.
- *Vocational training:* Special programs.
- *Preference for government jobs:* Yes, if received campaign ribbon.
- *On-base military medical care:* No.
- *VA medical care:* High priority, free.
- *VA dental care:* Yes.
- *VA disability compensation:* No, can't receive while drawing VA pension.
- *VA pension:* Yes, monthly payment.

Spouse's and Children's Benefits

- *VA pension for widows, widowers:* Yes, based on financial need.
- *Pension for children:* Yes, based on financial need for dependent children.
- *Educational benefits:* Special program for widows, widowers, and dependent children.

"BAD-PAPER" VETERANS

Not everyone who leaves the military is eligible for the full range of benefits that's available to the JPV vet.

People who get in trouble while on active duty often receive formal discharges that bar them from most veterans benefits. These are commonly called "adverse" discharges. Veterans advocates often refer to them as "bad-paper" discharges. Into this category fall dishonorable discharges, bad-conduct discharges, and discharges officially rated as "under conditions other than honorable." Also affected are discharges ordered by a general court-martial, discharges of conscientious objectors who refused military service, and discharges after 180 continuous days of unapproved absence, or AWOL.

The best news for bad-paper veterans is that they don't have to stay that way for the rest of their lives. The military can review discharges and issue better ones—called "upgrades"—to veterans long after they leave active duty.

Getting an upgrade is your responsibility. Discharges aren't routinely reviewed with that in mind. To get an upgrade, you have to begin the paperwork. The chapter titled "Tying Up Loose Ends with the Military" later in this book can get you started.

Not all bad-paper veterans are equal. Many benefits are determined on a case-by-case basis. Still, here's a summary of the major benefits as they apply to most bad-paper veterans:

Transition Benefits

- *Exit bonus:* No.
- *Final physical:* Yes.
- *Final dental checkup:* Yes.
- *Time off for job and house hunting:* No.
- *Job-hunting classes, counseling, data banks:* Yes.
- *Payment for unused annual leave:* No.
- *Government-paid move back home:* Yes, but very restricted. Vets may get a bus ticket home.
- *Government-paid storage of household goods:* No.

Back in Civilian Community

- *Unemployment compensation:* Frequently barred. Case-by-case decision.
- *Reemployment rights:* Frequently, no. Case-by-case decision.
- *Obligation toward reserves:* No, barred from service.
- *GI Bill education benefits:* No, not even if previously signed up for Montgomery GI Bill.
- *GI Bill home loans:* No.
- *Life insurance:* Case-by-case decision.
- *Preference for government jobs:* No.

- *On-base military medical care:* No.
- *VA medical care:* Case-by-case decision for treatment of service-connected problems.
- *Transition health insurance:* Yes.
- *VA dental care:* Case-by-case decision for treatment of service-connected dental problems.
- *Visit military commissary, exchange:* No.
- *Continuing job-hunting help:* Yes, through state-run programs, same as nonveterans.
- *Small business loans:* No.
- *VA disability compensation:* Not for discharge "under dishonorable conditions."
- *VA pension:* Not for discharge "under dishonorable conditions."

Other Veterans Issues

- *Replace medals:* Can request at any time.
- *Improve discharge:* Can apply at any time.
- *Correct military records:* Can apply at any time.
- *Homes for veterans:* Must meet local eligibility rules.
- *Burial in national cemetery:* Not if discharged "under dishonorable conditions."
- *Burial payments:* Not if discharged "under dishonorable conditions."
- *Burial flags:* Not if discharged "under dishonorable conditions."
- *Last honor guard:* Not if discharged "under dishonorable conditions."

Spouse's and Children's Benefits

- *VA pension for widows, widowers:* No.
- *Pension for children:* No.
- *Educational benefits:* No.
- *Appointment to military academy:* Applications considered alongside children of nonveterans.

MILITARY RETIREES

Military service takes a few years from the lives of many Americans. For some, however, it takes a career.

Military retirees have always been special members of the veterans community. They have devoted a large portion of their working lives to the nation's interests, and they have volunteered their families to join in sharing many of those hardships.

Traditionally, one of the hardships has been military pay. Although its purchasing power has increased substantially in recent decades, military pay still lags behind comparable salaries in the private sector, as measured by governmental and independent salary studies.

To offset this disparity, the government has historically offered military retirees a comprehensive package of programs. Civilian critics may argue it's too generous. But many veterans who have spent two or three years in uniform agree that military retirement benefits still don't make up for the hardships of two or three decades on active duty.

For much of the twentieth century, military retirement has been based on a minimum of twenty years on active duty. In 1993, as part of the 1990s drawdown, Congress approved full retirement benefits for selected—and that's a key word, *selected*— people who have spent at least fifteen years in uniform.

The fifteen-year retirement is a management tool to trim down the active-duty force. This early retirement is not something that a servicemember automatically has a right to get. He or she must be selected based on the needs of the military and the skills, rank, and other factors of the servicemember.

Fifteen-year retirees differ from the usual twenty-year retirees only in the size of their monthly retirement checks. All other benefits are equal. The military stopped offering fifteen-year retirements on January 1, 2002, but veterans who had already retired under the program kept their benefits.

Here's a summary of the major benefits for military retirees:

Transition Benefits

- *Exit bonus:* No.
- *Final physical:* Yes.
- *Final dental checkup:* Yes.
- *Time off for job and house hunting:* Yes, but limited by service.
- *Job-hunting classes, counseling, data banks:* Yes.
- *Payment for unused annual leave:* Yes.
- *Government-paid move back home:* Yes, to any home selected.
- *Government-paid storage of household goods:* Yes, for one year.

Back in Civilian Community

- *Unemployment compensation:* Varies by state.
- *Reemployment rights:* Yes, but with many legal subtleties.
- *Obligation toward reserves:* No, must forfeit retired pay to join reserves.
- *GI Bill education benefits:* Must meet eligibility rules based on date entered active duty.
- *GI Bill home loans:* Yes, must meet financial qualifications for loan.
- *Life insurance:* Yes, must sign up within 120 days after discharge, must pay regular premiums.
- *Preference for government jobs:* Yes, for enlisted and disabled. Other rules for officers.
- *On-base military medical care:* Lifetime eligibility, subject to space availability. Medicare becomes primary health provider at age sixty-five.
- *VA medical care:* Low priority, may have to pay fee.
- *Transition health insurance:* No, but may purchase for spouse and dependent children. Eighteen-month maximum duration.
- *VA dental care:* Yes, like any vet, within 180 days of discharge.

- *Visit military commissary, exchange:* Lifetime eligibility for self, also for spouse and dependent children.
- *Continuing job-hunting help:* Yes.
- *Small business loans:* Yes, like any vet.
- *VA disability compensation:* Yes, with complex rules for offsetting VA and DoD payments.
- *VA pension:* No.

Other Veterans Issues
- *Wear military uniform:* At appropriate events.
- *Wear medals:* As appropriate, usually as lapel pins.
- *Replace medals:* Can request at any time.
- *Improve discharge:* Can apply at any time.
- *Correct military records:* Can apply at any time.
- *Homes for veterans:* Must meet local eligibility rules.
- *Burial in national cemetery:* Yes, same as most vets, plus spouses and dependent children.
- *Burial payments:* Yes.
- *Burial flags:* Yes.
- *Last honor guard:* Yes, but may face scheduling problems.

Spouse's and Children's Benefits
- *Pension for widows, widowers:* Only if signed up—and paid—for Survivors Benefit Plan.
- *Pension for children:* Coverage available through retiree-paid Survivor Benefit Plan.
- *Educational benefits:* Must qualify in some other category.
- *Appointment to military academy:* Limited number of appointments.

SPECIAL VETERANS
Over the years, VA officials and lawmakers have come to realize that certain categories of veterans have special health problems related to their military service. They need VA-supervised medical care, even though they may not qualify for VA disability

compensation, which carries with it an increased priority for medical care.

For these special veterans, VA medical facilities offer free "baseline" examinations to determine the general condition of their health. They are later eligible for priority treatment in VA medical facilities for problems suspected of being related to their military service.

The following are "special veterans":

• Former POWs.
• Recipients of the Purple Heart Medal.
• Veterans exposed to Agent Orange.
• "Atomic" veterans.
• Gulf War veterans with undiagnosed illnesses.

The phrase "atomic veteran" refers to servicemembers exposed to ionizing radiation during atmospheric nuclear tests or during service in Hiroshima or Nagasaki immediately after World War II.

Vietnam veterans exposed to Agent Orange or Gulf War veterans must be seeking care for problems they believe are directly related to their service.

Recipients of the Purple Heart Medal do not have to pay for any inpatient or outpatient VA care, although they may pay a token amount for outpatient medication.

These special veterans are eligible to apply for VA disability compensation. In all other respects, they have the same basic benefits as just-plain-veteran veterans. Some may also be exit bonus veterans or even military retirees, qualifying for benefits appropriate for those statuses.

SPOUSES AND SURVIVORS

The wives and husbands of military veterans have had to make sacrifices and share in hardships because they were married to veterans. Every day, many spouses cope with a variety of problems related to the military service of their loved ones.

The government makes some important benefits available for the spouses and survivors of some veterans. Here are some highlights:

- *Health insurance:* For families of disabled vets and vets who die from disabilities. Called "CHAMPVA."
- *Monthly pensions:* For survivors of disabled vets, vets who die from disabilities, and military people who die on active duty. Called Dependency and Indemnity Compensation.
- *Education assistance:* For families of veterans who served after September 11, 2001, disabled vets, vets who die from disabilities, and POWs.
- *Home loans:* For families of POWs, vets who die from disabilities, and people who die on active duty. One-time benefit.
- *Federal job preference:* For spouses of veterans who die on active duty, spouses of 100 percent disabled veterans, and mothers of some disabled vets.
- *Help for caregivers:* As *Veteran's Guide to Benefits* was going to press, VA officials were creating a new package of benefits for the caregivers of seriously injured veterans. For the latest information about eligibility or benefits, call 1-877-222-8387, visit www.va.gov, or talk to officials at your nearest VA facility.

THREE

THE SOON-TO-BE VETERAN

In This Chapter:

- *Final Paycheck*
- *Final Physical*
- *Health Care*
- *Dental Care*
- *Time Off*
- *Getting Home*
- *Job Search*
- *Unemployment Compensation*
- *Veterans Preference*

All who have ever been in the military carry for the rest of their lives sharp memories of the experiences they had, the emotions they felt, and the lessons they learned during those first fateful days as they made the switch from civilian to soldier.

Those heading in the opposite direction—leaving the military world and reentering the private sector—face a transition that's nearly as great. Granted, they've been civilians before, so the "unknowns" aren't as formidable. Still, taking off the uniform can be difficult for some people precisely because they're so sure they know what to expect on the outside. Sadly, they're often wrong.

The civilian job market is changing at a dizzying pace. But there are other factors that make a transition difficult. Every upheaval in life is demanding, and people tend to lose their emotional resilience over the years. And everyone succumbs, from time to time, to pleasant fantasies about how effortless life is going to become after they cross some threshold.

Many emotional crises are natural and unavoidable. But some are completely preventable, especially the ones that can be eliminated by having sound plans and reasonable expectations built upon reliable information.

For the military member preparing to walk out the main gate for the last time, the government has provided a wide array of programs and benefits. Used successfully, transition benefits can ease a veteran's return to the private sector. Used smartly, they can save time, eliminate financial difficulties, and lessen the emotional price that's paid whenever people make major changes in their lives. The key to using these benefits smartly and successfully is to understand them and to incorporate that knowledge into realistic plans.

Some benefits, like exit bonuses, are available only to specific categories of people. Others, like veterans preference and post-discharge health care, have significantly different provisions for different kinds of veterans. Even those benefits available to all veterans have fine print in their rules governing deadlines and application procedures.

A smooth transition is a well-planned transition. And a well-planned transition begins with solid information.

FINAL PAYCHECK

The last check that most veterans receive from the military is a pleasant surprise. If they have accumulated leave time that hasn't been used, those days are converted into dollars and added to the check. For some, however, the final paycheck is a shock, for they discover the government is balancing the books for debts owed.

> The worst day to settle pay problems is your last day. Count on the government to remember—and settle—all debts you owe them. Plan as if they'll overlook all money they owe you.

Far more new veterans leave the military confused about their paychecks. Although the government gives everyone paperwork showing what's been done to the final paycheck, the paperwork isn't always clear. This section outlines some important information you should know about the final paycheck.

Details of Payment

For a final paycheck from the military, the government uses the same electronic transfer of funds to a financial institution that's used during active duty. Usually, that funds tranfer happens within three weeks after your last day in uniform.

Make sure you understand the exact timelines and procedures used by your service, especially if the final paycheck will go to a new bank account. Ensure that you have a financial cushion to fall back upon during any gap between your discharge date and the arrival of that final paycheck.

If you'll be in a tight fix, explore your service's rules for advance payment of the reimbursements for your final, government-paid travel home. Or see if you can get an advance on your last paycheck.

Rules for the method of payment vary by service and sometimes by installation. Again, don't wait until the last day to find out about the rules that affect your discharge from active duty.

Leave

Everyone in the military gets thirty days off each year. For most people, any leave that has not been used by the last day of service will be automatically "cashed in" in the final paycheck.

For each day of unused leave, veterans receive one-thirtieth of their monthly basic pay. Sixty days' leave is usually the most a servicemember can cash in. More may be allowed for folks coming directly from a combat zone.

Subtractions for leave can be made from the final paycheck if the servicemember was absent without leave or exceeded time-off limits for such transition-related items as house hunting or job hunting. For all subtractions from the final paycheck, finance offices again use the formula of one-thirtieth of the monthly basic pay for each day of unauthorized absence.

Not everyone is eligible to cash in unused leave. Cash-in privileges are denied to veterans with dishonorable discharges, bad-conduct discharges, and discharges that are officially labeled as "under other than honorable conditions."

Savings

If you took advantage of the government's Thrift Savings Plan, or TSP, you have some decisions to make. You can keep the money in TSP, transfer it to a qualified Individual Retirement Account, or cash out your TSP.

There are many advantages to keeping money in TSP. The government will administer the funds. Veterans can still transfer their money between different TSP investment accounts. And the money continues to grow, tax-free.

The government stops making its usual contribution to TSP accounts when people are discharged from the military. Otherwise, the TSP accounts of veterans are treated the same way as the accounts of active-duty folks.

Money that goes directly from TSP into your pocket will be treated as if it were regular income. That could kick you into a higher income tax bracket. Still, TSP funds that are transferred directly from the government to a qualified IRA shouldn't be taxed. A little advance research can save you money and worry.

Debts

Death and taxes are supposed to be the two certainties in life. Military people approaching the end of their active-duty stints can add a third: The government won't forget to collect for any debts.

Outstanding bills for damaged or missing equipment come due on discharge day if servicemembers haven't resolved the issue beforehand.

Reenlistment bonuses and some special education that carried an obligation for specific periods of additional active duty can also result in deductions if servicemembers haven't given the government all the time for which they were paid.

Taxes

Taxes are still a certainty for everyone taking off the uniform. You can count on the finance office to deduct federal and state income taxes, plus Social Security taxes, from the final paycheck, including exit bonuses. The amount of the withholding is determined by standard tax tables.

If a servicemember had no state tax withheld from the regular paychecks because he or she claimed residence in a state that doesn't have an income tax, then no state tax will be withheld from the final paycheck.

Veterans should be forewarned, however. Moving after discharge to a state that imposes a state income tax may put you in a position in which you owe state income tax on portions of the final paycheck.

There are no tax consequences for leaving savings in an account in a government-run Thrift Savings Plan, or TSP, after being discharged. TSP money that goes into your pocket will be fully taxed.

Study the fine print before transferring savings from TSP to an Individual Retirement Account, or IRA. Done properly, that transfer will protect your money from the taxman.

Health Insurance

Except for retirees, everyone leaving active duty can apply for a transitional health insurance plan. As with civilian health insurance, participants must pay premiums for the coverage. The first premium is due on the day of discharge. People who want the coverage can pay the premium by subtracting it from the final paycheck.

If a paycheck is smaller than a premium, which happens only for folks with unusually large families or sizable debts to the government, then the servicemember must write a check for the balance.

FINAL PHYSICAL

You were in top-notch physical condition when you entered the military. Otherwise, they wouldn't have taken you.

If your military service created or aggravated medical problems, you're entitled to compensation and treatment from the Department of Veterans Affairs.

VA compensation and care can begin years after your discharge. You don't have to be among the "walking wounded" limping out the main gate to qualify—eventually—for treatment for a service-connected medical problem.

> Insist on a final physical exam. Decades from now, your family's financial future may depend on VA benefits based on that physical.

What is a minor ailment at age twenty-three—for example, an occasionally painful back injury that happened on active duty—can become a disability that prevents you from earning an income when you're fifty-three.

VA offices routinely grant benefits to veterans decades after their original injuries, wounds, or illnesses in the military, but establishing the connection between those medical conditions and military service becomes more difficult for veterans who didn't receive a comprehensive physical examination when they left active duty.

Everyone has a right to a final physical. Transition counselors and veterans advocates urge that everyone leaving the military insist upon getting one.

Be sure to mention any injuries or serious illnesses that occurred on active duty, even ones that don't seem to have left any major aftereffects. Some ailments have a tendency to worsen over time.

And while you're at it, transition counselors recommend applying for VA disability compensation as part of the discharge process. A small legal subtlety becomes very important here. You don't need to have a disability in order to apply for disability compensation. You can even shout at the top of your lungs as you're signing the application form that you're a remarkable physical specimen.

Filing the application is a tactical move. By applying for VA disability compensation, you transfer a copy of your military medical files into the VA system and open up a file with the VA. Any later dealings with a VA office, even decades after your discharge, will be easier if those steps have already been taken.

And let's not forget a more immediate and traditional reason for getting a physical examination. Some folks have medical problems that haven't displayed major symptoms yet. The predischarge physical will be the last time for years that many soon-to-be veterans will see a doctor.

HEALTH CARE

Since the medical bills of many people in the United States are paid by health insurance plans offered by their employers, new veterans looking for civilian jobs once found themselves having to decide between two unfavorable options: They could gamble that they would stay healthy until they got a job with employer-provided coverage, or they could pay from their own pockets the exorbitant premiums demanded by many private health insurance plans.

Now, however, Congress and the Pentagon have rewritten the traditional rules about health care for veterans. The result is a government-sponsored health insurance plan for new veterans and their families.

Care Back Home

Nearly everyone leaving the military is able to purchase coverage from a special transitional health insurance plan, which offers veterans the low rates usually available only from group plans. It is called "Continued Health Care Benefit Program," or CHCBP.

> Health care rules are constantly changing. Make sure your medical plans are based on the latest, most detailed information.

The longest period of time for which coverage can be purchased for most veterans and family members is eighteen months; the shortest is three months. The coverage can be purchased only in three-month blocks, and the first payment is due on the date of discharge. Premiums for three months' coverage in the year 2010 were $988 for an individual and $2,213 for a family.

This program is operated by Tricare, the military's health insurance system, and it has the same basic rules as Tricare, The unmarried former spouses of military personnel and children of military folks are eligible for CHCBP when they become ineligible for Tricare.

Another transitional health insurance program, called "Transitional Assistance Management Program," or TAMP, applies to people involuntarily discharged from active duty under honorable conditions and to their families. For the first 180 days of civilian life, they can receive continued coverage under Tricare with no premiums, although they will have to pick up any deductibles and copayments. It is also available to National Guardsmen or reservists who leave active duty after at least 30 consecutive days supporting a contingency operation.

TAMP participants can sign up for the CHCBP health insurance after their TAMP eligibility period runs out.

Booklets with detailed information about these plans, including covered services and current rates, are available from transition offices and family support centers, and on the internet at www.tricare.com.

DENTAL CARE

Routine dental checkups shouldn't be put off until the last minute by military folks approaching their discharges. Under the best of circumstances, appointments are hard to get. And under the worst, if a checkup detects a problem that requires additional stretches in the dental chair, there may not be enough time left on active duty to schedule follow-up appointments.

Because of the difficulties many military members experience in getting dental care before their discharges, the government has created a unique benefit for new veterans: Most veterans are eligible for a one-time dental examination and treatment in any VA dental facility, without going through the normal hassles of filing for VA benefits.

To receive this one-time VA dental care, veterans must apply for it at a VA medical facility within 180 days of discharge. This one-time VA care will be denied to veterans who saw a military dentist within 90 days of discharge. Exceptions can be made for veterans whose treatments in active-duty dental facilities were incomplete at the time of discharge.

TIME OFF

A successful transition from active duty to civilian life takes planning. And some plans require your physical presence to find facts, discuss arrangements, and make deals. In fact, it's nearly impossible to find a home or a job by long distance. You need to be there. And that will require time away from the military before you're discharged.

Several different programs are on the books that make it easier for active-duty people to get away from their military duties during the last months in uniform. They all share one major trait: They're not absolute rights. Unit commanders have the final say in whether people get time away from their official duties.

Advance Leave

Commanders can grant up to an extra thirty days' leave (beyond the thirty days' leave everyone in the military receives) for people approaching the end of their military careers. This is called advance leave.

First, let's put advance leave in perspective. Everyone in full-time military service, regardless of rank or the time they've spent in uniform, receives 2.5 days of leave every month. Advance leave is permission to use leave that hasn't been earned yet but that will be earned by the time you are discharged.

If you leave the service early, previous advance leave can create confusion. Say you're scheduled to leave the military in December and your commander grants advance leave in August, knowing you'll be credited with at least seven more days of leave by your discharge date. If you suddenly leave the military in September, which is after you've taken the extra days away from work but before you've been credited with enough leave to fill the gap, then you would have to repay the government for the advance leave. In that case, you would see your final military paycheck shrink by one-thirtieth of your basic pay for each day of advance leave.

Permissive Temporary Duty

Time away from work that isn't charged against annual leave is called permissive temporary duty. Sometimes, commanders give people in their units permission not to report for work. Instead, they're supposed to use that time for specific, approved activities. House hunting and job hunting can fall into this category.

This time doesn't affect annual leave: Servicemembers won't see their final paychecks reduced because they've taken it.

Excess Leave

In unusual situations, commanders have the authority to grant folks "excess leave." This is time off from work when a servicemember isn't paid. This is an extreme measure. Commanders have considerable discretion in approving excess leave. Anyone contemplating it should think seriously about the consequences of going without pay for any length of time.

Terminal Leave

When you spend your last active-duty days on leave, you're said to be on terminal leave.

Many veterans find it convenient to take official leave time from their military jobs in the weeks before discharge. Then, instead of returning for a few days when their discharge date approaches, they go directly from "leave status" to civilian status.

Like so much in the military, terminal leave is subject to a swarm of restrictions. The first major hurdle is getting the approval of one's unit commander.

Still more complications can arise for people who use terminal leave for vacations or to travel to their new homes. These folks are still on active duty and drawing regular military pay, but the government won't pay extra mileage or per diem for vacations or extra travel. If you're traveling or vacationing while on terminal leave, make sure you've clearly discussed your plans with people from the local personnel office. Make sure you—and they—understand the portions of your trip that should be covered by government benefits and the portions that must be paid from your own pocket. This can prevent a rude surprise when you open your final paycheck. Odds are, the government will re-solve any discrepancies in its favor.

GETTING HOME

When you came on active duty, the military paid to move you away from home. At the end of your stint in uniform, the mili-tary will pay to send you back home.

That's the good news. The bad news is that the who-gets-what-and-how-much-of-it rules governing household moves in the military are complex. And they're not any simpler for the last move back to the civilian world.

In a nutshell, most of the same allowances and limitations that affect regular active-duty moves—what the services call permanent-change-of-station, or PCS, moves—are in force for the final move.

Where's Home?

Generally, the military will pay to send newly discharged ser-vicemembers, their families, and their worldly possessions back to their official home—called the "home of record"—or to the place they entered active duty.

Many veterans, however, don't want to go there when they walk out the main gate for the last time. They go to other parts of the country.

> Free booklets for a low-hassle last move are available from military transportation offices.

In those instances, the military figures out what your benefits would be if they sent you back to your home of record or the place you entered active duty. That calculation becomes a maximum payment. You can't get more by moving to a more distant part of the country.

If the place you actually settle is closer to your last assign-ment than your home of record, however, then your allowances and payments are based on the actual distance to your new home.

Those are the rules for most veterans. A more generous definition of "home" applies to military retirees. They can have their household goods moved to anywhere in the country.

Even for retirees, however, there can be a hitch getting the military to pick up the bills to move to Hawaii or Alaska.

If a veteran entered the military from either of those states or lists one as the official home of record, there should be no problem. Other retirees dreaming of a government-paid move to the Yukon or Waikiki should check the fine print in the rules at the nearest military transportation office.

Veterans with "bad paper," that is, with discharges that are officially rated as "under other than honorable conditions," typically get a bus ticket—or enough money to purchase one—returning them to their civilian homes.

Household Goods

The government promises to do more than put discharged veterans on an airplane. It will also make the necessary arrangements and pay the bills for the shipment of all the stuff in their homes.

Generally, personal property and household goods are treated in the last government-paid move under the same rules and benefits that apply to government-ordered moves while people are still on active duty.

The nearest military transportation office will make most of the arrangements with trucking companies to pick up your household goods and to deliver them.

As with normal PCS moves, folks returning home from active duty must keep an eye on the household goods weight table, the chart that specifies how many pounds the government will pay to move. Each rank has its own weight allowance, and there are different rates within each rank for single people and those with families. Trucking companies send their bills for

WEIGHT ALLOWANCES
(Limits in Pounds for Government-Paid Moving and Storage)

Rank	With Dependents	Without Dependents
0-6 to 0-10	18,000	18,000
0-5, W-5	17,500	16,000
0-4, W-4	17,000	14,000
0-3, W-3	14,500	13,000
0-2, W-2	13,500	12,500
0-1, W-1	12,000	10,000
E-9	15,000	13,000
E-8	14,000	12,000
E-7	13,000	11,000
E-6	11,000	8,000
E-5	9,000	7,000
E-4	8,000	7,000
E-3	8,000	5,000
E-2	8,000	5,000
E-1	8,000	5,000

these moves directly to the government. If discharged veterans go over their weight allowances, they must pay for the excess.

Payments
The government will also pay to get you and your family back home. At one time, that government obligation could be met by handing soon-to-be-discharged people a bus ticket. Later that was upgraded to an airplane ticket. In fact, a government-paid airline ticket is what single veterans who don't own a car will receive.

Usually, for family members to qualify for a government-paid move, they must meet all the official criteria for being "dependents." The general rule is that if the military will give them ID cards, it will pay to move them.

Most veterans driving their personal cars to postdischarge homes qualify for two separate payments: MALT and per diem.

MALT: MALT (which stands for "mileage allowance in lieu of transportation") is a payment to cover the expenses of operating the car. It's calculated at so many cents per mile—16.5 cents per mile in the year 2010. Two-car families can get that rate for each car.

Per Diem: Per diem (which means "by the day") is an allowance paid by the government for food and lodging expenses during a move. In the year 2010, the rates were $116 daily for the veteran, $87 for dependents 12 or older, and $58 for dependents younger than 12.

If travelers pay less for food and shelter than they receive in their per diems, they can pocket the savings. If they pay more, the government won't give them extra money.

Normally, the people receiving this per diem are the ones driving home after leaving the military. Partial payments may be offered to people using airplanes, buses, or trains.

The military has several things that are called "per diem." Perhaps the most widely known one, which can range up to several hundred dollars daily, goes to people on official duty for short periods of time in high-cost areas.

The per diem offered to discharged veterans has a single rate. It doesn't increase for people passing through expensive cities on their way home.

Storage

Quite often, home isn't ready when newly discharged veterans arrive there. Despite the best planning and precious days of annual leave spent in the new community long before discharge, many veterans still aren't able to occupy their new homes after the moving van pulls up at the curb. For them, the government will put property into storage at government expense. The usual limit is 180 days of storage, and most often, the government picks the storage facility. The government also pays to have the goods moved from storage and into the new home.

The time limit on government-paid storage is considerably longer for retirees who are entitled to one year's storage at government expense.

Stored goods also figure into the official weight table for household goods. The material put in storage *plus* the goods moved directly into the home must total fewer pounds than the amount listed on the table. Veterans must pay for any excess.

Calculating Days and Miles

The military has its own version of practically everything, including its own way of measuring time and distance. Veterans planning for their final government-paid move shouldn't assume that the military relies on the standard way of reading a map or the calendar.

Transportation offices have their own charts that give the official distance between two points. For computing the mileage used in the MALT formula, for example, officials will rely on the distance cited in those charts. A veteran's actual experience on the road doesn't carry any weight.

When it comes to per diem, which is based on the number of days a veteran spends on the road, the military also has its own calendar. Generally, for people traveling by car, per diem is computed on the basis that folks will travel 350 miles in one day. Put another way, one day equals 350 miles.

If you can cover more ground and consequently spend less time on the road, you can keep the extra per diem money. If you travel at a slower rate than 350 miles per day, you can't get extra per diem for the additional time.

The Bottom Line

In many ways, your discharge from active duty is the end of your relationship with the U.S. military. In one sense—the financial sense—the military wants to make your last day in uniform the end of its dealings with you.

The military wants to give you all the money you're owed, including all the travel-related payments for moving back home, on your last day on active duty.

Don't wait till the last minute to figure out what your travel benefits should be. And if you don't understand—or don't agree with what's offered—don't assume you can straighten it out after discharge.

Problems with pay and allowances get tougher to solve the closer you get to walking out the main gate for the last time.

JOB SEARCH

Leaving the military, for most people, is the second major problem confronting them as the day of their discharge approaches. The number one priority is finding a civilian job.

Military veterans return to the private sector with experiences, skills, and formal training they didn't possess when they first marched off to active duty. Many employers need people with the skills and knowledge acquired during years of service in the military. Supervisors value the personal traits—the reliability, trainability, maturity, and drug-free status—of people who have put in a few years in uniform. For these reasons, many jobs go to veterans instead of equally qualified—or perhaps even slightly better qualified—civilian competitors.

Don't wait for an invitation to use transition programs. Invite yourself. Learn about the job-hunting tools that the military offers.

Still, the first job search after taking off the uniform is a painful, perplexing time for many veterans. Too often, they don't have a realistic sense of their own value to employers. Few have much experience "selling" themselves to a potential boss, and most are hard pressed to translate their military skills, experiences, and training into terms meaningful to a nonveteran.

Fortunately, there are a variety of resources available to help veterans find private-sector jobs that are tailored to their interests, skills, and financial obligations. One resource is the book *Job Search: Marketing Your Military Experience*, 5th edition, by David Henderson (Stackpole: 2009).

State Employment Agencies

Perhaps the most valuable and underused resource for returning veterans is the employment agencies operated by every state. These offices charge no fees, and they're professionally staffed. They offer free, one-on-one counseling for job seekers. They hold their own free seminars on job search skills and resume writing. They also serve as clearinghouses for other private and governmental agencies with information of use to people seeking employment.

The staffs include people who work largely with veterans. Disabled veterans are a special priority, and everyone with an officially rated disability should make sure that his or her counselors at the state employment agency are aware of that. Often, it can make the difference at hiring time.

Of course, the most valuable tool at these agencies is the listing of available jobs. Many firms get most of their new employees through these state agencies.

Although each agency has slightly different procedures, at all offices job seekers are able to browse through the list of vacancies and see which employers are hiring, what jobs are open, and what skills are demanded for specific vacancies.

As the country becomes increasingly computerized, more state offices are linking themselves to a computer network only available to state employment agencies. This computer network has up-to-the-minute listings for jobs across the entire country, making it possible for servicemembers in the last months of active duty to find out about openings in their hometowns.

Transition Programs

For nearly two decades, the military has had formal programs to help servicemembers make the difficult move from active duty back into civilian life. Transition programs are available at most military installations, and for those installations where services are unavailable, it's possible to get the benefit of transition programs at another military base, even one operated by another service. Many transition services are also available to spouses.

Everyone within 120 days of leaving the military is eligible to attend a Transition Assistance Program (TAP) class. Run by professionals from the Department of Labor with assistance from the Department of Veterans Affairs, these multiday programs offer practical assistance with a wide range of issues facing newly discharged veterans—from resume writing and interview techniques to researching companies and translating military skills into civilian language. The classes are free, and everyone facing a discharge should attend one.

Mid- to large-sized military installations have transition centers that are usually located near the family support center. Usually staffed by full-time professionals, the transition center offers customized attention and long-term support for the military job seeker. Many will help folks leaving the military develop a personalized Individual Transition Plan (ITP), which identifies the important elements of a successful return to the private sector and establishes realistic milestones.

Another important item for transitioning military personnel is DD Form 2586, *Verification of Military Experience and Training*. The military services are supposed to provide this document to everyone who leaves active duty. Although not a substitute for a resume, it is an invaluable tool for those seeking civilian jobs, for it puts military experience, professional education, and training into terms that are meaningful to civilian supervisors.

A useful Internet tool to find out about transition programs, including the locations of TAP programs and transition centers, is www.dol.gov/vets/programs/tap.

Veterans Associations

Some of the best networking tools for new veterans, especially those who settle in a strange community after their discharge, are veterans associations.

Many of these organizations have programs to help recently discharged job seekers. Most of the formal programs are free, available to nonmembers, and even open to folks not eligible for membership. Local chapters of the groups are usually listed in the telephone book. The appendix of *Veteran's Guide* contains addresses and telephone numbers for national offices.

The Noncommissioned Officers Association (NCOA) is a major sponsor of job fairs for all veterans, even officers. The Military Officers Association of America (MOAA) and the Air Force Association offer one-on-one counseling and resume critiques.

Broad-membership veterans groups like the American Legion and the Veterans of Foreign Wars have their own job search programs. Disabled American Veterans and Paralyzed American Veterans offer specialized programs for people who leave active duty with lingering physical problems.

The major veterans groups have chapters in every community, with membership drawn from across the spectrum of industries, occupations, and skill levels. By joining one and taking an active role in its local activities, you begin the process of meeting people who can pass along information about good places to work, places to avoid, and job openings that haven't been publicized.

UNEMPLOYMENT COMPENSATION

Not everyone lands a job immediately after leaving active duty. Many new veterans spend their first weeks back in the private sector looking for work. Most of them are eligible for the same unemployment compensation paid to civilian workers who lose their jobs through layoffs and plant closings.

Although unemployment compensation is a nationwide program, each state administers it. States write their own rules within broad guidelines issued by the federal government.

Veterans shouldn't assume that some fact about unemployment compensation in one state will hold true in another. Ask direct questions to learn about the details for the state in which you plan to settle after taking off the uniform.

Eligibility

Most people leaving active duty are eligible for unemployment compensation. A few specific categories of people aren't eligible.

An unexpectedly pleasant rule for many veterans is the fact that there are no residency requirements for unemployment compensation. You can file for unemployment compensation in any state. It doesn't have to be your home state. It doesn't have to be the most recent state in which you've lived. It doesn't even have to be a state where you've ever lived. The only residency requirement is that you must file for unemployment compensation from the state where you live after leaving active duty.

While most veterans are eligible for unemployment compensation, a few groups may run into trouble. Here's the breakdown for those groups:

- *Retirees:* Usually ineligible.
- *Bad-paper veterans:* Frequently ineligible. Depends on specific discharge and the state.
- *Disabled veterans:* Not eligible if disability prevents veteran from holding a job.
- *Early outs:* May have trouble in a few states.

Leave and Government Checks

The basic idea behind unemployment compensation is to use taxpayer money to help folks without an income while they're looking for work. If people have an income—or something that looks like an income—then state officials become reluctant to approve them for the program.

To most states, "cashing in" leave time looks like income. Typically, if you cashed in twenty-one days of unused leave when you left the military, state officials will say you're ineligible for unemployment compensation for the first twenty-one days after discharge.

In a slightly different way, the same philosophy affects military retirees and those receiving some sort of disability pay. If the state law permits unemployment compensation for retirees and the disabled—and that's a big "if"—then the state may reduce unemployment compensation by one dollar for each dollar of retired pay or disability pay.

Details of the Program

Each state has its own rate for unemployment compensation. Amounts vary widely across the country. Rates for each person are determined by the individual's salary at the last job. In every state, unemployment compensation is less than half of a person's last weekly salary, and in most, it's significantly less than half.

States also have limits on the length of time that unemployment compensation will be paid. In most states, it's capped at twenty-six weeks. That has been increased by Congress during times of high unemployment, usually by the addition of another thirteen weeks per person.

Unemployment compensation comes with some strings. Recipients must be actively looking for work while receiving unemployment compensation. Most states require recipients to document their job-search efforts. Usually, that involves filling out a form that lists the specific places where someone has looked for work. Typically, those forms have blanks for the names, titles, and phone numbers of people talked to. Folks who falsify those forms, or who don't make the effort to find work, can lose their unemployment compensation.

Application
Unemployment compensation is administered by the same state employment agencies that maintain listings of job vacancies. Everyone—veterans, too—must apply in person for unemployment compensation. Former servicemembers should bring extra copies of their formal discharge papers, DD Form 214.

VETERANS PREFERENCE
Veterans should get a break when the federal government is hiring. That seems fair. And that's the way the federal civil service has been operating for a long time.

And for just as long, it's been misunderstood. Military service doesn't guarantee anyone a spot on the federal payroll. Your status as a veteran won't get you hired for a job for which you're not qualified.

What their time in the military gives veterans when hiring time arrives at a civil service office is an edge, an advantage, a slight nudge toward the front of the pack. It's called the "veterans preference," not the "veterans *guarantee*." Here are some of the basics:

Regular Preference
Qualified veterans receive an extra five points for any competitive examinations when they have honorable discharges and meet at least one of the following criteria:
- Served during wartime.
- Earned a campaign ribbon.
- Spent more than 180 days on active duty between January 31, 1955, and October 15, 1976.
- Spent at least 24 months on active duty, with at least one day between August 2, 1990, and January 2, 1992.
- Was a reservist or guardsman ordered to active duty between August 2, 1990, and January 2, 1992. (Must have served the full period for which brought on active duty.)

- Spent 180 consecutive days on active duty after September 10, 2001.

Ten extra points are added to examination results if the veteran was discharged with a disability or has a Purple Heart. Ten points can also be awarded, under certain circumstances, to the spouses and survivors of disabled veterans and of people who died on active duty.

Not eligible for any veterans preference are former servicemembers who don't have disabilities and retired in the rank of major, lieutenant commander, or higher.

VRA Preference

A special provision on the books of the U.S. civil service, called the "Veterans Recruitment Appointment," or VRA, permits veterans to be hired directly, without taking a competitive examination.

The VRA system has created an unusual amount of confusion and bad feelings. The first step in the process occurs when a federal manager decides to fill a vacancy using VRA. The manager doesn't have to use VRA. If the manager wants to use the usual civil service selection process, that's how it's done. There's no way to force a manager to use VRA.

Each major federal agency has its own guidelines for designating vacancies to be filled using VRA authority.

Generally, the program is open to veterans who have spent at least one day on active duty since August 4, 1964, have a total of 180 days on active duty, and have something other than a dishonorable discharge. The requirement for 180 days' active-duty service is waived for veterans with a campaign ribbon and people discharged with a service-connected disability.

Other Preferences

State, county, and municipal civil service systems frequently have their own versions of the veterans preference program. For details, check with the appropriate personnel office.

FOUR

HEALTH CARE

In This Chapter:

- *VA Health Care*
- *VA-Paid Hospital Care*
- *VA Nursing Homes*
- *VA-Paid Nursing Homes*
- *Care for Family Members*

- *Spina Bifida*
- *Children of Women Vietnam Veterans*
- *Gulf War Families*

When veterans take off their uniforms for the last time, many are unable to leave behind all of the consequences of military service.

Untold thousands have battlefield injuries that require life-long care. Many more have lingering health problems that didn't directly arise from combat but that can be traced to injuries and illnesses that began on active duty.

Helping these veterans is the central mission of the extensive medical system—the largest in the country—that's run by the Department of Veterans Affairs, or VA. More than 150 VA medical centers and 900 clinics are in operation, providing un-surpassed care with up-to-date medical technology and a cadre of trained professionals.

These facilities are located in every state in the union, plus a few other places. VA officials try to treat veterans in hospitals and clinics closest to their homes, but eligible veterans can be treated at any VA medical center. In fact, veterans are routinely sent to facilities away from home if those places have the medical hardware or the specialists best suited for treatment. And if the VA doesn't have the needed resources for an eligible veteran, the veterans agency will pay for treatment in a private-sector hospital.

It may come as a surprise to some veterans that care in a VA medical center is not free to all veterans. Limited resources have forced VA officials to put priorities on treatment for different categories of veterans. Those with medical problems not officially recognized as connected to their military service may have to pay for services and medication. Those charges, called "co-payments," are usually much smaller than private-sector health costs.

Veterans and family members curious about the eligibility rules for VA medical care must ensure that they're basing their health care decisions on the latest information.

There's no shortage of sources for the latest information. The best place to start is at a nearby VA medical center, where people known as "veterans benefits counselors" can explain recent changes in the rules. Regional VA offices and the major veterans organizations also are invaluable resources. The VA also posts information on its website, www.va.gov.

VA HEALTH CARE

If there's one segment of the federal government suffering from an unjustified image problem, it's the network of 153 hospitals and more than 900 clinics operated by the Department of Veterans Affairs.

Some media accounts have depicted VA facilities as antiquated and their staffs as uncaring, but patients, staffers, and other members of the medical community have personal experiences and hard statistics that prove the care in VA facilities is among the best in the nation.

About half of all physicians in the United States undergo some part of their training at a VA medical facility. For years, the independent commission that evaluates hospitals has given the average VA hospital a higher grade than the average private-sector hospital.

In many communities, even in some of the largest cities, the local VA medical center has state-of-the-art diagnostic and treatment hardware. Those VA resources are made available to private-sector hospitals.

Even students in medical colleges routinely go to VA medical centers to study the most advanced tools in the profession. VA hospitals have been the home for basic research that is advancing medical understanding in fields ranging from prosthetics to AIDS.

The full range of services from this medical powerhouse can be brought to bear in the diagnosis, treatment, and rehabilitation of that select group of people with the proud title of "veteran."

There is a downside, however. The doors of VA medical centers would be jammed if every veteran had an identical right to treatment. For years, the system has given priority to two special groups of former servicemembers—those with health problems directly related to their military service and those without the financial means to obtain care elsewhere. These people, along with a few other narrowly defined groups of veterans, receive their care without any charge.

Veterans who don't fit into one of these high-priority groups may be billed for their treatment. Generally, those expenses are lower than rates in private-sector hospitals. But even for the paying customers, no one gets treated unless there's room.

The trend for nearly two decades in the VA medical system has been a constant tinkering with the eligibility rules to make the budget fit the categories of veterans with an absolute right to care. Make sure you have the latest information about eligibility at these facilities.

Eligibility

More than any other veterans program, the VA medical system is governed by a balance between eligibility and access. "Eligibility" determines your legal right to treatment. "Access" occurs when there's a vacant bed or treatment room in which to put you.

Every veteran who has been officially discharged "under conditions other than dishonorable" is eligible for care in a VA facility.

In the year 2010, admission rules for VA medical centers were most likely to give access to veterans with one of these factors in their files:

- Service-connected disabilities.
- VA pension.
- Combat veterans discharged within the last five years.
- Former POWs.
- Recipients of the Purple Heart.
- "Catastrophically disabled" for reasons unrelated to military service.
- Agent Orange exposure.
- "Atomic" veterans.
- Gulf War illnesses.

The phrase "atomic veteran" refers to servicemembers exposed to ionizing radiation during atmospheric nuclear tests or during service in Hiroshima or Nagasaki immediately after the end of World War II. Vietnam veterans exposed to Agent Orange or Gulf War veterans complaining of undiagnosed illnesses must be seeking care for problems they believe are directly related to these events and must have entered their names on the appropriate list—known as a "registry"—maintained by the Department of Veterans Affairs to keep track of these former service-members.

Veterans with low incomes can receive free treatment if their incomes fall below certain limits. VA rules spell out the income restrictions based on family size. Those income levels change every year. In 2010, this category of veterans included people without immediate families with annual incomes of less than about $30,000 and veterans with a spouse and an annual income of less than about $35,000.

Higher-income veterans who don't fall into one of the groups mentioned above may still qualify for medical care. Check with the nearest VA facility or online at www.va.gov/health_elegibility to find out how the rules apply to you.

Service-Connected Problems

Top priority for care in VA medical centers goes to veterans with disabilities that are officially rated as "service connected."

Getting that official ruling can take months, perhaps even longer than a year. One of the best ways to ensure access to a VA hospital in the future is to do the work now to get a service-connected rating. That comes from applying for disability compensation, which is discussed in chapter 6, "Disability Pay."

Veterans with service-connected medical problems may also have ailments that aren't service connected. Expect different admission and reimbursement rules for non-service-connected ailments.

A service-connected medical problem is one that was caused by military service, that developed during military service, or that was aggravated by military service. Those lingering medical problems are officially known as "disabilities." Don't be put off by the term. Many veterans with VA disabilities aren't suffering from obvious handicaps. That's just the official label attached to their problems.

The severity of a disability is usually expressed as a percentage figure, ranging from 10 to 100 percent. Complex rules govern these ratings. For example, implantation of an artificial shoulder qualifies as a 100 percent disability immediately after the operation. Later the disability rating drops to 30 percent if there are no complications, or to 60 percent if pain and weakness in the arm continue.

Veterans who are concerned about getting access to inpatient VA services should keep their eyes on something called a "zero compensable disability." This arises when the official VA review of their medical files determines that, in fact, they do have a medical problem that is service connected, but this problem is not severe enough to justify the minimum monthly payment for VA disability compensation, which requires a 10 percent disability.

Veterans with zero compensable disabilities don't receive monthly disability checks, but their records note that they have a disability that meets the official definition of being service connected, which makes them eligible for free care in a VA hospital or clinic.

Be warned, though, that sometimes veterans with service-connected medical problems can get free care in VA medical centers only for those specific ailments. For example, even if your chronic foot problems have been officially rated as service connected, a VA hospital might expect payment to treat you for a cardiac problem that hasn't been rated as service connected.

Priority groups

For veterans new to the VA health care system, one of the biggest sources of misunderstanding is the "priority group." Every new patient is assigned to one of eight priority groups. Logically, that would mean the folks in the first priority group get seen before the patients in the second group. Right? No, that's wrong.

VA officials use the eight priority groups to identify the patients who must make minimal out-of-pocket payments for their VA health care, payments that are called "co-payments."

For determining the order in which patients are seen, VA doctors use the same system that their private-sector counterparts use—emergencies first, then other patients in the order they request appointments.

Emergencies

What if you are one of those emergency patients, and you're not sure if you're eligible for VA healthcare?

VA physicians, like all health care professionals, treat people with genuine medical emergencies and sort out the payment scheme later. Expect a bill for co-payments if the emergency isn't related to a recognized service-connected medical problem.

Costs

VA medical facilities don't charge anyone for treatment of an ailment that's officially rated as service connected, but, in order to hold down costs, officials will try to get reimbursed for treatments that aren't for problems directly related to military service. Veterans with service-connected disabilities shouldn't expect free care for non-service-connected medical problems.

Insurance companies may be billed by the Department of Veterans Affairs for treatment of a veteran for illnesses or injuries not related to military service.

For treatment of non-service-connected medical problems, the co-payments for veterans in 2010 were:
- For inpatient care, $1,100 for the first 90 days and $850 for each additional 90 days.
- For long-term care, $97 a day.
- For outpatient primary care, $15 a visit.
- For outpatient specialty care, $50 a visit.
- For outpatient medicine, $8 or $9 for a 30-day supply.

Admission

The VA medical system has its own identification card for singling out veterans who are entitled to medical care. You'll get one if you're approved for VA disability compensation or receive a percentage rating for disability pay.

Patients who don't have the card should bring some other documentation that proves they have a service-connected disability or that they've applied for a disability rating. The same holds true for veterans receiving VA pensions who seek inpatient care.

For your first visit to a VA medical center, it's a good idea to bring along a copy of your DD Form 214, your discharge papers.

Locations

An appendix at the back of this book has a state-by-state listing of VA medical facilities, and includes a summary of major services and specialties.

VA-PAID HOSPITAL CARE

Not all health problems can be treated in VA medical facilities. Sometimes veterans can receive more specialized care in a local, private hospital.

The rule is that veterans must be specifically approved to use another medical facility if they expect VA to pick up the bill.

Approvals are normally restricted to the following:

- Service-connected disabilities.
- Disabilities that caused a veteran's discharge from active duty.
- Disabilities associated with another service-connected disability.
- Disabilities of veterans in rehabilitation programs.

If veterans who are regular patients at a VA medical center require emergency treatment and they go to a non-VA facility, they must notify their "home" VA center within seventy-two hours after admission. Failure to meet the seventy-two-hour limit can result in the veteran having to pay the bill, even if it's one that VA officials would otherwise pay.

VA NURSING HOMES

Nursing homes are an integral part of the medical system operated by the Department of Veterans Affairs. With only a few exceptions, they're located on the grounds of VA medical centers.

VA nursing homes provide skilled nursing care, related medical services, and psychiatric treatment for veterans who don't need to be hospitalized but who do need institutional care.

Most residents of VA nursing homes come directly from hospitals. Some stay long enough to regain their health and return home, while others remain in the facilities for extended periods. In short, VA nursing homes serve both long-term and short-stay patients.

Eligibility

Traditionally, the eligibility rules for VA nursing homes have been identical to the rules for inpatient VA medical care. If you qualify for one, you qualify for the other.

One general rule is paramount. Even more than VA hospitals, nursing homes must make decisions based on the availability of space. If the nursing home doesn't have an empty bed, it cannot accept you.

VA nursing homes are principally medical facilities, not residential facilities. As with other medical resources, their operations have become uncertain during current increases in demand.

In the year 2010, admission rules for VA nursing homes gave top priority to veterans in need of the following treatment:

- Treatment of a service-connected disability.
- Any treatment when the veteran has a 70 percent or greater service-connected disability.

While these veterans have top priority for admission to VA nursing homes under the rules in effect in 2010, other veterans could be admitted if space was available and no high-priority veterans were on a waiting list.

Veterans with low incomes can receive free treatment in a VA nursing home, again assuming that space is available. VA rules spell out the income restrictions based on family size. Those income statistics change every year. In 2010, this category of veterans included people without immediate families with annual incomes of less than about $30,000, and veterans with a spouse and annual incomes of less than about $35,000.

Costs

Disabled and low-income veterans entitled to priority admission to VA nursing homes will have the government pick up the full costs for the stay, including all charges for medical services, rehabilitation, and even food.

Also exempt from charges are veterans with the following classifications:

- Former POWs.
- Eligible for Medicaid.
- "Atomic" veterans.
- Exposed to Agent Orange.
- Suffering from Gulf War illnesses.

Recipients of VA pensions who are admitted to VA nursing homes at the government's expense will have their monthly pensions reduced. The amount of the reduction varies, depending on the specific kind of VA pension received by the veteran, as does the effective date of the reduction. Those reductions leave recipients of VA pensions in nursing homes with between $30 and $90 per month.

Special rules go into play if the recipient of a VA pension has a spouse or another dependent. When those veterans are admitted to VA nursing homes, other family members can receive the rest of the VA pension.

But this doesn't happen automatically. The family member must take the initiative. Contact the veterans benefits counselor or some other official at the VA nursing home to start the paperwork.

If a veteran receiving VA disability compensation is admitted to a VA nursing home, there is no reduction in the amount of that monthly check.

Any veteran admitted to a nursing home who doesn't fall into one of the categories for priority care must pay for his or her treatment. Typically, those bills are lower than the costs in nongovernmental facilities.

Veterans not entitled to priority admission can use their private health insurance plans or the government's Medicare insurance to pay for care. In 2010, these nonpriority cases were charged a maximum of $97 per day, with the actual charge being determined on a case-by-case basis.

Details of the Facilities

VA nursing homes provide skilled nursing care and related health services to patients needing long-term nursing care and rehabilitation services. Since most VA nursing homes are located on the grounds of VA medical centers, the health care system's full resources are available for nursing home residents, including rehabilitative services.

Fine Print

The VA's nursing homes are often referred to as "NHCUs," a sort of verbal shorthand for "Nursing Home Care Units."

Locations

An appendix at the back of this book has a state-by-state listing of VA medical facilities. If a hospital or clinic has a VA nursing home, it is mentioned there.

VA-PAID NURSING HOMES

As veterans from the World War II era have grown older and encountered more health problems, the Department of Veterans Affairs has often found itself without enough of its own facilities to take care of these veterans' needs.

Fortunately, rules are on the books that authorize VA officials to subsidize the care of veterans in privately owned nursing homes. Called "community nursing homes," they are more convenient for some patients—and easier on families and friends—than VA-run facilities that are a long commute from home. VA money pays for some of the services offered to veterans who become patients under this program. If there's a gap between actual costs and VA reimbursement, however, the veteran is responsible for paying the difference. Patients can use private health insurance or Medicare.

The VA's community nursing home program isn't strictly for older veterans. It's for any qualified veteran who has health problems that require close medical supervision but who doesn't need to be hospitalized.

Eligibility

The VA's community nursing home program is open to a broad range of veterans. Here are some eligibility rules:

- Everyone eligible for treatment in a VA hospital, VA nursing home, or VA domiciliary is eligible for the community nursing home program.
- Active-duty military personnel and reservists being treated in a military hospital can use the community nursing home program for long-term convalescence.
- Veterans needing extended treatment for disabilities that are officially rated as service connected qualify.
- Veterans discharged from a VA facility who need home health services can be approved for community nursing homes.

Costs

Community nursing homes, unlike VA nursing homes and VA domiciliaries, may charge their patients for some services. Private health insurance plans may pick up those costs. Medicare and Medicaid are also used by many veterans to reduce their out-of-pocket expenses. Because of VA's financial support to these institutions, however, costs tend to be lower than in other private-sector facilities.

Veterans admitted to community nursing homes aren't subject to any automatic reductions in VA disability compensation, VA pensions, or military retired pay, but veterans whose VA pensions normally include a special payment called "Aid and Attendance" will lose that extra money while in the community nursing home.

Admission

Many veterans go directly into community nursing homes from VA facilities or military hospitals. For them, the government will take care of most of the paperwork and help family members prepare the rest.

But when veterans are going directly from their homes or private-sector hospitals into nursing homes, veterans advocates recommend that they get VA approval in advance. This may require a physical examination in a VA medical facility. However, civilian doctors under VA contract can also provide those examinations.

Time Limits

Just as VA nursing homes are generally for patients requiring less than six months' care, the six-month rule also applies to most patients under the community nursing home program.

If veterans require longer care, they are moved to other facilities. Frequently, Medicare or Medicaid will pick up the bills for that later care. If veterans needing longer care are able to look after most of their daily needs, they may be eligible for admission to a VA domiciliary.

A major exception to the six-month rule involves veterans with disabilities that are officially rated as service connected. They can stay as long as they need the care.

A more narrow exception involves veterans who are at the end of their six-month periods and have encountered glitches in their arrangements to transfer to another facility. VA officials can extend their stays in the community nursing homes for forty-five days to work out the problems.

Terminally ill veterans at the end of their six-month periods who have a life expectancy of less than six months can remain in the facilities. If the official diagnosis says they should live longer than six additional months, however, they can be transferred from the community nursing homes.

CARE FOR FAMILY MEMBERS

Veterans aren't the only ones with medical bills. Spouses and children have health care needs, too.

For a select group of spouses and children of veterans, the government offers a health insurance program called "CHAMP-VA." As with any other health insurance plan, CHAMPVA participants may have deductibles and co-payments. When they need medical care, they are expected to pay a small portion of the bill, but the health insurance plan picks up the lion's share. Because it has government backing, CHAMPVA costs less than most commercial health insurance plans.

Vietnam veterans with children born with spina bifida, a crippling deformity of the spine, should be aware that these children are eligible for a unique array of VA benefits. These children were given special benefits after scientific studies showed a link between spina bifida and Agent Orange, a powerful defoliant used in Southeast Asia during the Vietnam War.

As this book went to press, VA officials were writing rules to provide government-paid health care for the caregivers of some veterans. Look for the latest updates on VA's website, www.va.gov.

Sponsors

Like many benefits for active-duty families, the most important eligibility rules for CHAMPVA don't involve the family members, but the veteran.

In this case, this government-backed health insurance can be purchased by the spouse or dependent child of the following kinds of veterans:

- Those officially rated by VA officials as having a "permanent and total" disability that's service connected.
- Deceased veterans rated at the time of their death by VA officials as having a "permanent and total" disability that was service connected.
- Veterans who died as the result of a service-connected disability.
- People who died on active duty.

Spouses

Spouses of deceased veterans and the spouses of people who died on active duty lose their right to CHAMPVA if they remarry. They may be able to regain their CHAMPVA benefits if that new marriage ends, however. This is decided on a case-by-case basis.

Children

As commonly happens in defining "child" for the sake of determining eligibility for VA benefits, the term covers people who are unmarried and who meet one of the following criteria:

- Are under the age of eighteen.
- Are older than eighteen but became permanently incapable of self-support before reaching age eighteen.
- Are older than eighteen but less than twenty-three and enrolled in a full-time educational program approved by VA officials.

They can be natural children, legally adopted children (including those adopted less than two years after the adoptive parent's death), stepchildren residing at home, or illegitimate children officially recognized.

Medicare

CHAMPVA participants who become eligible for Medicare or Tricare lose CHAMPVA, but if they later lose eligibility for Medicare or Tricare, they can resume CHAMPVA.

Costs

CHAMPVA is like many private health insurance programs. Participants have minimal payments called "deductibles" that they must make each year before coverage begins. And they frequently must pay a portion—called "co-payments"—of medical bills. Unlike with private health insurance, however, CHAMPVA participants don't pay annual premiums.

For 2010, the deductible is $50 per beneficiary or $100 per family. For most medical services, CHAMPVA will pay 75 percent of the costs, with the veteran responsible for the remaining 25 percent.

Application

The latest information about CHAMPVA is available at VA regional centers or from benefits counselors at VA medical centers. Those interested can also contact the CHAMPVA center directly: CHAMPVA Center, P.O. Box 469028, Denver, CO 80206. Information is also available by calling 1-800-733-8387 or going to VA's Internet page at www.va.gov/hac/champva/champva. html.

SPINA BIFIDA

The children of some Vietnam War veterans and veterans with peacetime service in Korea can receive government-paid health care if they have been diagnosed with spina bifida.

Congress authorized these unique benefits after several scientific studies noted increased birth defects in the families of people who served in Southeast Asia during the Vietnam War and in Korea. Researchers believe the birth defects stem from veterans' exposure to Agent Orange, a powerful spray used by the U.S. military to strip foliage from the jungles.

Eligibility

Like many other VA benefits for the families of veterans, the spina bifida benefits have eligibility rules for the veteran and for the family members.

The veteran must have served in the U.S. military in the Republic of Vietnam between January 9, 1962, and May 7, 1975. This can include service off the Vietnam coastline. There is no minimum period for which the veteran must have been in Vietnam. Service in other parts of Southeast Asia during the war doesn't count, with the exception of service in Korea between September 1, 1967, and August 31, 1971.

The child must be the natural child of a veteran and must have been conceived after the veteran served in those countries. The child must be diagnosed with spina bifida.

Spina bifida victims who are the children of two Vietnam or Korean veterans are not eligible for any extra benefits.

Health Care

The U.S. Department of Veterans Affairs will pay for the health care and supplies needed to treat spina bifida and medical problems unrelated to spina bifida. Coverage for non–spina bifida medical problems began in October 2008 when Congress changed federal law.

VA acts, essentially, like a health care insurance company. In the vast majority of cases, the health care provided to spina bifida sufferers will be given by private-sector facilities and doctors, not by VA doctors or VA hospitals.

People receiving coverage under this program don't have out-of-pocket expenses, such as copayments or deductibles. But as with any health insurance program, there is fine print concerning how much VA will pay for specific services, which the insurance industry calls "allowable expense." Patients may find themselves billed for a portion of their medical bills.

Application

Any Vietnam or Korean veteran with a child suffering from spina bifida will have to go through an administrative process with VA before receiving any benefits for the family member.

Although any VA health care facility can point a veteran in the right direction, the application is actually made to a VA regional office, not to a hospital or clinic. Regional offices are included in a list of VA facilities at the back of this book. People can also reach regional offices through a toll-free number, 1-800-827-1000.

Coverage for VA benefits begins when the veteran applies for spina bifida-related benefits. VA will not assume responsibility for medical payments that go back to a child's birth. Rules that stipulate how far back VA can go to pay medical bills are written into federal law. VA doctors and administrators cannot change that.

More information about benefits can be obtained by writing VA Spina Bifida, P.O. Box 469065, Denver, CO 80246, by calling 1-888-820-1758, or going online to www.va.gov/hac.

Other Benefits

When the children of veterans qualify for spina bifida-related health care, they also become eligible for a monthly allowance from the VA. The size of the allowance is based upon the severity of the child's disability.

In the year 2010, federal law put all spina bifida victims into one of three categories. Each category had its own monthly allowance from the VA. Those monthly amounts were $286, $984, and $1,678. Other income doesn't affect eligibility for this monthly allowance, nor does it affect the amount paid.

CHILDREN OF WOMEN VIETNAM VETERANS

After Congress established special benefits in 1997 for some veterans' children with spina bifida, additional research pointed to a link between birth defects and the service of female veterans in Vietnam. So lawmakers authorized VA to provide benefits to the offspring of these veterans.

Like the spina bifida program, this broader program began after researchers found a high incidence of certain birth defects among the children of women who served in Vietnam during the war. Researchers are uncertain whether the birth defects are linked to Agent Orange, a powerful defoliant used during the war, or something else these women were exposed to while on active duty.

Eligibility

Like the benefits for children with spina bifida, the program for the children of women Vietnam veterans has eligibility rules for the veteran and the child.

The mother must be a female veteran who served in Vietnam between February 28, 1961, and May 7, 1975. The program does not cover the offspring of male veterans.

The child must be the natural child of the female veteran. The child could have been born at any time since the veteran's service in Vietnam. Covered birth defects are identified by a case-by-case determination. Covered birth defects do not include familial disorders, birth-related injuries, and fetal or neonatal infirmities with well-established causes.

Health Care

The U.S. Department of Veterans Affairs will pay for the health care services and supplies needed to treat the birth defect, including psychological care, medication, and prosthetics.

Unlike VA's spina bifida program, this benefit only applies to the treatment of identified birth defects. Medical problems unrelated to the birth defect are the responsibility of the veteran.

Under this program, most health care is provided by private-sector facilities and professionals, although some care may come from VA doctors or VA hospitals. Although the benefit resembles health care insurance, there is no annual premium for eligible veterans and their families, and no deductibles or copayments for covered services.

Application

Women Vietnam veterans who have natural children with birth defects must go through an administrative process with VA before their children can receive any benefits.

Initial application for coverage can be made at the nearest VA medical center or by contacting VA's Health Administration Center (HAC) toll-free at 1-888-820-1756; by writing to HAC, P.O. Box 469065, Denver, CO 80246; or by visiting www.va.gov/hac.

Other Benefits

When the children of women Vietnam veterans qualify for health care coverage for birth defects, they also become eligible for other benefits. VA will provide vocational rehabilitation if the child has a feasible job-related goal. VA will also pay a monthly allowance that in 2010 ranged from $131 to $1,678, depending on the nature and severity of the birth defect.

GULF WAR FAMILIES

Since the end of the first Gulf War, there have been stories about the health-related concerns of people who served in the Middle East during the war. Some of the stories dealt with spouses and children who believe they became ill because of something the veteran in the family brought home from overseas. Some doctors concur that this has happened.

But as this book goes to press, the consensus within the medical community was that Gulf War veterans do not experience a higher incidence of birth defects in their families. Nor have doctors found anything—a bacteria, a virus, or a toxic substance—that veterans spread to their families after the war.

In order for the ill spouses and children of Gulf War veterans to receive health care or some type of disability payment from the government, Congress will have to pass a federal law specifically giving those benefits to them.

FIVE

CARE FOR CHRONICALLY ILL OR ELDERLY VETERANS

In This Chapter:

- *VA Domiciliaries*
- *State Veterans Homes*
- *Adult Day Care*
- *U.S. Retirement Homes*
- *For Spouses*

For a young country, the United States has many traditions. One custom that goes back to colonial days involves special homes provided by communities for veterans who are unable to care for themselves, either because of their war wounds or because of simple old age.

In those settings, the men—and now increasingly, the women, too—who have served their country in uniform are given an extra measure of protection and care.

Those facilities have come under conflicting pressures in recent years. The nation's World War II veterans have, as a group, passed into retirement, and the "Old Soldiers' Homes" are receiving unprecedented numbers of applications.

At the same time, governments and charitable organizations are finding themselves squeezed financially. Revenues aren't increasing fast enough to keep up with responsibilities.

Former servicemembers should be aware that rules and services for veterans homes and other facilities treating ill or elderly veterans are likely to change as these traditional facilities are fitted into the nation's medical system for the new century.

VA DOMICILIARIES

Under the medical system operated by the Department of Veterans Affairs, a special kind of facility is available for people who need long-term care but who have some ability to take care of themselves.

Called "domiciliaries," these VA facilities offer rehabilitation, long-term residency, and so-called maintenance care for many former servicemembers. They are, in short, the veterans' homes.

Like VA nursing homes (see chapter 4), VA domiciliaries are part of the overall medical system operated by the Department of Veterans Affairs.

Eligibility

Perhaps the most important rule for VA domiciliaries involves the availability of space. No one is admitted to a VA domiciliary unless it has the room for one more resident. And like many other facilities catering to the nation's aging population, the domiciliaries are finding their resources put under great pressure as their waiting lists expand.

The eligibility rules are broadly written and depend on a number of factors.

Military Service: Everyone admitted to a VA domiciliary must have served in the military, either on active duty or in the reserves. They don't have to have served in wartime or to have served for any specific period of time.

Discharge Status: Only a narrow range of discharges make a veteran ineligible for admission to a VA domiciliary. Those are discharges officially rated as "under other than honorable conditions." These discharges shouldn't be confused with dishonorable discharges. They're two different things.

Income: In most cases, to be eligible a veteran must also meet a very specific income standard: The veteran's annual income must be less than the rate set up for people receiving a VA pension, plus the additional VA payment known as "Aid and Attendance."

The figure for VA pensions plus "Aid and Attendance" changes annually. For 2010, it was about $20,000 for people without dependents, slightly higher for those with families.

Special Cases: Federal law gives the secretary of the Department of Veterans Affairs broad authority to admit people to domiciliaries when they have "no adequate means of support." Usually, this applies to veterans who exceed the income limitation by relatively small amounts.

Nevertheless, veterans admitted under this special-case rule must be able to take care of themselves. That means they must be able to feed themselves, dress with minimal assistance, and bathe without help.

Those special-case veterans also must be able to make "competent and rational decisions," especially concerning their admission to the domiciliary. VA domiciliaries are not for the long-term care of mental patients.

Spouses: Some long-term care facilities in the private sector permit spouses to live in their facilities with patients. Under VA rules, however, only veterans can be admitted.

Costs

Low-income veterans are entitled to have the government pay all the bills for their stays in VA domiciliaries. "Low income" means people who earn less than the amounts detailed in the "Eligibility" section above.

Nevertheless, recipients of VA pensions will have their monthly pensions reduced if they're admitted to VA domiciliaries. The amount of the reduction varies, depending on the specific kind of VA pension received by the veteran, as does the effective date of the reduction. Those reductions leave recipients of VA pensions in domiciliaries with between $30 and $90 per month.

Special rules apply if the recipient of a VA pension has a spouse or another dependent. When those veterans are admitted to VA domiciliaries, other family members can receive the rest of the VA pension.

But this doesn't happen automatically. The family member must take the initiative. Contact the veterans benefits counselor or some other official at the VA domiciliary, who can start the paperwork.

If a veteran receiving VA disability compensation is admitted to a VA domiciliary, there is no reduction in the amount of that monthly check.

Veterans who earn more than the income limit can still be admitted to VA domiciliaries, but they will be billed for their care. Typically, those bills are lower than the costs in nongovernmental facilities.

Veterans not entitled to priority admission can use their private health insurance plans or the government's Medicare insurance to pay for care.

Details of the Facilities

For many of the nation's veterans, VA domiciliaries are—in a word—home. They are places where veterans live and pursue their own interests, with many of the day-to-day responsibilities of running a household left to others.

Domiciliaries provide their residents not only with food and shelter, but also, if needed, with clothing and toiletry items.

Medical care by VA professionals is another service offered to the residents of VA domiciliaries. In fact, most of those facilities are located on the grounds of VA medical centers.

Many of the ingredients for a useful, interesting life are offered at the facilities, from recreational and social events to a safe, secure place to meet with family and friends.

To the extent permitted by any health problems, residents are expected to help the staff by performing light housekeeping chores.

Unlike VA nursing homes, which generally limit stays to six months, there is no time limit for residency in a VA domiciliary.

Again, domiciliary residents have to be able to take care of many of their own needs. The facilities simply don't have the staffs to meet all of the needs for all of their residents. Residents of a VA domiciliary who become unable to care for themselves may be transferred to a private or state-run facility that provides the needed level of care.

Locations

A state-by-state listing of VA medical facilities appears at the back of this book. If a hospital or clinic has a VA domiciliary, it is mentioned there.

STATE VETERANS HOMES

Not all the nursing homes and domiciliaries for veterans are operated by the Department of Veterans Affairs. In 2010, state governments operated nearly 140 of their own facilities. Although they go by many names, they're generally known as "state veterans homes."

State veterans homes are operated by the state governments under a special, close arrangement with the VA system. They receive some VA funds for operation, follow VA admissions rules, pass periodic VA inspections, and receive VA money for construction.

Many residents of state veterans homes come directly from VA nursing homes. Unlike VA nursing homes, the state facilities rarely have a time limit on stays.

> **C**onsumer tip: A nursing home can call itself anything it wants. Ask if it "has VA recognition." If it does, you know it meets VA standards.

Some of these state facilities are allied with state-run hospitals for veterans. Like the VA system, states operate both domiciliaries and nursing homes. Domiciliaries tend to be for people who can take care of most—if not all—of their needs. State nursing homes are for patients who require long-term care but who don't need the full services of a hospital.

It's not always clear from the name of a state veterans home whether it's a domiciliary or a nursing home. But to receive VA financial support, it must be one or the other or both.

Eligibility

Each state has its own detailed eligibility rules for its state veterans homes.

As with VA facilities, sometimes the most important rule is that no one will be admitted unless there is room. Waiting lists for state veterans homes are common.

The federal government has set down broad rules for domiciliaries and nursing homes, within which the states must operate if they want to keep their federal funding. Remember, these are minimum requirements. States can open their facilities to other categories of veterans, who may have to pay more for their care.

Domiciliaries: Eligibility rules are the same as for VA domiciliaries.

Nursing Homes: Residents must fall into one of the following categories:

- Service-connected disability.
- Disabled by a condition not related to military service and unable to pay for private nursing.
- Discharged with a disability.

- Receiving VA disability compensation.
- Eligible for VA disability compensation but receiving military retired pay instead.

Costs

Unlike VA nursing homes and domiciliaries, state veterans homes don't provide free care to their patients.

The costs for their services tend to be lower than costs at private-sector facilities, however, because the Department of Veterans Affairs is subsidizing the facilities for some expenses.

There are no automatic reductions in VA Disability Compensation or VA pensions following admission to a state veterans home.

Details of the Facilities

State veterans homes provide a complete array of services for the long-term resident, ranging from medical and rehabilitative care to recreational facilities and social events.

A few state veterans homes are located on the grounds of state-owned hospitals, assuring quick access to a full range of medical services.

Some state veterans homes are actually part of larger facilities, but VA rules require them to house veterans in areas set apart from civilian patients.

Locations

An appendix at the back of this book has a state-by-state listing of state veterans homes. The list includes state veterans hospitals. Information is also available online at www.nasvh.org.

ADULT DAY CARE

As the average age of the nation's veterans gets higher, new ways are being found to take care of their needs. A program in the VA system is called Adult Day Care. As the name implies, it is similar to day-care programs that have been around for many years for children.

Veterans taking part in Adult Day Care may live in their own homes, with their children, or in a group setting, but they spend many of the daylight hours in an Adult Day Care center.

Increasingly, Adult Day Care programs are opening up in VA medical centers, but not all the care is provided within these facilities. There's a separate, but related, program that uses VA money to subsidize the treatment of veterans in Adult Day Care programs run by the private sector.

VA's Adult Day Care is primarily a health care program designed to improve the well-being of frail elderly patients. It is distinguished from private-sector programs that mostly provide a social outlet for elderly people who may be isolated from others.

Eligibility

The two versions of the program—in VA facilities and in private facilities—are governed by the same eligibility rules.

> VA officials will help families find facilities offering long-term care in the private sector. That's a service they offer all veterans. Family members shouldn't hesitate to ask for help.

Admission is limited. Not everyone eligible for care in a VA domiciliary, for example, qualifies for admission to the Adult Day Care program. Generally, eligibility for both the VA-run and private-sector programs is determined by the needs of the patient, with the highest priority going to frail and elderly veterans who are most likely to benefit from the program's services. Active-duty personnel who are released from military hospitals whose doctors say they need Adult Day Care are also eligible.

Costs

Adult Day Care in a VA facility is free. It doesn't affect a veteran's disability compensation, VA pension, or military retired pay.

Private-sector facilities charge for their services, and the individual veteran is responsible for paying those bills. Programs such as Medicare and Medicaid can reimburse veterans for some—perhaps even all—of those expenses.

Details of Facilities

A proper Adult Day Care facility does more than provide food and shelter for part of each day. It offers medical care, some physical therapy, limited rehabilitative services, recreational outlets, and reliable nutrition.

Whether run by VA or the private sector, each facility is under the overall supervision of a physician and provides assistance with eating, bathing, and toileting. Records are kept on each patient.

The private-sector facilities must meet certain minimum standards laid down by the Department of Veterans Affairs.

Locations

An appendix at the back of this book has a state-by-state listing of VA medical facilities. If a hospital or clinic has an on-site Adult Day Care center, it is mentioned there.

U.S. RETIREMENT HOMES

For more than a century, two places have offered special care and attention for older veterans. The U.S. Soldiers' and Airmen's Home in Washington, D.C., and the U.S. Naval Home in Gulfport, Mississippi, provide long-term care for men and women who once served their country in uniform and who are now in their retirement years.

Residents have the best that a grateful nation can offer to its older veterans—from a full range of up-to-date medical facilities in a secure environment to every imaginable recreational opportunity and the companionship of fellow veterans.

Veterans come in two basic varieties—male and female—and these two U.S. veterans homes have long accepted women veterans as residents.

Despite their names, both facilities accept people who have served in every branch of the military.

Eligibility

For most of their histories, the two homes operated independently, with their own eligibility rules. Now they have identical admissions procedures.

One major rule weeds out most officers. To be accepted in the homes, veterans must have been enlisted personnel or warrant officers during their entire time on active duty, or they must have been officers who spent at least 50 percent of their active-duty time as enlisted people or warrant officers.

Once veterans meet this basic requirement, they must also fit into one of these five categories:

- Retired with twenty years on active duty and at least sixty years old.
- Unable to earn a livelihood because of a disability that's officially considered service connected.
- Have served in an official theater of war and unable to earn a livelihood because of a disability not connected to military service.
- Have once received hostile fire pay or combat pay and now unable to earn a livelihood because of a disability not connected to military service.
- Be a female veteran who served in uniform before 1948.

Coast Guard veterans can qualify for admission, if they meet the admission rules above and if at least some of their active-duty service was during wartime when the Coast Guard operated under the control of the Department of the Navy.

Costs

Many of the basic necessities of life—food, shelter, and medical care—are part of the services offered to the residents of the U.S. veterans homes. But they're not completely free. Residents give up between 35 percent and 65 percent of their income, depending on the services they need.

Details of Facilities

With renovations steadily in progress, the U.S. veterans homes are on their way to offering private rooms and baths to all residents.

Everyone on active duty automatically contributes fifty cents each month for the U.S. veterans homes. The facilities also receive all fines imposed by courts-martial.

Virtual cities-within-cities, they offer a wide array of arts and crafts, hobby shops, libraries, social events, indoor recreation facilities, and outdoor exercise areas.

Extensive medical services are part of the leases. At no cost, residents are eligible for hospital care, assisted living arrangements, specialized medical care, and rehabilitation and physical therapy.

As this book went to press in 2010, the U.S. Naval Home in Gulfport, Mississippi, was preparing to reopen after temporarily closing in 2005 due to extensive damage from Hurricane Katrina. The closure permitted major improvements in the facility.

More Information

More information about the Washington and Gulfport campuses can be obtained by writing to the Armed Forces Retirement

Home, 3700 N. Capitol Street, N.W., Washington, DC 20011, or by visiting www.afrh.gov.

AND SPOUSES, TOO

The "Old Soldiers' Homes" discussed earlier in this chapter are for veterans. Unlike some private-sector facilities for the elderly, which admit the spouses of the people needing care, these homes don't have the room to permit spouses to stay, too.

But some special facilities, sponsored and financially supported by veterans groups, keep families together when one spouse needs special care. In most cases, they're also open to the widows and widowers of veterans.

Knollwood

Formerly known as the Army Distaff Hall, Knollwood is located in Washington, DC, and is open to retired officers from all services, and their spouses and female relatives, including widows, mothers, daughters, sisters, and mothers-in-law. Retired Reserve and National Guard officers are also eligible for admission, along with their female relatives.

For more information, write to the Army Distaff Foundation, 6200 Oregon Avenue, N.W., Washington, DC 20015. Their website is www.armydistaff.org.

Vinson Hall

Located in McLean, Virginia, Vinson Hall was founded by the Navy-Marine-Coast Guard Residence Foundation and is open to retired officers of all services and their spouses, widows, and parents, as well as other relatives of retired officers on a case-by-case basis. Vinson Hall consists of three campuses in McLean, each dedicated to a special level of care—independent living, assisted living, and dementia support.

For more information, write to Vinson Hall Corp., 6251 Old Dominion Drive, McLean, VA 22101. Their website is www.vinsonhall.org.

Air Force Villages

Retired officers from all services and their widows or widowers are eligible for residency at the Air Force Villages in San Antonio, Texas. The homes are also open to young widows and children of Air Force officers for one year.

For more information, write to Air Force Village Foundation, 5100 John D. Ryan Boulevard, San Antonio, TX 78245. Their website is www.airforcevillages.com.

Air Force Enlisted Village

The Air Force Enlisted Village in Shalimar, Florida, is open to widows and widowers of enlisted personnel who have retired from the Air Force, Air Force Reserve, or Air National Guard, as well as to a limited number of survivors from other services, retired couples, and younger widows.

For more information, write to Air Force Enlisted Village, 92 Sunset Lane, Shalimar, FL 32579. Their website is www.afenlistedwidows.org.

SIX

DISABILITY PAY

In This Chapter:

- *Military Disability Retirement*
- *Temporary Disability Retirement*
- *Disability Compensation*
- *Disability Severance Pay*

Military service is dangerous, even during peacetime. Veterans are eligible for some sort of financial payment from their government for injuries and illnesses that resulted from time in uniform, or for medical problems that were aggravated by military service.

The people at the heart of the government's system of disability pay were permanently crippled while serving their country. But most recipients of disability pay—especially the VA's disability compensation—aren't in that category. They are former servicemembers with physical ailments incurred during active duty or reserve service.

Both the military and the Department of Veterans Affairs provide monthly checks to veterans who can pass through all the legal hoops necessary to qualify for disability payments.

For a hundred years, federal law prohibited people from collecting both veteran's disability pay and military retired pay. Those barriers began to crumble in the early twenty-first century.

Also crumbling as this book went to press was the very concept of two government-run systems that provide payments to former service personnel with medical problems. Make sure you have up-to-the-minute information before making any major decisions.

DISABILITY COMPENSATION

Most veterans drawing pay for the lingering effects of illnesses or injuries related to military service are receiving—to use the precise term—"disability compensation" from the Department of Veterans Affairs.

Disability compensation is made in monthly payments to qualified veterans. Usually, Congress increases the amounts each year to keep pace with inflation. Payments are fully exempt from federal, state, and local income taxes.

Eligibility

Disability compensation can be paid to anyone who has served in the military, including members of the reserves and National Guard. There is no minimum time that a person must spend in uniform to qualify.

Two major groups of veterans are ineligible:

- Veterans who receive discharges officially rated as "under dishonorable conditions."
- Veterans with disabilities caused by "willful misconduct," such as those incurred during commission of a crime or during unauthorized absences, or because of drug or alcohol abuse.

Details of the Program

VA disability compensation is a monthly payment designed to offset the lost earning power caused by military-related health problems.

The severity of the disability is expressed as a percentage. The percentages start at 10 percent and go in increments of 10 percent up to 100 percent. There is a fixed amount of disability pay for each level of disability. In 2010, for example, the monthly payments ranged from $123 for a 10 percent disability to about $2,673 for a 100 percent disability. The amount usually increases each year by the same rate as the Consumer Price Index.

Not normally included in the rates for disability compensation are special payments for the loss of specific body parts—like eyes, hands, or legs—or the loss of the use of body parts, all for reasons connected with military service. These financial additions to regular VA disability compensation are called special monthly compensation, and can range up to $8,150 per month.

VA disability pay is not affected by a veteran's earnings or savings. This includes the $100,000 lump-sum payments to the most severely injured combat veterans under the military's Servicemember's Group Life Insurance Traumatic Injury protection Program, commonly known as TSGLI.

Application

The earliest you can apply for VA disability compensation is during your final days in uniform. Application may be made at any time after leaving the military. Most applications are made years—even decades—after a veteran's discharge.

Application is made by filling out VA Form 21-526, "Veteran's Application for Compensation or Pension." A copy can be obtained from any VA facility.

Claims are retroactive to the date of discharge only when made within a year of discharge.

Other Benefits

Veterans who receive VA disability compensation are also eligible to apply for several other benefits:

- Free lifetime VA medical care for the disability.
- Vocational rehabilitation.
- Dependents' allowance (if the disability is rated at 30 percent or higher).
- Financial help for spouses unable to care for themselves (if the veteran's disability is rated at 30 percent or higher).

Veterans rated with 100 percent VA disabilities may be eligible to use exchanges and commissaries at military installations, plus on-base recreational facilities, as may their spouses and dependent children.

To obtain access to on-base facilities, veterans and their family members must have a military identification card.

Military Retirees

Traditionally, military retirees have given up one dollar of their military retired pay for each dollar of VA disability pay they receive. Many veterans perceive that as an inequity, and they successfully lobbied Congress to change the 100-year-old prohibition.

Unfortunately, lawmakers didn't eliminate the old system. They modified it, allowing certain categories of military retirees to collect portions of both payments, while introducing a third payment into an already confusing situation.

Two things are clear: The new rules apply only to military retirees, and some military retirees still lose some of their VA disability pay.

Currently, military retirees with disabilities caused directly by combat or combat-related training receive "combat-related special compensation." Technically, they still lose their VA disability pay, but this new payment equals the amount of lost VA money. Eligible for this benefit are people with regular, length-of-service retirements and disability retirements. Payments under this program are tax-free.

A second system—called "concurrent retirement and disability payments"—provides extra money to all military retirees with disabilities rated 50 percent or more, not just those with combat- and training-related medical problems. Again, folks lose their VA disability pay, but this second system provides extra money which in 2010 ranges from $194 a month for a 50 percent disability to $974 monthly for a 90 percent disability. Those rates will increase 10 percent each year, until they equal VA disability pay by the year 2014. Retirees with 100 percent VA disabilities began receiving their full rates for both military retirements and VA disability pay in January 2005. Payments under this program are taxable.

Note that under these two programs, some military retirees still lose one dollar of retired pay for each dollar of VA disability pay, without receiving a financial offset from the government, specifically:

- People who received medical retirements after less than 20 years in uniform and who don't have VA disabilities based upon combat injuries, and
- Veterans discharged with disability ratings of 40 percent or lower which aren't based upon combat injuries.

Fine Points

The foundation for a successful claim for VA disability compensation is laid in a military member's last weeks on active duty, specifically in the physical examination that everyone on active duty should receive before being discharged.

Sometimes military physicians will offer to waive the physical or to conduct an abbreviated exam. If you're still on active duty, insist on a thorough examination. You have a right to it. Besides, it may be the last time you receive a physical in a while. Many employer-paid health plans don't cover routine physicals.

In fact, you also have a right to apply for VA disability compensation as part of your out-processing from active duty. Many transition counselors advise servicemembers to apply for compensation for a minor problem—say, a hurt back that bothers you only some days or an injured joint that you feel only if a storm is coming. By filing a claim, even one that you know is going to be rejected, you're ensuring that the VA will preserve your medical records. Decades later, if that back problem or tricky joint worsens, it will be much easier to prove a connection between that problem and your military service.

Finally, whether you're approaching your discharge or you've been a civilian for decades, to ensure that you supply the proper details and documentation when applying for VA disability compensation, you should discuss the procedure beforehand with a VA counselor or a professional service officer from a veterans group.

MILITARY DISABILITY RETIREMENT

Long before the United States had the Department of Veterans Affairs or the Veterans Administration, it had people who were permanently disabled while serving their country in uniform. To protect the financial needs of those veterans, the military devised its own programs offering lifelong income and other benefits.

The military's disability retirement system has undergone many changes throughout the years. Usually, servicemembers are covered by the rules in effect on the day they came into the military.

The general provisions now in effect date to 1949. The specific details that follow cover the disability retirement rules for people who joined the military on or after September 7, 1980. Slightly different rules apply to veterans whose service began earlier.

> Both VA and Department of Defense disabilities are expressed as percentages. Beware comparing them. A 30 percent VA disability isn't the same as a 30 percent Department of Defense disability.

As always, keep in mind that minor changes in the rules are made frequently by the laws that Congress passes, by interpretations made by the courts, or by policies established by the military. Before taking major action affecting a disability retirement from the military, make sure you have an up-to-the-minute understanding of the rules.

Eligibility

A military disability retirement is available to everyone in the military—active-duty and reservist—who becomes unable to perform military duties because of a permanent injury or illness.

To be eligible, servicemembers must meet two basic criteria:

1. The disability must be permanent.
2. The disability cannot result from "intentional misconduct," "willful neglect," or an unauthorized absence.

People with less than twenty years in the military—who are thus ineligible for a normal retirement—must be officially rated as being at least 30 percent disabled before they can qualify for a disability retirement from the military.

Details of the Program

Two formulas are used to compute the size of a disability retirement check from the military. Veterans are entitled to use the formula that results in the most generous disability payment for them.

1. They can multiply the average basic pay from their highest-paying 36 months in uniform by 2.5 percent for

each year of service. This monthly payment is called a "disability retirement based upon length of service."

2. Under a second option, veterans multiply the average basic pay from their highest-paying 36 months in uniform by the percentage assigned to their disability. That's what they would receive as disability retired pay. This is called a "disability retirement based upon percentage of disability."

These formulas apply to people who first joined the military after September 8, 1980. Veterans who joined before that date use the amount of basic pay in their last military paycheck.

Payments for a disability retirement from the military cannot exceed 75 percent of the servicemember's monthly basic pay. Payments usually increase every year with cost-of-living adjustments, or COLAs, that typically offset purchasing power lost to inflation.

Application

Generally, servicemembers don't have to take any action to apply for a disability retirement from the military. If medical problems make a servicemember unable to perform his or her official duties, the military will begin a detailed review of the person's fitness for service that may end up with the servicemember receiving a disability retirement.

Technically, a veteran also can apply for a military disability retirement at any time after leaving active duty. There is no time limit for applications.

For postdischarge applications, veterans first must petition their service's Board for the Correction of Military Records to change their discharge to a disability retirement. That petition is made by filling out DD Form 293, "Application for Review of Discharge from the Armed Forces of the United States," obtainable from any military personnel office, military retiree affairs office, or VA benefits office.

Second, if the corrections board rules in favor of a veteran, then a medical board must review the veteran's records and make the basic decision about eligibility for a disability retirement and set the level of the disability.

Anyone trying to correct a discharge—to obtain a military disability retirement or for any other reason—should take advantage of the free, expert advice obtainable from a military retiree affairs office, a veterans group, or a VA office.

Other Benefits

Veterans with military disability retirements are like other military retirees, even if they haven't spent 20 years in uniform. They retain their own military ID cards, and they continue to get access to on-base services and facilities. They keep these benefits even if they later apply for VA disability compensation and waive all their taxable military retired pay for the VA's tax-free payments.

Veterans eligible for disability retired pay from the military can have their spouses treated in military hospitals and clinics, under the same rules that apply to the spouses of other military retirees. The rights of a spouse to treatment in a military medical facility aren't taken away if a retiree waives all taxable military retired pay to receive tax-free VA disability compensation.

Again, like veterans with regular military retirements, an ex-servicemember eligible for disability retired pay from the military can provide an income for a spouse after the ex-servicemember's death by enrolling in the military's Survivor Benefit Plan (SBP).

Fine Points

Once the military rates a disability by assigning it a percentage, that figure cannot be changed at another time. By contrast, veterans with VA disability compensation frequently have the government increase the percentage rating given to a disability.

It helps to understand why that happens. The military gives disability retirements to people because they cannot perform their most recent duties. If the disability worsens after discharge, the military expects veterans to turn to the VA system for redress. The military's disability rating system is, basically, a one-time deal.

As for the tax status of military disability retirements, this section has focused on the rules that apply to people leaving the military at the beginning of the twenty-first century. Veterans of an earlier era are covered by different rules.

Military disability retirements are tax exempt for veterans who meet one of the following criteria regarding September 24, 1975:

- Were in the military on that date.
- Were already receiving disability retired pay on that date.
- Were in the military before that date.
- Became eligible for a disability retirement after that date because of a combat-related injury.

Veterans who entered the military after September 24, 1975, and who are leaving service with disabilities that are only partially based on combat-related injuries will be able to shield from taxes only that portion of their total military disability retirement pay that is based on the combat injuries.

TEMPORARY DISABILITY RETIREMENT

Not all disabilities are permanent. Even with the latest medical technology, doctors aren't always able to tell which patients will recover or how much of their health they will regain.

When military people enter that fuzzy medical realm—with disabilities that make them incapable of serving but that might not be severe or permanent enough to justify a discharge—they are placed in a special status. The Temporary Disability Retired List, or TDRL, is an administrative category to which military people are assigned until their medical conditions stabilize. About 10,000 people on active duty end up on the TDRL each year.

As this book went to press in 2010, the TDRL was a likely candidate for a major overhaul. If you're injured on active duty and wonder whether you're eligible for the TDRL, check with your personnel office to ensure you have the latest, most comprehensive information.

Eligibility

Personnel are placed on the TDRL after a lengthy, formal medical screening. Military people who are placed on the TDRL fall into two basic categories:

1. Disqualified from active duty because of a disability that may not be permanent.
2. Disqualified from active duty because of a disability that may be permanent, but whose severity (the percentage rating assigned to the disability) is unknown.

Details of the Program

Servicemembers on the TDRL have no active-duty responsibilities, but they must report for periodic medical examinations at least every eighteen months. Those examinations or other formal reviews of medical records can result in a decision at any time to have the person return to active duty or be discharged.

Pay for people on the TDRL is at least 50 percent but cannot exceed 75 percent of their most recent basic pay.

Servicemembers can choose between two formulas to determine their pay while on the TDRL:

1. They can multiply the amount of basic pay in their last monthly paycheck by 2.5 percent for each year of service. The resulting figure is their pay while on the TDRL.
2. Under a second option, veterans multiply the amount of basic pay in their last monthly paycheck by the percent-

age assigned to their disability. That's what they will receive as temporary disability retired pay.

Remember: Whichever formula is used, service members are guaranteed at least 50 percent of their last basic pay. The longest anyone can spend on the TDRL is five years. There is no legal provision for waivers of the five-year limit.

Application

Servicemembers cannot directly volunteer to go on the TDRL, but they can make their cases to be placed in that category if their medical fitness to remain on active duty is being considered by a Physical Evaluation Board (PEB).

Military people who are being evaluated by a PEB can also argue to avoid the TDRL and seek instead to be returned to active duty or to be discharged with a disability.

Other Benefits

While on the TDRL, military members and their families have access to the same on-base facilities that are open to other active-duty retirees.

Especially important to many families is continuing eligibility of family members to military medical care, either on base or through Tricare.

TDRL recipients are also eligible for treatment in VA medical facilities and for VA disability compensation. VA medical treatment doesn't affect eligibility for military medical care, but accepting VA disability compensation makes people ineligible for TDRL pay.

Fine Points

Since TDRL recipients have the same benefits as other military retirees, they also encounter the same restrictions.

A major benefit that's lost is eligibility for on-base housing. Military retirees don't continue to live in military housing and, as a general rule, neither do TDRL families. Base commanders have some authority to permit TDRL recipients to stay in on-base quarters for periods up to 180 days. That's the commander's call. Don't expect special treatment if an installation has a long line of active-duty families waiting for government quarters.

For servicemembers returned to active duty from the TDRL, their TDRL time counts toward pay purposes, but not toward retirement.

Take the case of an E-6 who goes into TDRL status after twelve years on active duty. If that enlisted person spends four years drawing TDRL pay, then returns to active duty, basic pay will be calculated as an E-6 with sixteen years. But that enlisted member will need to spend eight more years on active duty to qualify for retirement at twenty years' service.

DISABILITY SEVERANCE PAY

If the disability retired pay administered by the military and the VA's disability compensation were the only financial payments made to active-duty people, reservists, and National Guardsmen with medical problems, however, thousands of people every year would fall through a huge crack in the rules.

A large number of servicemembers have injuries or illnesses that make them unfit for continued service on active duty, but they don't have enough time to meet the eight-years-in-uniform requirement for a military disability retirement.

To meet the financial needs of the military folks who have less serious medical problems, the armed forces maintain something called "disability severance pay." It is also often called "medical severance pay" or "medical separation pay."

Disability severance pay is among the items that will probably change as a result of a DoD review of benefits still underway as this book went to press in 2010. Your personnel office will have the latest details. Check with them before making any important decisions.

Eligibility

When military people are unable to perform the duties appropriate for their rank, they may be discharged with disability severance pay. Eligibility is based on both length of service and the severity of the disability, as determined by the usual rating system for disabilities.

To qualify for disability severance pay, military people must have less than twenty years of military service. Their disability must be rated as less than 30 percent, and three conditions affecting the disability must be met:

1. It cannot result from "intentional misconduct" or "willful neglect."
2. It cannot have occurred during a period of unauthorized leave.
3. It cannot have existed before the servicemember comes on active duty.

On this last point, there is a small loophole. If a medical condition exists before the person entered the military, but the problem was aggravated by military service, then people may qualify for disability severance pay. Of course, they must meet all the other eligibility conditions for the payment.

It's important to note that two major groups of military people are ineligible for disability severance pay because they qualify for other payments. Not eligible are people with twenty years in uniform (who qualify for regular military retirements) and people with disabilities rated at 30 percent or more (who qualify for military disability retirements or VA disability compensation).

Details of the Program

Disability severance pay is a payment made on a person's last day in the military. Unlike the other disability pays discussed above, which result in monthly checks, disability severance pay is a onetime payment.

The amount is determined by a specific formula. For each year on active duty a servicemember is entitled to receive two months' basic pay. In this formula, months are rounded to the nearest year. Thus, someone with nine years and seven months on active-duty would be credited with ten years. Someone with nine years and five months would be credited with just nine years.

Despite the formula, everyone paid for injuries or illness in a combat zone receives disability severance pay equal to at least twelve months of their basic pay. Folks with diabilities based upon non-combat service qualify for severance pay worth at least six months of basic pay.

For most people, the figure for basic pay that's used in the formula is the amount appropriate for their rank and years of service during the last month on active duty.

For people who have satisfactorily held a temporary higher grade on active duty, disability severance pay can be computed using the basic pay currently given to military folks in that higher rank and years-of-service category.

Disability severance pay based on noncombat injuries is taxable. When the injuries or illness were received in a combat zone, the benefit is nontaxable.

Application
As happens with the other DoD-administered disability pays, servicemembers cannot directly volunteer for disability severance pay. The closest they come to genuine input occurs if their medical fitness to remain on active duty is being considered by a Physical Evaluation Board.

For most people, disability severance pay is a benefit of last resort. It's better than being discharged with nothing, but it's usually inferior to a military disability retirement, or even assignment to the Temporary Disability Retirement List.

Other Benefits
Recipients of disability severance pay have cut their relationship with the military. They aren't entitled to any ongoing, special benefits from the armed forces.

Usually, they are ineligible to join the reserves or National Guard. The rationale is that if they're physically incapable of serving on active duty, they're physically incapable of serving in the reserves. People with special skills, however, may be able to wiggle into a reserve assignment at a lower rank. Since disability severance pay is specifically based on the inability to perform duties at one's active-duty rank, highly skilled veterans may be able to argue that they can perform reserve duties at a lower rank.

Recipients of disability severance pay, like other disabled veterans, are eligible for medical treatment in VA facilities. Because their disabilities are officially rated as service connected, it should be easier for them to receive treatment than veterans without disabilities or veterans with medical problems not related to military service.

Veterans who get the military's disability severance pay can also receive VA disability pay. However, when the military severance was for a non-combat-related medical problem, veterans must reimburse the government for their severance pay before they can receive VA disability compensation. That repayment is made through a monthly deduction from the VA disability pay.

That may sound like a high price to pay for the VA benefit, but most veterans discover it's a good deal. Years of a regular monthly check from the VA quickly dwarf the one-time military payment.

Beware the trap of "overcomparing" benefits, then assuming that you're entitled to all the perks of a similar benefit. Disability severance pay is a specific program, with clearly defined benefits set by federal law. It may be similar to a disability retirement, but you're not considered a military retiree if you receive disability severance pay. It also may seem quite similar to the exit bonuses that got heavy use during the 1990s. But don't count on getting continued access to exchanges and commissaries like recipients of the Voluntary Separation Incentive or Special Separation Benefit. Those were separate programs, operating quite differently from disability severance pay.

SEVEN

VETERANS PENSIONS

In This Chapter:

- *Improved Pension*
- *Old-Law Pension*
- *Section 306 Pension*

Military veterans were the beneficiaries of the original social safety nets that were erected by the federal government and by the states. At the time of the nation's first wars, veterans who were unable to take care of themselves were given a hand by their communities.

With the creation of the Veterans Administration and later the Department of Veterans Affairs, that legacy was systematized and continued. Today, the VA pension program is the major benefit that helps veterans who are unable to take care of themselves for reasons unrelated to their military service.

The VA pension program gives regular monthly checks to former servicemembers with limited incomes and health problems that prevent them from earning a living. Unlike recipients of VA disability compensation, recipients of a VA pension don't have to show a link between their medical problems and their military service.

It's often called "live pension" by specialists in veterans affairs, to distinguish it from the so-called death pension paid to the widows, widowers, and other dependents of some veterans.

Recipients of VA pensions are eligible for a variety of other benefits, including a high priority for VA medical care, vocational training, death benefits, and continuing payments to widows, widowers, and dependent children.

Like many government programs, VA's pension program has undergone fundamental changes over the years, and its rules have been completely rewritten several times. Currently, veterans are receiving VA pensions under three different versions of the pension program: the Improved pension, the Old-Law pension, and the Section 306 pension.

Since January 1, 1979, the Improved pension is the only one open for applications. People who received pensions under one of the earlier versions of the program have the option of switching to the current Improved pension.

IMPROVED PENSION

The Improved pension plan is open to veterans with low incomes, meager financial resources, and poor health.

Recipients must have disabilities that aren't connected in any way with active duty. Those with health problems that stem from their military service are eligible for VA disability compensation.

Pension recipients get monthly checks from the government. The size of the checks varies, depending on the number of dependents and the severity of restrictions upon day-to-day living caused by the veteran's medical condition.

Eligibility

Veterans must pass through a series of very specific legal hoops to qualify for a VA pension. Here are some of the major requirements:

- Service must include at least one day on active duty during wartime.
- Veterans who joined the military before September 7, 1980, must serve at least 90 days. Those who joined afterward must serve 24 months.
- The veteran's discharge must be rated as "under other than dishonorable conditions" or better.
- The veteran must have limited income and net worth. (Income must be less than the rates listed below, in "Details of the Program.") The size of allowable assets isn't specified by law, but veterans advocates say pensions are usually granted to people with less than $30,000 in assets.
- The veteran must have a disability officially rated as "permanent and total." VA rules outline very specific conditions that must be met before a disability can be given this rating.
- The disability cannot be due to "willful misconduct," which traditionally applies to cases of alcoholism, drug addiction, and venereal disease.

Veterans who are sixty-five years of age or older can qualify for a VA pension solely on the basis of income, without having a permanent and total disability.

Recipients of the two oldest VA pension programs—the Old-Law pension and Section 306 pension—have the option of switching to the Improved pension at any time. Once they make that choice, they cannot return to an Old-Law pension or Section 306 pension at another time.

Two other eligibility rules for the Improved pension are worthy of note:

- Veterans will lose their pensions if their income or net worth exceeds certain levels. Usually, the pension will be restored if income or worth falls back to a qualifying level.
- No one can receive a VA pension while he or she is also being paid VA disability compensation. Anyone eligible for both programs will have to pick one.

Details of the Program

The Improved pension provides a monthly income for qualified veterans. The exact amount varies with several factors, including the veteran's level of self-sufficiency and whether a spouse or other dependents live with the veteran.

The amount of the pension increases annually to keep up with inflation. Annual increases are the same amount and are given at the same time as increases in Social Security.

Below are listed the amounts of pension during the year 2010 for veterans fitting the major categories of the pension program. Remember that rates are approximate yearly maximums. Many veterans who qualify for VA pensions never receive the full amount because if they have additional income, their pensions are reduced by one dollar for each dollar from another source.

- *Without a spouse or child:* $11,800.
- *With one dependent (spouse or child):* $15,500.
- *Without dependents and unable to care for self:* $19,700.
- *With one dependent (spouse or child) and unable to care for self:* $23,400.
- *Without dependents and housebound:* $14,500.
- *With one dependent and housebound:* $18,100.
- *Two eligible veterans married to each other (total payment to couple):* $15,500.
- *Extra for each additional child:* $2,100.

Two other common conditions affect payments of Improved pensions: hospitalization and incarceration.

Hospitalization: Pensions for veterans receiving pensions at a with-spouse or with-dependents rate aren't affected by hospitalizations, even in a VA facility, or by admissions to domiciliaries or nursing homes; neither are the pensions of veterans without dependents or spouses who are hospitalized at VA expense.

Veterans without dependents or spouses who are admitted to a domiciliary or nursing home at VA expense have their checks reduced to a fixed amount monthly, which was $90 in 2010. The reduction begins four months after they enter the facility.

Incarceration: As a rule, veterans without spouses or other dependents cannot receive their Improved pensions if convicted and confined to a federal or state prison or to a local jail. Payments end on the sixty-first day of their confinement. After their release, veterans can resume receiving the pension if they still meet the eligibility rules.

For incarcerated veterans paid Improved pensions at the with-spouse or with-dependents rates, the monthly checks can continue to the spouse or children, but VA officials first must calculate what the spouse or children would receive under the VA's death benefit. The death benefit is compared with the Improved pension, and the spouse and children receive whichever monthly amount—Improved pension or death benefit—is smaller.

When a veteran's spouse or child is the one imprisoned, the Improved pension is recalculated. The veteran receives the pension at the rate applicable for people without a spouse or child.

To lose their pensions, veterans must be convicted. Payments are unaffected by pretrial confinement.

Income Restrictions

VA's Improved pension is primarily for low-income veterans. Generally, for each dollar of outside income, veterans lose one dollar of their Improved pension.

Unfortunately, the dollar-for-dollar reduction is only a general rule. Some kinds of income will affect the size of an Improved pension. Other kinds of income have no effect on a pension check. VA officials verify eligibility by checking the amount of income reported to the Internal Revenue Service on the veteran's annual income tax return.

Here are some sources of income that will *reduce* the size of an Improved pension check:

- Wages, dividends, and interest.
- Income of spouse.
- Income of children under legal age.
- DoD exit bonuses.
- Military retired pay or civil service retirement, even if a veteran has waived rights or refused to accept military retired pay or civil service retirement.
- Social Security's Old Age, Survivors, and Disability Insurance.
- Social Security death benefits.
- Commercial annuities.
- Insurance dividends.
- Pay for jury duty.

The following sources of income *don't* reduce the size of an Improved pension:

- Social Security's Supplemental Security Income.
- Value of property owned and lived in by veteran.
- Financial gifts from relatives and friends.
- Profit from sale of property.

Application

Veterans can apply for the Improved pension at any time after leaving active duty.

The formal method for requesting an Improved pension is submission of VA Form 21-526, "Veteran's Application for Compensation or Pension," which can be obtained from any VA facility.

Veterans may not know some of the precise information requested by the form, such as monthly Social Security benefits or exact periods of military service. When in doubt, applicants should provide their best understanding of the right information, followed by the notation "approx.," to indicate approximations.

Veterans filing their first request for VA benefits should include a copy of their discharge papers, typically DD Form 214. If the discharge papers have been lost, veterans can request new copies by filling out Standard Form 180, "Request Pertaining to Military Records," which is also obtainable from the nearest VA office and on the internet at www.archives.gov/veterans.

The applications can be submitted without discharge papers and using approximate information in order to get the paperwork moving. However, before they actually begin receiving VA's Improved pension, veterans will have to provide VA officials with exact figures and the appropriate discharge papers.

Benefits can be paid retroactively to the date the application was received, but veterans usually have to request retroactive payments when they first file their VA Form 21-526. There is a block on the form for that request.

Certification that a veteran has a "permanent and total" disability can be done through a written statement by a private physician. The odds of VA officials accepting these statements improve when doctors back up their judgment with diagnostic results (e.g., X-rays, lab tests) and submit their evaluations on a standardized form called FL 21-104, "Request for Medical Evidence from Non-VA Physician."

As you can see, the application procedures are very precise. This blizzard of paperwork can overpower many veterans. Before giving up, they should contact the nearest VA office or a professional veterans service officer working for a major veterans group. These professionals are paid to help. They understand the procedures, and they already have all the necessary forms.

Other Benefits

The Improved pension alone will not solve the financial problems of many veterans and their families. For people with additional needs, there are additional programs.

- *VA health care:* High priority for free inpatient and outpatient VA medical care.
- *Aid and Attendance:* Increase in pension check for people in nursing homes or in need of care. May also take the form of an increase in permitted additional income. The rates for Aid and Attendance include the housebound benefit described below.
- *Death pension:* Monthly payment to spouses of veterans eligible for—though not necessarily receiving—a VA pension at time of death.
- *Housebound benefit:* Increase in pension check for people permanently confined to their homes but otherwise capable of taking care of themselves.
- *Vocational training:* Up to twenty-four months of vocational training, followed by another eighteen months of job-placement help.

Fine Points

VA pensions are closed to people with employment and health problems caused by alcoholism, drug abuse, and venereal disease. Those three conditions come under the category of "willful misconduct," which federal law says makes veterans ineligible for pensions. Veterans with AIDS or HIV have been able to receive VA pensions. The "willful misconduct" restriction hasn't been applied to people with this illness.

In the hands of an experienced advisor, however, many veterans with those problems have been able to qualify for VA pensions. For example, skilled advocates have been able to argue successfully that cirrhosis of the liver—not the alcoholism that caused the cirrhosis—has made a particular veteran disabled, unemployable, and therefore eligible for an Improved pension. Since cirrhosis isn't officially listed as "willful misconduct," the veterans have received their pensions.

Winning these borderline cases takes experience and skill. Veterans and family members should rely on attorneys and service officers from the major veterans groups who have successfully split these legal hairs before.

Pensions can be paid retroactively to the date of the application. Sometimes a letter can constitute that first official "application." Letter-applications must clearly specify who the veteran is—by name and Social Security number, service number, or VA identification number. They must state that the veteran is applying for a pension and include the dates of military service. Letter-applications must be followed up as soon as possible by the formal applications on the forms mentioned above.

A final fine point of great importance: Pension recipients must stay below the income limits discussed earlier. At one time, they had to file annual income reports. Now, VA computers automatically check the tax returns veterans file with the Internal Revenue Service.

OLD-LAW PENSION

VA pensions first became available to veterans after World War I. The initial pension program, now called the Old-Law pension, continued almost until the start of the Vietnam War.

The Old-Law pension was closed to new applications in 1960. Everyone who has been receiving it can continue to receive it but these veterans also have the option to switch at any time to the newer Improved pension.

Most of the rules listed above for the Improved pension also apply to the earlier Old-Law pension. The information in this section deals only with areas in which the Old-Law pension differs from the Improved pension.

Eligibility

Eligibility rules are the same as for the Improved pension, with these two exceptions:

- Recipients must be veterans of World War II, or the Korean War.
- Recipients must have filed for the Old-Law pension before June 30, 1960.

Details of the Program

The details for the Old-Law pension are the same as for the Improved pension, with these exceptions:

- Pensions are reduced, usually by 50 percent, when a veteran who is receiving the Old-Law pension at the without-dependents rate is admitted to a VA facility. Reductions begin after seven months.
- Most veterans receiving Aid and Attendance lose that monthly payment two months after entering a VA facility. Instead, they begin receiving the smaller "housebound benefit."
- Most veterans without families who receive Aid and Attendance have their housebound benefit cut in half seven months after being admitted to a VA facility.

Income Restrictions

The following are exceptions to the income restrictions for the Improved pension:

- In determining a veteran's income, the incomes of a spouse and children under age eighteen aren't included. Also not figured into those calculations are separation pay, exit bonuses, any federal retirement pay that the veteran can receive but has refused to accept, and dividends from commercial insurance.
- Net profit from the sale of personal property or most real property (i.e., land, buildings) is counted as income.
- Net profit from the sale of a veteran's home isn't counted as income if the money is used to purchase another home within the same calendar year or the next calendar year.

- Net profit is calculated as the sales price, minus the value of the property on the day the veteran began receiving a VA pension.

Application
New applications for the Old-Law pension haven't been accepted since June 30, 1960. All new veterans must apply for the Improved pension. Everyone receiving the Old-Law pension is eligible, at any time, to switch to the Improved pension. Once made, that decision cannot be reversed.

Other Benefits
Other benefits for the Improved pension also apply to recipients of the Old-Law pension. VA officials may require Old-Law pension recipients who apply for Aid and Attendance or the housebound benefit to switch to the Improved pension before the additional benefits are approved.

Fine Points
Recipients of the Old-Law pension who lost this VA benefit because their income exceeded official limits, and who later become eligible again for a VA pension because their income dropped below the limits, are given the Improved pension, not the Old-Law pension.

People who erroneously lost their Old-Law pensions because their income exceeded the official limits, but who are able to prove their income was within the limits all along, can have their Old-Law pensions restored.

SECTION 306 PENSION
Between the original VA pension program, called here the Old-Law pension, and the current Improved pension, another pen-

sion program was on the books. It's commonly called the "Section 306 pension," a name derived from the section of the federal law that created it.

> The Old-Law pension and Section 306 pension are sometimes called "protected pensions." That's because recipients were protected from changes in their pensions after the newer Improved pension began in 1979.

Section 306 pensions were closed to new applications in 1978. Everyone who has been receiving the Section 306 pension can continue to receive it. They also have the option to switch at any time to the newer Improved pension.

Most of the rules listed above for the Improved pension also apply to the Section 306 pension. The information in this section deals only with areas in which the Section 306 pension differs from the Improved pension.

Eligibility

The eligibility rules for this pension are the same as for the Improved pension.

Details of the Program

All of the rules for the Improved pension apply, with this exception:

Some veterans will have their pensions reduced three months after admission to a VA domiciliary and four months after entering a VA medical facility or nursing home. This applies to veterans without dependents and to veterans who are paid Section 306 pensions at the without-dependents rate because they are not living with their spouse or supporting their children.

Income Restrictions

Income restrictions are the same as for the Improved pension with these exceptions:

- In determining a veteran's income, wages of family members under age eighteen aren't counted; neither are dividends from commercial insurance.
- Some medical expenses can be subtracted from total income to reduce the amount of income listed on annual VA reports.
- In determining the net worth of Section 306 pension recipients, VA rules exclude home furnishings, personal effects, and a personal automobile.

Other Benefits

Section 306 pension recipients are eligible for the other benefits of the Improved pension, except that federal rules prohibit payment of Aid and Attendance to Section 306 pension recipients who need help taking care of themselves at home. Veterans who are eligible for the extra monthly payments must switch to the Improved pension to receive Aid and Attendance.

Application

Applications for the Section 306 pension were accepted only between July 1, 1960, and December 31, 1978. Everyone receiving a Section 306 pension is eligible, at any time, to switch to the Improved pension. Once made, that decision cannot be reversed.

Although the Section 306 pension was created after the Old-Law pension, recipients of an Old-Law pension are not entitled to switch to a Section 306 pension.

EIGHT

PAYMENTS TO FAMILIES

In This Chapter:

- *Dependency and Indemnity Compensation*
- *Death Pension*
- *Birth Defects*

The government's responsibility to individual veterans often lingers long after a former servicemember has been laid to rest in a national cemetery. A little-known fact about the Department of Veterans Affairs is that it sends checks every month to hundreds of thousands of people who never served in uniform.

Like all VA programs, the ones available to widows, widowers, and the children of veterans have very specific eligibility rules. If the rules often sound bureaucratic, it's because they are based on very specific language that has been written into federal law.

This chapter, as its title says, is about *payments* to family members who aren't veterans themselves. Many other programs that don't involve a monthly check from the government are available to spouses, widows, widowers and dependent children. Check the index at the back of this book to learn about these other programs.

DEPENDENCY AND INDEMNITY COMPENSATION

When people die while serving in the military, their spouses and children—and sometimes even their parents—become eligible for a variety of benefits from the government. Many of the same benefits are also offered to the survivors of disabled veterans who died years after their discharge.

The principal financial benefit for these family members is Dependency and Indemnity Compensation, commonly known by the acronym DIC.

DIC provides a monthly income for survivors. Like many government programs, it changes constantly. In 1993, a fundamental change legislated by Congress took effect. For people receiving their first DIC payments in 1993, the rates changed from amounts based on the highest military rank of the veteran to a standard amount that everyone would receive. Survivors receiving DIC before 1993 will keep their old rank-based rates, unless they would receive more under the new system.

At least two other VA benefits are similar to DIC. The Death Pension is the principal VA program for the survivors of wartime veterans who died of medical problems that weren't related to their military service. Death Compensation goes to the parents of people who died before 1972, either on active duty or with service-connected disabilities.

Eligibility

In order for a widow, widower, dependent child, or parent to receive DIC, the deceased veteran and the family member applying for DIC each must meet very specific eligibility rules.

The deceased veteran must have met one of the following criteria:

- Died on active duty, active duty for training, or inactive duty for training.
- Died after leaving the military as a result of medical problems caused or aggravated by situations officially rated as

"in the line of duty" while on active duty, active duty for training, or inactive duty for training.

- Died for reasons unrelated to military service, as long as he or she left the military with a disability that was officially rated as total and service-connected and that existed continuously for at least ten years immediately before death.
- Died for reasons unrelated to military service, as long as he or she left the military with a disability that was officially rated as total and service-connected and that existed at least for the first five years after discharge.

When a claim for DIC is based on a death that occurred after a veteran was discharged from the military, the discharge must be rated as "under conditions other than dishonorable."

If the person applying for DIC is a widow or widower, that person also must meet one of these conditions:

- Have been married to the veteran for at least one year, if the marriage was childless.
- Have a child by the veteran if the death occurred less than a year after the marriage.
- Have lived with the veteran continuously from the time of the marriage, except if a separation was through no fault of the spouse.
- Have not remarried.

Some subtleties about remarriage are important. Normally, survivors lose DIC if they remarry after a veteran's death. But if the new marriage ends by death or divorce, the veteran's spouse can often qualify to receive DIC again. And surviving spouses who remarry after December 16, 2003, can have their DIC reinstated on their fifty-seventh birthday.

Spouses can lose DIC if they live with another person in an undeclared, common-law marriage after the veteran's death.

If the person applying for DIC is a child of the deceased veteran, that child must be unmarried and meet one of these other criteria:

- Not have reached his or her eighteenth birthday.
- If older than eighteen, be incapable of supporting self because of a physical or mental disability incurred before his or her eighteenth birthday.
- Not have reached his or her twenty-third birthday and be attending a VA-approved school.

If the person applying for DIC is a parent of the deceased veteran, that parent must have little income. In the year 2010, a maximum monthly payment of $569 went to parents with incomes of less than $9,600 a year.

Details of the Program

DIC provides a monthly income for qualified survivors of people who die on active duty or after being discharged with service-connected disabilities.

Since three basic groups of people are eligible for DIC—spouses, children, and parents—let's look at each group separately.

Spouses: If a veteran's death occurred on or after January 1, 1993, qualified spouses receive a fixed monthly amount which in the year 2010 was $1,154. Normally, that amount will increase annually to keep pace with inflation.

That figure will be increased by another amount (in 2010, $233 monthly) if the veteran was totally disabled from an illness or injury that was officially rated as service connected. That disability must have existed for at least eight years before the veteran's death.

Generally, DIC isn't affected by the income of spouses, but DIC will cause a decrease in another important federal benefit: Spouses who receive monthly payments from the military's Survivor Benefit Plan, or SBP, will lose one dollar in SBP for each dollar in DIC they receive.

Children: Sons or daughters of veterans who qualify for DIC can qualify for $286 monthly in 2010 if they are under eighteen, or if they are between ages eighteen and twenty-three and attending school.

Parents: Parents who depended financially upon a deceased veteran or military member who died can sometimes qualify for DIC benefits designed to guarantee a minimum income. Amounts vary by income, the number of surviving parents, whether they live together, and whether they have divorced and remarried.

In 2010, the monthly rates were a maximum of $569 for a single parent, $412 for each parent if separated, and $387 each for parents living together.

Application

The application procedure differs slightly for each category of applicant.

> Do you think the government doesn't keep promises to veterans? In 2010, VA was paying pensions to three children of Civil War veterans.

Spouses and dependent children should submit VA Form 21-534, "Application for Dependency and Indemnity Compensation or Death Pension by a Surviving Spouse or Child." For a child with no surviving parent, submit VA Form 21-4183, "Application for Dependency and Indemnity Compensation by Child." A parent should submit VA Form 21-535, "Application for Dependency and Indemnity Compensation by Parent(s)." These forms are all available at VA offices and online at www.va.gov/vaforms.

Survivors should get help from a VA counselor or a trained professional from a veterans organization when submitting an application for DIC. Errors in paperwork can delay payments by months.

Effect upon SBP

Some survivors are eligible for both DIC and a military-run program for survivors. Called the Survivor Benefit Plan, or SBP, this DoD benefit provides a monthly income to survivors of military retirees and people who die on active duty. At the same time, DIC is available for all spouses of people who die on active duty and spouses of military retirees who die from service-related medical problems.

As this book went to print in 2010, spouses eligible for DIC and SBPS couldn't receive full payment for both benefits. If they decide to get DIC, they could only receive $70 from SBP. That minimal payment was scheduled to increase gradually to $310 in October 2017. The minimal payment is called the Special Survivor Indemnity Allowance, or SSIA.

Activists are fighting to eliminate this quirk in federal law, which is known as the "DIC offset." If you're making financial plans for yourself or your family, make sure you have the latest information about the DIC offset.

Other Benefits

DIC alone will not meet the financial needs of many spouses and children of veterans. For people with additional needs, there are additional programs:

- *Aid and Attendance:* Increase in check for surviving spouses and parents who are in nursing homes or in need of care. In 2010, this benefit added about $286 to monthly DIC payments.
- *Housebound benefit:* Increase in monthly check for people permanently confined to their homes, but otherwise capable of taking care of themselves. This benefit applies to surviving spouses only, and in 2010 added about $135 to monthly DIC payments.

Eligibility for DIC and DIC rates aren't affected by receipt of Social Security, nor is there an impact on Social Security when people receive DIC.

Fine Points

If a DIC recipient is imprisoned after being convicted of a felony, the DIC will be reduced to a token amount, usually about $50 monthly.

If that person has dependents who would be hurt financially by the loss of DIC, VA officials have the authority to make a reduced DIC payment directly to the dependents.

DIC is restored to its full amount after a beneficiary has been released from prison, begins participation in a work-release program, or enters a halfway house.

DEATH PENSION

The death pension is the principal VA program for the survivors of low-income veterans whose deaths weren't related to their military service. Many of these veterans received a VA pension, as is discussed in the chapter titled "Veterans Pensions."

Eligibility

In order for a widow, widower, or dependent child to receive the death pension, the deceased veteran and the family member applying for the death pension must meet very specific eligibility rules. The veteran must have:

1. Spent at least ninety days on active duty, at least one day of which must have been during an official period of wartime.
2. Received a discharge that was officially rated as "under other than dishonorable conditions."
3. Died of a disability that was not related to military service.

If the person applying for the death pension is a widow or widower, that survivor also must meet the following conditions:

1. Meet the income limits discussed below.
2. Have documentary proof that the marriage began more than a year before the veteran's death. The proof may be a public record of marriage, an affidavit from a clergy-

man, certified statements from two eyewitnesses to the ceremony, or other documentation.

If the person applying for the death pension is a child of the deceased veteran, that survivor must meet the following conditions:

1. Meet the income limits discussed below.
2. Be unmarried and under eighteen.
3. If a stepchild, be living in the veteran's household.
4. If older than eighteen, must have become permanently incapable of self-support before his or her eighteenth birthday.
5. If between eighteen and twenty-three, must be enrolled in training or education at an institution approved by the Department of Veterans Affairs.

Details of the Program

The death pension provides a monthly income for qualified survivors of wartime veterans. The exact amount varies with several factors, including the survivor's income and whether dependents live with the survivor.

The amount of the pension increases annually to keep up with inflation. Annual increases are the same amount and given at the same time as increases in Social Security.

Below are listed the amounts at the start of 2010 for survivors fitting the major categories of the death pension. These amounts are totals for the year:

- *Without a child:* $7,900.
- *With one dependent:* $10,400.
- *Without dependents and unable to care for self:* $12,700.
- *With one dependent and unable to care for self:* $15,100.
- *Without dependents and housebound:* $9,700.
- *With one dependent and housebound:* $12,100.
- *Extra for each additional child:* $2,000.
- *Payment to each surviving child:* $2,100.

DIC underwent a major change in 1993. Descriptions of this program written before 1993 may be inaccurate, especially about rates.

Again, these rates are yearly maximums and usually change every year to keep up with inflation. Many people who qualify for the death pension never receive the maximum annual amount. That's because if they have income from other sources, their monthly death pension check is reduced by one dollar for each dollar from another source.

Income Restrictions

The VA's death pension is primarily for the low-income survivors of veterans. Generally, for each dollar of outside income, survivors lose one dollar from the maximum payable death pension.

Until recently, recipients had to fill out annual reports that set down their income. Now, VA computers automatically check income as reported to the Internal Revenue Service.

Application

Survivors can apply for the death pension at any time, even years after a veteran's death. The formal method for requesting the death pension is submission of VA Form 21-534, "Application for Dependency and Indemnity Compensation or Death Pension by a Surviving Spouse or Child," which can be obtained from any VA facility or on the Internet at www.va.gov/vaforms.

If the application is made within forty-five days of the veteran's death, payments will be retroactive to the day of death. If the application is filed more than forty-five days after the veteran's death, payment will be retroactive only to the day of the application.

Other Benefits

The death pension by itself will not solve the financial problems of many veterans and their families. For people with additional needs, there are additional programs that can help, including Aid and Attendance and the housebound benefit, as discussed on page 114.

Fine Points

Spouses who have been receiving a death pension lose the monthly payments if they remarry. Those payments can be restored if the marriage is legally voided or annulled, but the death pension isn't restored if a marriage ends in divorce.

BIRTH DEFECTS

Since 1997, the children of some Vietnam veterans can receive monthly payments and government-paid health care. These benefits go to children diagnosed with birth defects who had a parent who served in Vietnam during the Vietnam War.

The child must be the veteran's natural child and have been conceived after the veteran served in Vietnam.

The payment is called a "monetary allowance." It is paid in different amounts, depending upon the severity of the child's disability.

In the year 2010, those monthly amounts for children with Spina Bifida were $286, $984, and $1,678. For other qualifying birth defects the monthly rates were $131, $286, $984, and $1,678. Other income doesn't affect eligibility for this monthly allowance, nor does it affect the amount paid.

People apply for this benefit by contacting the nearest VA regional office. Those offices are included in a list of VA facilities at the back of this book. People can also reach VA regional offices through a toll-free number, 1-888-820-1756.

HELP FOR CAREGIVERS

As *Veteran's Guide to Benefits* was going to press, VA officials were creating a new package of benefits for the caregivers of seriously injured veterans. For the latest information about eligibility or benefits, call 1-877-222-8387, visit www.va.gov, or talk to officials at your nearest VA facility.

NINE

LIFE INSURANCE

In This Chapter:

- *Veterans Group Life Insurance*
- *Servicemember's Group Life Insurance*
- *Service-Disabled Veterans Insurance*
- *Veterans Mortgage Life Insurance*
- *Programs for Pre-1974 Discharges*

Financial obligations don't disappear while new veterans are reestablishing their civilian careers. Risks to life and limb aren't suspended while former servicemembers readjust to the private sector.

Bad things can happen to good people who've just taken off their uniforms and who haven't been able to build up their resources. And some of those bad things can jeopardize the financial welfare of families. To help protect against that, the government has backed a special life insurance program that veterans can purchase immediately after they leave the military.

It isn't a "freebie." To get the coverage, veterans must pay for it through regular contributions called "premiums." The rates, however, are at the low levels that are only available through large group policies.

Like many veterans programs, life insurance for veterans has changed many times over the years. About a dozen different programs are on the books, each with its own rules. Only four life insurance programs have been open to people leaving the military since the mid-1990s.

The latest information about VA's life insurance program is available on the Internet at www.insurance.va.gov.

VETERANS GROUP LIFE INSURANCE

Most people leaving active duty can purchase coverage at low, group rates under a program called Veterans Group Life Insurance, or VGLI.

The current VGLI program is open to most people who have left active duty since August 1, 1974. Other programs, discussed later in this chapter, provided similar coverage for those discharged before that date.

VGLI has been substantially improved over the years. It has gone from being "term" insurance, which veterans could purchase only for the first five years after leaving the military, to a plan they can renew periodically for the rest of their lives.

Although the military has a program offering life insurance to the spouses and dependent children of active-duty personnel and ready reservists, there is no similar benefit for the families of veterans.

Eligibility

Many veterans programs have elaborate eligibility rules, but to qualify for VGLI, you must meet at least one of the following criteria:

- Had coverage under the Servicemember's Group Life Insurance (SGLI) Plan when left active duty or the reserves.
- Be a member of the Individual Ready Reserve (IRR) or Inactive National Guard (ING).

- Be a disabled reservist with a disability incurred while on inactive duty for training or while on active duty for less than thirty-one days.

What are the eligibility rules for military retirees? For recipients of exit bonuses? For veterans with early releases or continued obligations for time in the reserves?

The answers to all those questions—and more—lie in the first, broad eligibility criterion. So long as veterans left active duty with SGLI coverage, they are eligible for VGLI.

> Life insurance is a low-cost, high-benefit investment for married veterans. Single people without children may find better uses for their money.

Improvements that officially took place September 1, 1993, created their own eligibility rules. Before that date, new veterans could sign up for VGLI for five years. After that date, veterans could have VGLI for the rest of their lives.

The 1993 change applies to people who left active duty after September 1 of that year and to veterans who had VGLI coverage in force on that date.

Dual Eligibility

VGLI is the insurance program for people who have left the military. A similar program, Servicemember's Group Life Insurance (SGLI), which is discussed in greater detail later in this chapter, has comparable coverage for folks who are still in uniform.

But many ex-servicemembers don't stay in the "ex" category forever. There's a constant movement of reservists, National Guardsmen, and discharged veterans back into active duty.

From time to time, many veterans will find themselves back in uniform and eligible again for SGLI, the active-duty insurance program. For them, it's possible to be covered by both VGLI and SGLI. The major restriction is that the combined coverage can't exceed the cap ($400,000 for 2010).

Rates and Rules

Coverage can be for as little as $10,000, as much as $400,000, or any amount in between. Those "in between" coverage amounts, however, must be in $10,000 increments.

Some veterans may face restrictions on the amount of coverage that they can obtain. In the year 2010, for example, the amount of VGLI couldn't be greater than the amount of SGLI coverage that people had on active duty.

As with any private insurance program, veterans must make regular contributions, called "premiums," to obtain the coverage. The government doesn't pay these premiums for veterans.

The amount of the premiums is determined by two factors: the age of the veteran and the amount of coverage. In 2010, for example, here were the monthly premiums for $10,000 in coverage for the major age groups:

- *Age 29 or younger:* $.80.
- *Age 30 through 34:* $1.00.
- *Age 35 through 39:* $1.30.
- *Age 40 through 44:* $1.70.
- *Age 45 through 49:* $2.20.
- *Age 50 through 54:* $3.60.
- *Age 55 through 59:* $6.70.
- *Age 60 through 64:* $10.80.
- *Age 65 through 69:* $15.00.
- *Age 70 through 74:* $22.50.
- *Age 75 and older:* $45.00.

Each block of $10,000 has the same monthly premiums as those listed. VGLI participants who choose to pay in one lump sum each year get a discount.

Thus, for a thirty-two-year-old veteran, coverage for the full $400,000 would cost $40 per month. That's $1 for each of forty blocks of $10,000.

Older veterans can obtain "decreasing term coverage" at age sixty. For them, the amount of their premiums remains the same as they age, but the amount of coverage decreases.

Beneficiaries

A VGLI beneficiary may be any person; it doesn't have to be a relative. It may also be a firm, corporation, the veteran's own estate, or any legal entity.

> **V**GLI veterans decide whether their beneficiaries will receive one lump-sum payment or thirty-six equal monthly payments.

To avoid legal complications, however, that decision should be submitted to the VGLI administrator on the official beneficiary designation forms provided by the administrator. The administrator is the office to whom the premium checks are mailed.

VGLI participants are permitted to change their beneficiaries at any time.

Application

Veterans receive VGLI coverage only if they apply. There are two deadlines for applications for most veterans:

- Within 120 days after discharge: Qualify simply by paying your first VGLI premium.
- Between the 121st day after discharge and one year after discharge: Qualify by paying the first VGLI premium and demonstrating that you're in good health, which often requires a recent physical examination.

Veterans who qualify for VGLI by membership in the Individual Ready Reserve or Inactive National Guard have two similar deadlines. They can apply for VGLI within 120 days of joining the IRR or ING, along with paying the first premium.

At the end of that 120-day period, IRR and ING members have another year in which to apply, although for the extended application period they will have to submit proof that they are good insurance risks, a process often requiring a recent physical.

Veterans qualifying for VGLI because of a reserve-related disability have within a year of their discharge to apply for VGLI. Ironically, to qualify, they will have to prove that they are, in fact, poor risks for conventional insurance because they have disabilities.

Terminally Ill Veterans

Since February 1999, veterans who are terminally ill can receive half of the value of their life insurance before they die. The other half is paid to beneficiaries after their death.

This special payment is called the "accelerated benefit" option. To qualify, veterans need an official diagnosis from their doctor that says they have less than nine months to live.

SERVICEMEMBER'S GROUP LIFE INSURANCE

The same government-backed insurance program that goes to active-duty people—Servicemember's Group Life Insurance, or SGLI—is also available to many members of the reserves and National Guard.

SGLI participants are also eligible to purchase coverage for spouses and dependent children.

Eligibility

SGLI is available to a wide spectrum of the military population, including the following:

- Everyone on active duty.
- Cadets and midshipmen at the four military academies.
- Members of the Ready Reserve.
- Reservists with part-time coverage.

The term "Ready Reserve" also has a precise definition, usually reservists who are assigned to units and who take part in weekend drill periods every month.

Some reservists and National Guardsmen who don't meet the general membership provisions of SGLI are covered by this insurance plan during specific periods, usually lasting only a few days. This part-time SGLI coverage applies to people who have orders specifying that, for a period of less than thirty-one days, they will be on active duty or active duty for training. They have SGLI coverage during those days of service, plus during travel to and from the training site.

A more narrow kind of part-time coverage goes to folks who aren't members of the Ready Reserve but who are scheduled for brief periods of military service, such as attendance at a drill period. They have SGLI coverage from the moment they leave home until the moment they return home.

Dual Eligibility

There is a perpetual flow of people from active duty to the Selected Reserve to the IRR to the civilian population and back again.

A VGLI reservist who becomes eligible for SGLI for a period may want to drop VGLI in favor of the less costly SGLI policy. Or the reservist can choose to keep both government-backed insurance policies. As noted before, the combined coverage can't exceed $400,000, as of the year 2010.

Rates and Rules

The minimum amount of SGLI coverage available is $50,000; the maximum is $400,000. Between those two figures, people can obtain coverage in multiples of $50,000.

Although SGLI is government backed, it isn't government paid. People have to make monthly contributions for the coverage.

Those contributions are made through withholdings from the military paycheck. Traditionally, a single SGLI rate applies to everyone. In 2010, the rate for most SGLI recipients was $0.65 monthly for each $1,000 in coverage.

For an additional monthly premium of $1.00 SGLI participants also can receive up to $100,000 in compensation for traumatic injuries, such as the loss of a limb.

Coverage for Spouses

SGLI participants can also insure their spouses for up to $100,000 under a program known as Family SGLI, or simply FSGLI. Coverage under this program comes in blocks of $10,000.

Monthly premiums are based on the age of the spouse, from 55 cents for $10,000 in coverage for a spouse under 35, to $5.20 for $10,000 in coverage for a spouse 60 or older.

Beneficiaries

An SGLI beneficiary may be any person; it doesn't have to be a relative. It may also be a firm, corporation, the veteran's own estate, or any legal entity. To avoid legal complications, however, that decision should be submitted to the SGLI administrator on the official beneficiary designation forms, which can be obtained from military personnel offices or VA regional offices. SGLI participants can change their beneficiaries at any time.

Application

When people become eligible for SGLI, a key provision of the insurance program goes "on automatic pilot." Everyone eligible for SGLI is automatically enrolled in the program at $400,000 of coverage. To obtain less coverage, or no coverage, folks have to request it.

Under legislation that took effect in May 2005, servicemembers with dependents must get written approval from their beneficiaries—usually a spouse—to choose anything except the maximum coverage.

To obtain the forms necessary to change the amount of SGLI coverage, contact the nearest military personnel office. Many family support centers also have information about the program.

After Discharge
Active-duty members with SGLI and most reserve SGLI participants are covered by their insurance policies—at no cost—for 120 days after discharge.

SERVICE-DISABLED VETERANS INSURANCE
To give veterans with permanent disabilities related to their military service an extra measure of financial protection, the government has put together a special insurance program called Service-Disabled Veterans Insurance, or SDVI. It's also known as the "RH" program, a name based on the letters at the beginning of individual policy numbers.

Eligibility
SDVI is available to veterans who have left the military since April 24, 1951, and have disabilities that are officially rated as being service connected.

People discharged at earlier dates may be eligible for one of the insurance programs discussed in the section below, "Programs for Pre-1974 Discharges."

For SDVI, eligible veterans fall within two broad groups, each having slightly different policies:
1. Those who are officially rated as having a service-connected disability but are otherwise in good health.
2. Those who are totally disabled.

Possession of VA disability compensation isn't necessary to qualify for this insurance coverage. In fact, many SDVI participants are so-called zero-compensable disabled veterans, people with disabilities caused by military service that aren't severe enough to warrant disability compensation. But the official determination that a disability is service connected is necessary to be eligible for SDVI coverage.

Details of the Program

Traditionally, SDVI coverage has been for much smaller amounts than the government-backed insurance plans for active-duty people and other veterans.

In the year 2010, the basic coverage was capped at $10,000. Participants could receive less coverage, in multiples of $500, to a minimum of $1,000.

Disabled veterans who are otherwise in good health must pay for the coverage from their own pockets. Government backing holds their insurance premiums to the same amounts normally paid by people without disabilities.

Totally disabled veterans can receive the basic coverage— $10,000—at no cost. To get the free coverage, however, they must ask for it. They must apply in writing to the Department of Veterans Affairs for a waiver of premiums.

If they receive the waiver, they become eligible for an additional $20,000 in coverage. But, this time, they must pay for that additional coverage. Government support keeps premiums within the financial reach of many veterans.

Application

Veterans must apply for SDVI coverage within two years after being notified that they have a service-connected disability.

A legal guardian can apply on behalf of an incompetent veteran. That application should be made within one year after the guardian has been appointed.

Beneficiaries

Veterans with SDVI coverage have the same freedom in designating their beneficiaries as holders of other government-backed insurance policies.

To avoid legal complications, veterans should use the forms maintained by VA offices to designate beneficiaries, and they should file that paperwork promptly at a VA regional office.

When the veteran isn't competent enough to name a beneficiary, the veteran's estate automatically becomes the beneficiary.

VETERANS MORTGAGE LIFE INSURANCE

Veterans Mortgage Life Insurance, or VMLI, provides an extra measure of financial protection for the families of some disabled veterans who are buying homes. VMLI can help a family to keep its home if the veteran dies before the mortgage has been paid.

Eligibility

This insurance policy is narrowly focused. It's for veterans with the most extreme disabilities. Relatively few recipients of VA disability compensation qualify.

To be eligible for VMLI, a veteran must first be eligible for the VA's Specially Adapted Housing program, which provides grants to veterans with severe disabilities requiring extensive modifications to their homes.

Among the veterans entitled to the special housing program are those who have suffered these injuries:

- Blindness in both eyes.
- Loss of both legs or the use of both legs.
- Loss of one leg or the use of one leg, plus blind in both eyes.
- Loss of one leg or the use of one leg, plus disease or injury that affects the sense of balance, confining the veteran to a wheelchair.
- Loss of one leg or the use of one leg, plus loss of an arm or the use of an arm, affecting balance and requiring special aids to movement.
- Loss of both hands or the use of both hands.

Rules and Rates

The amount of VMLI coverage a veteran can obtain is linked to the value of the home the veteran is buying. The insurance policy cannot be worth more than the amount due on the home, up to a maximum of $90,000 in 2010. As the veteran pays off the mortgage and the principal decreases, the amount of VMLI coverage will decrease, too.

Like most of the veterans insurance programs, VMLI coverage isn't free. Participants pay for it, usually by the government withholding a certain amount from their monthly VA disability compensation checks.

The exact amount of the premium is based on complex formulas that include the veteran's age, the unpaid principal due on the home, and the remaining length of the mortgage.

Despite the out-of-pocket premiums, VMLI coverage is a very good deal. The government pays for the administrative costs of the program, and the formulas to calculate the size of premiums use standard life-expectancy projections for the general population, not those for disabled people.

Application

VMLI coverage is like the active-duty SGLI program in its automatic sign-up provision. If you're eligible and you don't want to have VMLI, then you must take action. If you do nothing, you get the coverage.

Fine Points

It's possible for veterans to have more than one piece of property that makes them eligible for VMLI coverage. When that happens, the overall coverage limits and rules apply to a combination of all the property. According to the rules as of the year 2010, the total coverage will be held to $90,000, regardless of the value of all the property. And when the principal due on all mortgages, added together, falls below $90,000, the VMLI coverage will drop to that amount.

PROGRAMS FOR PRE-1974 DISCHARGES

The U.S. government has offered insurance to its active-duty people, reservists, and veterans since World War I.

At least one feature of those earlier programs still causes problems today. Many of the earlier insurance policies provide annual dividends to veterans. The news media frequently reports the amounts of those dividends, making newer veterans wonder what they're missing.

None of the government-backed life insurance plans now available to people who are leaving the military—or, generally, who have left the military since the mid-1960s—pay annual dividends.

> Some scam artists target veterans. If you're eligible for a dividend, you don't have to pay anyone to get your money.

This section highlights of some of the earlier government-backed life insurance programs. Rather than using their formal names, which can get quite confusing when all the programs are mentioned in a short space, we'll refer to them by the "policy letter."

Each individual insurance policy has an identification number. In front of those numbers is a letter or several letters. Each of the various life insurance plans used its own distinctive letter, called the policy letter. It's a useful, shorthand way of identifying which policy we're talking about.

Dividends

On the anniversary of a veteran taking out a life insurance policy, most of the older, pre-1960 programs will offer dividends. These can be paid directly to the veteran or kept in the VA insurance program and used to purchase more coverage.

The Internal Revenue Service has ruled that veterans do not have to pay taxes on the dividends when paid directly to the veteran. Dividends that are left with the VA and used to buy more insurance are also not taxable.

Dividends go regularly to veterans with policies in the following programs: K, V, RS, W, J, JR, and JS.

Not eligible for dividends are policies under VGLI, SGLI, or VMLI. Also not eligible are H and RH policies.

Loans

Veterans can borrow up to 94 percent of the cash value of their insurance policies, while continuing to earn dividends for those policies. Like any other loan, a loan on the insurance policy must be repaid. Also like any other loan, the repayment includes an interest charge.

Veterans can learn about the repayment schedule and interest rates when applying for the loan. Generally, since November 2, 1987, there has been a variable interest rate for loans taken out against V and H policies. That interest rate changes annually. The government guarantees that the interest rate on these policies won't be more than 12 percent or less than 5 percent.

Interest on loans for all K policies is fixed for the life of the loan. That's also the rule for loans taken out before November 1987 that were based on V and H policies.

As with any loan, veterans should make sure they can handle the repayment schedule. Failure to keep up with the repayment scheme can result in the loss of the policy.

Disabilities

Government-backed insurance programs have a variety of rules that come into play when policyholders become disabled.

For example, people with V and H policies can keep their life insurance without paying any more premiums if they become disabled before their sixty-fifth birthdays and if the disability is permanent.

Veterans with K policies may be eligible to receive the cash value of their insurance coverage if they become permanently and totally disabled.

Whatever the policy, veterans with government-backed life insurance should get some up-to-date, professional advice if confronting a disability that's likely to last several months. They should contact the nearest VA regional office, a benefits counselor at a VA medical facility, or a professional service officer for one of the major veterans groups.

Disability Riders

Many commercial life insurance companies offer "riders," or special provisions to their policies that offer extra protection for a slightly larger premium.

A popular rider for many policyholders, both veterans and members of the general public, guarantees that the policyholder will receive an extra income if the policyholder becomes disabled.

Disability riders are available for many of the government-backed insurance policies, especially the K, V, and H policies. They are not available for RH, JR, or JS policies.

Another popular rider that's related to disabilities allows policyholders to keep their life insurance without having to pay any more premiums in the event of permanent disabilities.

Other Policies

Not all the government-backed insurance programs for veterans were mentioned above. Here are the identifying letters and summaries of a few other programs:

- *A:* The bonus to World War I veterans that was the focus of the famous "Bonus March on Washington" in 1932. Some bonuses may still be unclaimed.
- *T:* Term insurance for World War I veterans, which ended in 1925.
- *AN:* Special free coverage for World War II veterans who didn't purchase any coverage and who later died before April 20, 1942.

- *N:* Term insurance for World War II veterans. It converted, over the years, into V policies. No N policies are still in force.
- *ARH:* A free version of the RH policy for people who were mentally incompetent because of a service-connected disability at the time of their discharge or within a year after discharge.
- *K:* Term insurance for active-duty personnel from 1919–1940.
- *V:* Permanent insurance for active-duty servicemembers from 1941–1951.
- *RS:* Issued to veterans discharged between April 25, 1951, and January 1, 1957.
- *W:* Term insurance that began in 1959 and ends on a veteran's fiftieth birthday.
- *J:* Permanent insurance for disabled veterans, which closed to new applicants in May 1966.
- *JR:* Same as J program, but for severe disabilities.
- *JS:* Same as J program, except disability must be rated as non–service connected.
- *H:* Policies for people who served on active duty between October 8, 1940, and September 2, 1945, and who had service-connected disabilities.
- *RH:* Permanent insurance for veterans discharged after April 25, 1951, with service-connected disabilities.

TEN

HOME LOANS

In This Chapter:

• *VA Home Loans*

Home ownership is still part of the American dream. Financial help from the government in purchasing a home is one of the most important benefits of military service.

That help comes in the form of a guaranty from the government to a financial institution that if the veteran stops making regular payments on a home loan, then the government will repay the lender for some of its losses.

No payments are made directly from the government to veterans under this program.

VA HOME LOANS

Home loan guaranties are one government benefit for which people outside the government have a prominent voice in making some basic decisions about eligibility. Remember that the actual loans that veterans receive come directly from a bank, savings and loan, or mortgage company. Those financial institutions have the right to decide whether someone applying for a home loan—veteran or nonveteran—is a good financial risk.

Veterans who believe they've been unfairly turned down for a home loan because of race or gender or because they are veterans should notify the nearest office of the Department of Veterans Affairs.

> There was no VA home loan program for World War I veterans or for veterans between the two world wars.

Unlike the GI Bill educational program, there's no deadline specifying that a veteran must use the home loan guaranty by a certain time after discharge. Eligible veterans may obtain a VA-backed home loan at any time after their discharge. They may even use it more than once to buy more than one home (but only one at a time).

Following are the eligibility rules for veterans of different eras.

Now on Active Duty: Current servicemembers must meet the following criteria:

- Served at least 90 days of continuous active duty.
- Not a six-month enlistee on active duty for training.

Now in Selected Reserve: Members of the Selected Reserve must have completed at least six years in the reserves or National Guard and meet one of following conditions:

- Still in Selected Reserve.
- Discharged under honorable conditions.
- Retired.
- Transferred to Ready Reserve.

Spouses: To qualify for a VA home loan, a person must be the spouse, widow, or widower of one of the following:

- Someone who died on active duty.
- Someone who died after discharge from service-connected causes.

- Someone officially listed as missing in action or prisoner of war for ninety days or longer.

Note: Spouses of deceased veterans generally lose eligibility when they remarry. However, spouses who remarry after their fifty-seventh birthdays and after December 16, 2003, may still be eligible.

Gulf War Vets: Veterans of the Gulf War must have served on active duty between August 2, 1990, and the formal end of conflict, which hadn't been set when this book went to press, and meet one of these other conditions:

- Served at least twenty-four months with discharge under conditions other than dishonorable.
- Served at least 90 days and discharged with a disability, for a hardship, for convenience of the government, or during a formal reduction in force.
- Was a reservist or guardsman called to active duty during the official period of conflict who served at least ninety days and was discharged honorably.

Most Peacetime Vets: Veterans who served on active duty between July 26, 1947, and June 26, 1950, or served between February 1, 1955, and August 4, 1964, or enlisted between May 8, 1975, and September 7, 1980, or were commissioned as officers between May 8, 1975, and October 16, 1981, must meet one of the following criteria to qualify for a VA home loan:

- Served at least 181 days continuous active duty and discharged under conditions other than dishonorable.
- Served less than 181 days and discharged under conditions other than dishonorable for service-connected disability.

Other Peacetime Vets: Those who enlisted between September 7, 1980, and August 1, 1990, or were commissioned as officers between October 16, 1981, and August 1, 1990, must meet one of the following requirements:

- Served the full period of active duty in the stated time span.
- Completed twenty-four months of continuous active duty or the full period (at least 181 days) for which called to active duty and discharged under conditions other than dishonorable.
- Completed at least 181 days on active duty and discharged for hardship or early-out.
- Discharged for service-connected disability, regardless of length of time on active duty.

Other Wartime Vets: Also qualifying for VA home loans are people who served at least one day during the Vietnam War, from August 5, 1964, to May 7, 1975; the Korean War, from June 27, 1950, to January 31, 1955; or World War II, between September 16, 1940, and July 25, 1947, and meet both of the following conditions:

- Served at least ninety days on active duty or discharged with less than ninety days for a service-connected disability.
- Discharged under conditions other than dishonorable.

Note: The eligibility rules don't require these veterans to have served in a combat theater, only to have been in uniform during these periods.

Qualifying Homes

Homes that veterans wish to purchase with a government-backed loan must pass two tests—a specific test and a general test.

> VA loans cannot be used for investment property. Veterans must use the homes as their primary residences.

The specific test involves a VA-approved appraiser establishing the market value of the home. The goal is to ensure that, since the government is being asked to repay if the veteran defaults, the home itself is a reasonable financial risk for the government.

And here, things can get murky. The government assumes no responsibility for a veteran's choice of a home. It cannot act as an attorney or real estate agent for the veteran, nor can it guarantee that a home is free of defects.

But the government can refuse to back a loan if a home is in disrepair, and it can refuse to guarantee a loan if it is in excess of the fair market value.

There's also a general test to identify qualifying homes. Not every type of home or transaction can qualify for a government-backed VA home loan. Here are the major uses:

- To buy a home.
- To buy a townhouse or condominium.
- To buy a manufactured or mobile home.
- To buy a lot for a manufactured home.
- To build a home.
- To repair, alter, or improve a home.
- To make energy-efficient improvements.
- To simultaneously purchase and improve a home.
- To purchase a manufactured home and improve the lot.
- To refinance an existing home loan.
- To refinance an existing home loan in order to reduce the interest rate.
- To refinance a manufactured home loan and acquire a lot.

Additionally, VA home loan guaranties can be used to purchase or build residential property containing more than one family unit. There cannot be more than four family units, however, and the veteran must occupy one of them.

If the veteran intends to use income from the other units to repay the mortgage, then VA rules require that the veteran must have a background that provides him with some qualifications to be a landlord. The veteran also must be able to repay the mortgage for at least six months without any rental income.

For a farm to qualify for a VA home loan, it must have a home in which the veteran will live. If the veteran intends to farm, he or she must show that the operation has a good chance of being successful. If nonfarming income permits the veteran to qualify for the loan, then farming operations aren't considered in the loan application process.

Businesses cannot be financed through the VA home loan guaranty program.

Cooperatively owned apartments rarely qualify for VA loans. To pass muster, all the cooperative members must be veterans who are using their own VA home loan benefits for the purchase.

VA home loans cannot be used to purchase homes overseas. To qualify, a home must be in one of the fifty states, the District of Columbia, Puerto Rico, Guam, the Virgin Islands, American Samoa, or the Northern Mariana Islands.

Details of the Program

The government's promise to mortgage lenders is not to repay the entire mortgage if the veteran defaults, but to repay a portion. That bit of partial financial protection to lenders significantly reduces their costs for a default and makes them eager to deal with veterans looking for government-backed home loans.

The amount of money the government will pay to lenders for each defaulted mortgage is called the veteran's "entitlement." In most cases, the size and other details about the entitlement have no practical effect on veterans who want to buy a home.

The amount of the entitlement is calculated by a formula that uses the value of the home and, sometimes, its location. The numbers used in the formula usually change every year.

To find the latest formula, go to www.homeloans.va.gov/XXXX_county_loan_limits.pdf. Where "XXXX" appears in this Internet address, insert the current year.

Application

Veterans seeking a VA home loan must take their formal discharge papers, the DD Form 214, to the nearest office of the Department of Veterans Affairs and obtain a second document called a "Certificate of Eligibility." This document can be issued on the spot, often in less than an hour.

Occupancy

Everyone obtaining a VA home loan guaranty must certify in writing that he or she intends to use the home as the primary residence. This rules out the use of VA loans to purchase rental property and vacation homes.

There don't seem to be any written provisions that stipulate how long a veteran must live in a home before putting it up for rent. Again, VA rules give officials wide discretion. But, in general, it's permissible for veterans to retain their home loans if they move out and rent the property.

Interest Rates

The government doesn't set the interest rate. That's between the veteran and the mortgage lender.

VA home loan guaranties can be obtained for a fixed rate or an adjustable rate which can rise by up to five percentage points over the life of the loan.

Down Payments

Most people with VA-backed home loans don't make down payments. That's a major advantage of the program. Still, VA rules require a down payment for a small number of specific kinds of purchases.

Who may have to make a down payment? The government requires them for the purchase of manufactured or mobile homes, for lots for manufactured or mobile homes, and for loans that exceed the government's appraisal of a property's fair market value.

With these exceptions, the government doesn't require veterans to make a down payment. Some veterans mistakenly believe that VA rules mean that lenders cannot require down payments. That's not the case.

Lenders make their own appraisals of the risks involved in making a loan to a specific veteran. They can decide to ask a veteran for a down payment.

Funding Fee

Most veterans purchasing a home with a VA-backed home loan must pay a small amount, called a "funding fee," to offset the government's cost of running the program and to make up for some of the government's losses when veterans default on their loans. Veterans receiving VA disability pay don't pay the funding fee.

The size of the funding fee is a percentage of, and can be included in, the overall home loan. Thus, if a veteran purchases a $100,000 home and the funding fee is $1,500, then the veteran might include the funding fee in the total loan and take out a loan for $101,500.

Here are the 2010 funding fee rates for specific categories:

- *Loans with no down payment or down payments less than 5 percent:* 2.15 percent for active-duty veterans; 2.40 percent for reserve veterans.
- *Loans for refinancing, home improvement, and home repair:* 2.15 percent for active-duty veterans; 2.40 percent for reserve veterans.
- *For second or subsequent use:* 3.3 percent with no down payment.
- *Loans for purchase or new construction with down payment of at least 5 percent but less than 10 percent:* 1.5 percent for active-duty veterans; 1.75 percent for reserve veterans.
- *Loans for purchase or construction with down payment of at least 10 percent:* 1.25 percent for active-duty veterans; 1.50 percent for reserve veterans.
- *Manufactured or mobile home:* 1 percent for both active-duty and reserve veterans.

• *Interest-rate reduction loans:* 0.5 percent for both active-duty and reserve veterans.

Closing Costs

Incidental expenses are paid by everyone buying, building, or refinancing a home. Many of these incidental expenses are commonly lumped together and called "closing costs."

Closing costs may include title search, recording fees, a VA appraisal, credit report, survey fees, hazard insurance premiums, prepaid taxes, and a loan-origination fee.

Unlike the VA funding fee, which was discussed above, these closing costs cannot be included in loans for the purchase or construction of homes using VA-backed guaranties.

When a veteran refinances a home loan using the VA guaranty, however, these closing costs can be included in the overall loan.

Along with closing costs, veterans can also include in the overall loan up to $6,000 for home improvements made for energy efficiency.

Discount "Points"

Frequently, home purchases include up-front payment of additional amounts to the lender. These amounts, called "discount points," or more simply "points," are computed as a percentage of the loan amount.

Except for what are formally known as "Interest Rate Reduction Refinancing Loans," points cannot be included in an overall VA-backed loan. Like closing costs and interest rates, details about the payment of points are worked out between the borrower and the lender.

Prepayments

One of the commitments that the lender makes to the government is that there will be no penalty for veterans who pay off their mortgages early. That legal protection includes veterans who pay a little more each month than the required mortgage payment.

Selling

The VA-backed home loan isn't a onetime deal. Veterans can buy several homes using VA guaranties, but they can own only one at a time.

Veterans who closed on a home loan after February 29, 1988, must formally notify the VA if someone else is assuming responsibility for the loan, and the VA must approve the transaction in writing. Application forms for that notification, called "a release from liability," can be obtained from the bank, mortgage company, or savings and loan association that made the loan.

A buyer who closed on a home before March 1, 1988, doesn't have to receive the VA's approval before letting someone else assume the home loan.

If a VA-backed loan is assumed by a nonveteran, the original veteran-owner may not be able to use VA benefits to buy a second home until the mortgage on the first one has been paid up. That's because the government is still liable if the new owner defaults.

One simple way to avoid this problem is for veterans not to let nonveterans assume a VA-backed loan. The veteran can avoid this trap by selling the home and repaying the original loan in full.

But if another veteran assumes a VA-backed loan, including the substitution of "entitlement," then the original owner may be free to seek a VA home loan guaranty to purchase another house.

Once property has been sold or a VA-backed loan has been assumed by another veteran, veterans don't automatically regain the right to seek another VA home loan. They must apply for the right in a process called "restoration of entitlement."

Any VA office has the forms necessary to apply for a restoration of entitlement. This review guarantees that the veteran isn't responsible for any debts to the government and that the veteran is still eligible for VA-backed loans.

Financial Problems

If a temporary setback like a job loss or unusual expense results in a veteran being unable to pay the regular monthly mortgage, there is some limited protection for people with VA-backed loans.

To participate in VA's home loan program, lenders must formally agree with the Department of Veterans Affairs to offer "reasonable forbearance and indulgence" for veterans in temporary financial difficulty.

Usually, that means that lenders can't threaten to drive veterans out of their homes because a mortgage check was a day or two late.

ELEVEN

EDUCATION AND TRAINING

In This Chapter:

- *Post-9/11 GI Bill*
- *Montgomery GI Bill*
- *Montgomery GI Bill (Selected Reserve)*
- *Reserve Educational Assistance Program*

- *Veterans Educational Assistance Program*
- *Vietnam-Era GI Bill*
- *Vocational Rehabilitation*

Since the end of World War II, government help in paying for education has been a major benefit of military service, designed to help people leaving the military make the adjustment back to civilian life. While the name "GI Bill" has remained on the books since the end of World War II, the program has been changed enough to justify slightly different names.

Three major wartime versions of the GI Bill—the World War II, Korean War, and Vietnam War programs—have expired. If you haven't already used your benefits under one of those programs, you can't get any government financial help now. Some veterans of the Vietnam War, however, can obtain government help in paying for civilian education by qualifying for the current program, called the Post-9/11 GI Bill.

POST-9/11 GI BILL

For people now on active duty, the Post-9/11 GI Bill is the government's way of helping pay their educational bills. Like earlier versions of the GI Bill, the Post-9/11 program reduces soldiers' and veterans' out-of-pocket expenses for attending undergraduate and graduate institutions, vocational and technical training, and even some tutors and certification tests. Also like the earlier programs, the government gives wide latitude to participants to make their own decisions about what to study and where to go to school.

Unlike the Montgomery GI Bill, its immediate predecessor, the Post-9/11 program doesn't require people to have a $100-a-month reduction in pay during their first year in uniform.

Other differences are also significant. In contrast to most earlier versions of the GI bill, the Post-9/11 benefit does not have a one-size-fits-all payment. In fact, it has a complex system of payments, with most people qualifying for three separate payments or reimbursements, and some having as many as five. It also allows veterans and service members who don't use their full benefits to transfer some to their spouses or children.

The program's complexity can lead to frustration and confusion. But veterans should take heart. The Post-9/11 GI Bill is more generous than any other version of this valuable educational benefit in more than fifty years.

The Department of Veterans Affairs began making payments under the Post-9/11 GI in the summer of 2009. It was a rocky start. Folks eligible for this program shouldn't be deterred by the events of those first months.

The GI Bill has always been a major "thank you" to the men and women who serve in uniform. Those eligible for the Post-9/11 GI Bill will find themselves better off than their fathers and mothers who may have relied upon earlier versions of this benefit.

Eligibility

The Post-9/11 GI Bill is the government's basic educational benefit for military service since September 10, 2001. Active-duty personnel, reservists, National Guardsmen, and veterans can qualify for the program.

Four broad categories of people are eligible for this program:
1. People who have been on active duty at least 90 days after September 10, 2001.
2. Those who got an honorable discharge after that date. This includes:
   a. Most veterans who left the military since the magic date;
   b. People who retired or went on the Temporary Disability Retirement List (TDRL) since that date;
   c. Members of the Fleet Reserve or Marine Corps Reserve after September 10, 2001; and
   d. People released from active duty to a reserve component after that date.
3. People who were medically discharged since September 10, 2001, as long as:
   a. The medical problem for which they were discharged is officially recognized as a "service-connected disability;" and
   b. They have an honorable discharge; and
   c. They served at least 30 consecutive days on active duty.
4. Some spouses and dependent children of active-duty members, reservists, or National Guardsmen.

Not eligible for the Post-9/11 GI Bill are people who attended service academies at Annapolis, West Point, or the Air

Force Academy. Also ineligible are active-duty personnel assigned to full-time education that is "substantially the same" as courses routinely offered to civilians. For this last group, the military has other programs that pay for the civilian education of full-time students who are on active duty.

As this book went to print, Congress was looking at a variety of proposals to extend benefits to other groups—mainly reservists and National Guardsmen with little time on active duty—who were originally ineligible for the basic program.

A couple points about the eligibility date are important. First, some publications about this educational benefit say it affects folks "on or after September 11, 2001." This book uses a slightly different way—"after September 10, 2001"—to say the same thing.

Second, the date of September 10, 2001 is important for calculating the amount of time in uniform to qualify for educational assistance. But that date isn't used to decide when educational expenses are covered. The Post-9/11 GI Bill covers the costs of classes and other approved instruction that began no earlier than Aug. 1, 2009. Education expenses accumulated between September 11, 2001 and July 31, 2009 won't be paid by this program.

Time Limits

The government will provide benefits for 36 months of full-time education. For a student going to school at only the half-time rate, the coverage will last for 72 months. Similar adjustments are made for students going at a three-quarters rate or a one-quarter rate.

Generally, the government stops writing checks for educational expenses on the fifteenth anniversary of a veteran's discharge from active duty. This "fifteen-year clock" can be reset if a veteran returns to active duty for at least ninety days.

VA officials can also reset the fifteen-year clock for people prevented from using their Post-9/11 GI Bill benefits by a disability or by being detained by a foreign power.

Veterans with discharges from active duty that weren't good enough to qualify for educational benefits can have the fifteen-year limit extended if their discharges are upgraded to honorable.

Approved Courses

To receive payments from the Post-9/11 GI Bill, veterans and active-duty people must enroll in classes or training approved by the Department of Veterans Affairs.

In general, the following types of education and training are covered by the Post-9/11 GI Bill:

- College and university courses leading to an associate, bachelor's, or graduate degree
- Accredited independent study leading to a standard college degree
- Courses leading to a diploma or certificate from an approved business, technical, or vocational school

Payments

The Post-9/11 GI Bill covers educational expenses that arose after July 31, 2009. It will not cover educational expenses incurred before that date.

An earlier date—September 10, 2001—is used to determine whether a service member or veteran is eligible for coverage under the Post-9/11 GI Bill. Don't let that date confuse you. The program didn't actually begin paying for educational expenses until after July 31, 2009.

Although participants receive a single monthly check from VA for the approved costs of their schooling, several different items make up the check. And the most important part of the benefit—the payment for tuition and fees—goes directly from VA to the school.

Here are the things that make up benefits under the Post-9/11 GI Bill:

- *Tuition and fees.* The amount the government will cover depends upon the amount charged to the student. The maximum is the largest amount charged within the state by any state-run school for undergraduates at the in-state tuition rate—so it varies from state to state. The same formula applies to fees. This payment is made directly by the government to the school.

  Note: this is a maximum. If your actual tuition and fees are lower than the maximum, you won't get the difference between your actual expenses and the maximum.

- *A housing allowance.* A monthly housing allowance is paid directly to veterans. The amount is the same as the basic allowance for housing for an E-5 with dependents within the zip code of the school. The military's housing allowance rate for the area in which the student actually lives is irrelevant.

  Everyone receives the E-5 rate, regardless of their actual rank. Folks using GI Bill benefits while on active duty are ineligible for this benefit. Nor is the housing allowance paid to people who are attending school at half-time or less. More about this later.

- *Stipend for books and supplies.* Veterans receive up to $1,000 annually. Active-duty personnel using their GI Bill benefits don't receive this special payment.

- *Relocation.* Some people leaving areas defined as "highly rural" to attend school qualify for a one-time $500 relocation payment. Check with the school office administering GI Bill benefits to find out if you qualify.

Like many earlier versions of the GI bill, how much a veteran or service member actually receives is also based upon the amount of time spent in uniform.

For the Post-9/11 GI Bill, folks who spent 36 months on active duty receive the maximum payments outlined above for tuition and fees, the housing allowance and the stipend for books and fees. Also receiving the maximum are people with at least 30 continuous days on active duty who are discharged because of a medical problem that's officially recognized as a "service-connected disability."

People with at least 30 months, but less than 36 months, on active duty receive 90 percent of the maximum. That shrinks to 80 percent for those with 24 months on active duty, 70 percent for 18 months, 60 percent for 12 months, 50 percent for 6 months, and 40 percent for 90 days.

People with 89 days or less are ineligible for any benefits under the Post-9/11 GI Bill unless they were discharged because of a service-connected medical problem.

Tabulating time on active duty cannot include boot camp and skills training for folks with less than 24 months in uniform. People with 24 months or more can have their boot camp and initial skills training counted as time toward their educational benefits.

Also affecting payments is something called the "Yellow Ribbon Program." It's offered by private schools and other private institutions where tuitions are larger than the highest tuition at the in-state rate in public colleges and universities.

In the Yellow Ribbon program, participating schools volunteer to accept some students with GI Bill benefits and not charge the students the school's higher, normal rate. Typically, private schools will select a specific number of students that they will accept each semester or quarter under the program. Those lower rates aren't offered to everyone. Again, this is a voluntary program for the schools.

If your plans include enrolling in private institutions, it's a good idea to find out if they participate in the Yellow Ribbon program. Also find how many students they're likely to accept under that program and for which courses of study.

Transferring Benefits

Earlier versions of the GI Bill allowed some family members of disabled veterans and some survivors of deceased veterans and military personnel to qualify for educational benefits. The Post-9/11 GI Bill is the first that permits active-duty people to transfer their own educational benefits to a spouse or children.

In fact, military personnel can transfer benefits to several family members at the same time. An important distinction is that veterans are unable to transfer their benefit to a family member, although a loophole is discussed below.

The benefit: Spouses and children receive the same benefits under the Post-9/11 GI bill as their military sponsor. They are getting, in effect, the portion of the service member's GI bill benefit that the service member didn't use.

Here's how it works: If a soldier only uses 20 months of his benefit and he's entitled to the maximum 36 months of coverage, then he can split the remaining 16 months among his spouse and children.

Eligibility:
- The service member must have at least six years in the military to transfer benefits to a spouse, and ten years in uniform to transfer benefits to a child.
- A child must be 18 years of age or must have a high school diploma or equivalent certificate.

Time Limits:
- Service members must officially notify the military of their intention to transfer educational benefits to a family member while still in uniform. So long as that requirement is met, family members can still receive the benefit after their sponsor leaves the military.
- A spouse has 15 years to use the educational benefits.
- Chilrden must use benefits before their twenty-sixth birthdays. The 15-year time limit doesn't apply to children, but they lose all eligibility for benefits after the twenty-sixth birthday.

- Spouses and children continue to receive their educational benefits even if their military sponsor dies.
- Sponsor can stop or change the spouses' and children's educational benefits at any time.

An Irrevocable Choice

Most people who were on active duty when the Post-9/11 GI Bill began on September 11, 2001 were also covered by earlier versions of the GI Bill. They must choose whether to use the new GI Bill or the version they originally qualified for; they cannot use both the Post-9/11 GI Bill and an earlier version of the GI Bill. This decision is irrevocable. Once made, it cannot be undone.

As this book went to print, people who switched from earlier versions of the GI Bill to the Post-9/11 GI Bill were able to use their earlier benefits for certain kinds of training not available under the Post-9/11 program. The types of education and training for which coverage is only available to folks switching to the Post-9/11 program from other versions of the GI Bill include flight training, apprenticeships, on-the-job programs and correspondence course.

MONTGOMERY GI BILL

The major program from 1985 to 2009 to pick up the tab for veterans in civilian colleges and trade schools was the Montgomery GI Bill. Like earlier versions of the GI Bill, it was open both to veterans who had been discharged and to people on active duty. And also like earlier versions, both groups had to meet very specific eligibility rules. Unlike the major wartime versions of the GI Bill, however, the Montgomery GI Bill required participants to make a contribution before they could receive any benefits.

Trivia item: It's easy to understand how the Vietnam-Era GI Bill got its name. But where did the "Montgomery" in the Montgomery GI Bill come from?

G. V. "Sonny" Montgomery was a congressman from Mississippi who chaired the House Veterans Affairs Committee for many years during the final quarter of the twentieth century. He shepherded through Congress the GI Bill version that now bears his name. Until then, it had been simply called "the New GI Bill."

Eligibility

The Montgomery GI Bill was the government's basic educational benefit for people who came on active duty from 1985 to 2009, served their tours, then left with an honorable discharge.

Over the years, eligibility was extended to different groups of veterans and active-duty people. That created a confusing layer of rules. Let's try to examine one layer at a time.

Who: The Montgomery GI Bill was open to all enlisted members of all the armed services. It was also available to all officers who received their commissions through officer candidate school, direct commissioning, or as nonscholarship ROTC cadets.

In effect, this meant the program was usually closed to graduates of a U.S. military academy and officers who received commissions as scholarship cadets in ROTC. Nevertheless, even these normally barred officers could sign up if they were discharged with separation pay, Special Separation Benefit, or Voluntary Separation Incentive.

When: Participants were required to have entered the military for the first time after June 30, 1985. The phrase "for the first time" is important. It means what it says.

People who first came on active duty before that date may be eligible for more generous benefits under VEAP (see the section titled "Veterans Educational Assistance Program," later in this chapter). Or they may be eligible to convert some benefits from the Vietnam-Era GI Bill into benefits under the Montgomery GI Bill.

People officially serving on full-time National Guard duty qualified if they assumed full-time status after November 29, 1989.

How Long: Montgomery GI Bill recipients must meet one of these minimum time-in-uniform rules:

- Continuous service for at least three years if the initial military obligation was for three years or for a longer period.
- Continuous service for at least three years, regardless of length of obligation.
- Continuous service for at least two years if the initial military obligation was for less than three years. This results in a reduced benefit.
- Continuous service for at least two years—regardless of length of obligation—followed by at least four years in Selected Reserve.

The normal required time periods for length of service can be shortened for certain involuntary discharges.

High School Diploma: If a person comes on active duty without a high school diploma, within the initial period of obligated service he or she must meet one of these three conditions:

- Earn a high school diploma.
- Earn an officially recognized equivalent.
- Complete twelve credit-hours toward a college degree.

Discharge: Regardless of the reason for the discharge or the time on active duty, a veteran must have an honorable discharge to take part in the Montgomery GI Bill.

Approved Courses

Veterans and active-duty people using the Montgomery GI Bill must enroll in classes or training that has been approved by the Department of Veterans Affairs.

In general, the types of education and training covered by the Montgomery GI Bill are the same as for the Post-9/11 GI Bill. The following are programs available under the Montgomery GI Bill that are not covered by the Post-9/11 GI Bill:

- Cooperative training programs (for discharged veterans only, not for active-duty people).
- Approved correspondence courses.
- Apprenticeship and on-the-job training (for discharged veterans only, not for active-duty people).
- Flight training for veterans who already have a private pilot's license; must pass a physical for a commercial license.

Time Limit

The time restrictions for the Montgomery GI Bill work the same way as for the Post-9/11 GI Bill, except that the Montgomery GI Bill has a ten-year clock for using benefits.

Payments and Contributions

Before servicemembers can receive any benefits from the Montgomery GI Bill, they must make a contribution. Normally, this takes the form of a nonrefundable monthly deduction from the paycheck. The deduction was $100 per month for twelve months.

The basic benefit under the Montgomery GI Bill varies by the amount of active-duty and reserve time. Following are the major categories, plus the typical maximum payment rates in effect for 2010:

- $1,368 monthly for thirty-six months to veterans with three years or more on active duty.
- $1,368 monthly for thirty-six months to veterans with two years on active duty, followed by four years in the Selected Reserve.
- $1,111 monthly for thirty-six months to veterans with less than three years on active duty.

Up to $50,000 in addition to one of these basic rates is available for people who enlisted or reenlisted in hard-to-fill jobs. This extra money is known as a "kicker." If you're eligible for a kicker, you already know it. You were officially notified when you enlisted or reenlisted.

Accelerated Payment

The Montgomery GI Bill also allows recipients to make "accelerated payments." With accelerated payments, recipients receive substantially more than their monthly benefits. Monthly educational expenses must be more than twice the monthly payments under the Montgomery GI Bill.

What's an accelerated payment? It happens when folks receive more than the normal monthly payment, but for less than the usual time. Take the example of a veteran eligible for thirty-six months of benefits at $1,138 monthly. Under the accelerated program, he might receive $2,276 (double the usual rate) for eighteen months (half the usual term). Or triple the monetary payment for a third of the time. Or some other balance between payment size and time.

This provision usually affects people enrolled in expensive courses for technical skills. In fact, accelerated payments cannot apply to any program leading to an associate, bachelors, masters, or any other degree. And the course of study cannot last longer than two years.

If you think you may qualify for accelerated payments, check with your nearest VA benefits office or with your school's financial office. They should have the latest rules affecting this unique feature.

An Irrevocable Choice

Generally, once a servicemember decided to participate in the Montgomery GI Bill, that decision could not be changed.

A major exception involves servicemembers and veteran who are also eligible for the new Post-9/11 GI Bill. They can choose to get benefits under the newer educational program. But once they accept Post-9/11 GI Bill benefits, they cannot switch back to the Montgomery GI Bill.

Veterans cannot request refunds of their money contributed toward the Montgomery GI Bill. Even if they never enroll in a single class, the government will keep their $1,200.

Refunds are made only when participants die before receiving $1,200 in educational assistance and the death occurs on active duty or within one year of discharge. In such a case, the government will pay the veteran's survivors for the unused portion of the veteran's out-of-pocket contribution.

MONTGOMERY GI BILL (SELECTED RESERVE)

Not everyone performing invaluable service for the U.S. military wears a uniform for forty hours each week. Reservists and National Guardsmen are an indispensable part of the military.

To recognize their contributions, Congress has extended the Montgomery GI Bill to the men and women who serve the nation's defense needs as members of the reserve component. The reserve version of the Montgomery GI Bill is sometimes referred to as the "Chapter 1606" program. The name comes from the section of federal law that created it.

There are two major differences between the active-duty and reserve versions of the program. First, active-duty service-members have $100 withheld monthly from their paychecks for a year in order to qualify, while reservists don't have any reduction in salary.

Second, many people taking part in the active-duty version of the Montgomery GI Bill don't begin using their benefits until they leave the military. For most reservists, eligibility for the Montgomery GI Bill ends when they leave the Selected Reserve.

Eligibility

Most people in the reserves and the National Guard have served on active duty, where they may have earned Montgomery GI Bill benefits. If you qualified for this educational program through active-duty time, then you don't have to requalify as a reservist. For these people, all benefits and rules are the same as for active-duty personnel.

Not all reservists and guardsmen are eligible. Only participants in the Selected Reserve can qualify for the Montgomery GI Bill. The Selected Reserve consist of reservists and guardsmen who are assigned to units or to the trained manpower pool called the Individual Mobilization Augmentation (IMA) program.

Here are some other eligibility rules:

- Enlisted members must have first enlisted after June 30, 1985, or they must have reenlisted or extended an enlistment after that date.
- Enlisted people must enlist or extend for not less than six years.
- Officers must have agreed to serve six years in addition to the original obligation.
- Participants must have completed initial active duty for training (IADT).
- Servicemembers must have earned high school diplomas or the equivalent before finishing IADT.

- Participants must remain in good standing with the Selected Reserve.
- People who received scholarships under the ROTC program may not use the reserve version of the Montgomery GI Bill.

Here are some technical nicknames for educational programs for veterans:

- Chapter 30 = Montgomery GI Bill.
- Chapter 31 = Vocational rehabilitation.
- Chapter 32 = Veterans Educational Assistance Program (VEAP).
- Chapter 33 = Post-9/11 GI Bill.
- Chapter 34 = Vietnam-Era GI Bill.
- Chapter 1606 = Montgomery GI Bill (Selected Reserve).

The nicknames come from the sections of federal law that created them.

Time Limits

Unlike the active-duty version of the Montgomery GI Bill, most reservists and guardsmen lose eligibility for their educational benefits when they leave the Selected Reserve.

- People who joined the Selected Reserve after September 30, 1992, must use their benefits within fourteen years of becoming a selected reservist.
- People who joined the Selected Reserve before October 1, 1992, must use their benefits within ten years of becoming a selected reservist.
- People who were discharged from the Selected Reserve because of a medical disability or a formal drawdown program must use their benefits within ten years of their discharge.

Payments and Contributions

Unlike active-duty personnel, reservists and guardsmen don't have money withheld from their paychecks in order to qualify for their version of the Montgomery GI Bill. What they receive from the government to pay for their educational bills was placed, in 2011, at a maximum of $333 monthly. Generally, that figure should increase yearly at the same rate as inflation.

Reservists attending class full time can receive the maximum payments for thirty-six months. Besides full time, there are three other ways of measuring educational time for the Montgomery GI Bill: three-quarters time, half time, and one-quarter time.

Accelerated Payment

Reservists and National Guardsmen are also eligible for accelerated payment of their benefits. The rules are similar to the ones discussed in "Accelerated Payments" in the section above for the Montgomery GI Bill for active-duty personnel.

If you think you may qualify for accelerated payments, check with your nearest VA benefits office or with your school's financial office. They should have the latest rules affecting this unique feature.

Fine Points

Some reservists are eligible to participate in both the active-duty and the reserve versions of the Montgomery GI Bill. There are limits on what they can do. For example, federal law prohibits them from being paid twice for the same class.

Nevertheless, it may be possible for some people to use all their benefits under the active-duty program, then to use their benefits under the reserve version, or vice versa. For them, there's a forty-eight-month limit.

Other reservists are eligible, simultaneously, for the reserve version of the Montgomery GI Bill and the Veterans Educational Assistance Program, or VEAP.

They may be able to qualify for payments from both programs at different times, but they cannot use the same period of active duty to qualify for both VEAP and the reserve version of the Montgomery GI Bill.

RESERVE EDUCATIONAL ASSISTANCE PROGRAM
Reservists and National Guardsmen "ordered to active duty in response to a war or national emergency" are eligible for an educational benefit called the Reserve Educational Assistance Program, or REAP.

Since November 2004, the program has provided educational assistance to reservists and Guardsmen who were not on active duty long enough to qualify for benefits under the Montgomery GI Bill for the Selected Reserve.

Still, many REAP participants are also eligible for the Post-9/11 GI Bill, the Montgomery GI Bill or the Montgomery GI Bill for Selected Reservists. As is usually the case with government benefits, folks cannot be paid twice by the government for attending the same class. However, REAP can blur that line because of an unusual feature involving retroactivity. More about that later.

Eligibility
The REAP program is available to reservists and National Guardsmen who were called to active duty from the Selected Reserve since September 11, 2001. They must remain on active duty for at least ninety continuous days to qualify for minimal benefits. They also can qualify with less than ninety days if discharged for an illness or injury the government officially classified as "service connected."

What happens to people after leaving active duty can be crucial for getting REAP benefits. With the exception of those discharged with medical disabilities, people who get REAP benefits as veterans have served the total number of years called for in their service contracts, both on active duty and as reservists.

In most cases, participants have to return to the Selected Reserve after leaving active duty. Then, in order to qualify for REAP, they must receive their discharges from the Selected Reserve, not from the Individual Ready Reserve, or IRR. Transferring into the IRR after leaving active duty can make them ineligible for REAP.

Payments

Recipients of REAP benefits receive monthly payments from the VA for their education. Those payments are really reimbursements. Participants cannot receive more than the amount of the tuition and fees charged by an institution of higher learning, vocational course, or any other approved course of study.

The amount of each payment is determined by a two-step process.

Step One: Find out the maximum monthly payment under the Montgomery GI Bill. In 2010, it was $1,368.

Step Two: Do a little math.

- Folks who served continuously for at least ninety days on active duty can receive 40 percent of the Montgomery GI Bill rate per month;
- People discharged from active duty with less than ninety days because of "an injury, illness or disease incurred or aggravated in the line of duty" also get 40 percent of the maximum rate for the Montgomery GI Bill.
- Reservists and Guardsmen who served on active duty for at least one year are eligible for 60 percent of that rate;
- Those who served two continuous years on active duty receive 80 percent of the current monthly rate under the Montgomery GI Bill;

- Qualified reservists and National Guardsmen who spend a total of three years on active duty—not necessarily continuously—also can receive the 80 percent rate.

The periods in uniform mentioned above must have been accumulated since September 11, 2001.

Keep in mind, there are two "maximums" here. One is the maximum monthly payment for the Montgomery GI Bill mentioned in Step One. The other is the individual maximum from Step Two that's based upon a person's time in service. Veterans, reservists and Guardsmen will receive less than Step Two's individual maximum if their tuition and fees are less.

Generally, REAP benefits are more generous than those offered under the Montgomery GI Bill for Selected Reserve.

Time Limits

People who qualify for REAP have ten years to use their benefits after being discharged from the Selected Reserve. The ten-year limit after discharge also applies to reservists and Guardsmen who leave active duty because of medical problems that are officially labeled as service-connected disabilities.

REAP participants receive thirty-six months of full-time benefits. If they combine REAP with another version of the GI Bill, the total coverage is limited to forty-eight months.

Accelerated Payment

Reservists and National Guardsmen taking part in the REAP program are also eligible for accelerated payment of their benefits. The rules are similar to the ones discussed in "Accelerated Payments" in the section above for the Montgomery GI Bill for active-duty personnel.

If you think you may qualify for accelerated payments, check with your nearest VA benefits office or with your school's financial office. They should have the latest rules affecting this unique feature.

Approved Courses

As with many government-funded education programs, people have considerable latitude in choosing their own schools and their own courses of study under REAP. However, the government won't fund study in schools that fail to meet minimal professional standards. Nor will it pay for all kinds of education and training.

Fortunately, REAP benefits apply to the widest variety of courses, the same as the approved courses for the Montgomery GI Bill.

Retroactive Payments

Technically, the REAP program will cover educational expenses incurred since September 11, 2001. But there's a hitch. The bill didn't pass Congress until late in 2005, and the government needed several years to get all the legal gears in motion. And not every eligible person became instantly aware of the new benefit. So now what?

REAP is retroactive. Even if an eligible veteran, reservist or Guardsman has already paid the bill for educational expenses, he or she may be able to receive reimbursement from REAP. REAP also covers situations where veterans or service members used another educational benefit, but still had some out-of-pocket expenses. REAP will make up the difference.

Take the example of a former, REAP-eligible reservist who took six months of a full-time course of instruction costing $500 per month. Assume that veteran used the full benefits of the Montgomery GI Bill for the Selected Reserve, which was $297 per month. Under REAP, the government can reimburse him for the $203 per month in tuition and fees not paid by the Montgomery GI Bill for Selected Reserve. The combined payment under REAP and the other government program cannot exceed the larger of the two educational benefits.

Folks who think they may be eligible for retroactive payments should work with their nearest VA office or the office at their school that handles GI Bill questions to make sure they're eligible. Significant fine print comes into play, especially involving the timing of the class and whether a student was eligible for REAP when taking the class.

Irrevocable Choices

Except for people taking advantage of REAP's retroactive rule, service members and veterans can only receive benefits under one of the government's major educational programs for military personnel and veterans—the Montgomery GI Bill, the Montgomery GI Bill for the Selected Reserve, the Post-9/11 GI Bill, or REAP.

Once people select the benefit they'll use, they can't change their minds.

Transfer to Family

Reservists, Guardsmen and veterans can transfer some—or all—of their REAP benefits to a spouse or a child, or divide them between a spouse and children. The family member receives the same benefits under the same rules, including the same payment scheme, that apply to military personnel.

The fine print is identical to the rules for transferring benefits under the Post-9/11 GI Bill. And, as happens with the Post-9/11 GI Bill, you cannot initiate the process for transferring benefits after you leave the military, although family members can still use REAP benefits if their sponsor set up the transfer while still in uniform.

VETERANS EDUCATIONAL ASSISTANCE PROGRAM

Between the end of the Vietnam-Era GI Bill and the creation of the Montgomery GI Bill, a program was put on the books with the name of the Veterans Educational Assistance Program.

Although commonly called VEAP, it is sometimes referred to in legal shorthand as the "Chapter 32" program. By any name, it was a milestone for veterans. VEAP was the first educational program for veterans that required an out-of-pocket contribution from participants.

Although no one has been able to sign up for VEAP since 1987, veterans are still receiving benefits under this program.

Eligibility

As with all versions of the GI Bill, VEAP's participants are defined by the period during which they came into the military. To be eligible, people must have first joined the military between January 1, 1977, and July 1, 1985. The word "first" means what it says. If you came on active duty during the eligibility period, then left the military, then returned after the eligibility window had closed, you still could receive financial help for education under the VEAP program.

VEAP participants who were on active duty on October 9, 1996, were given the option of switching to the Montgomery GI Bill. They had to make a $1,200 contribution to be eligible.

There's another important eligibility criterion for late users of VEAP benefits, however. In order to get benefits *now,* they must have made some sort of financial contribution before April 1, 1987: Remember that VEAP required military people to make an out-of-pocket contribution before they would receive any benefits from the government.

Contributions

Essentially, VEAP is a matching program: For every dollar contributed by a servicemember, the government adds two dollars to be used to pay educational bills.

The maximum contribution by a servicemember toward VEAP is $2,700. After the government adds its share, the most the majority of veterans will receive from VEAP is $8,100.

Some Army veterans, however, receive more. That service's Army College Fund offered improved VEAP benefits to soldiers who enlisted in some high-skill or hard-to-fill jobs. Those benefits, known as kickers, could be worth as much as $18,300. Everyone who received a kicker signed a written contract with the Army at the time of enlistment that spelled out those rights and benefits.

Payments

The easiest way to figure out how much a veteran will receive from VEAP is to multiply that person's total contribution by the number three.

Payments to veterans are made monthly. Usually, veterans receive VEAP payments for the same number of months that they contributed money into the program.

Time Limits

Payments for education under VEAP end ten years after a veteran's discharge.

For veterans who have broken service—that is, they've been discharged at least once and returned to active duty—VEAP payments end ten years after the most recent discharge.

The ten-year limit can be extended if a veteran is unable to attend class or take training courses because of a disability.

Refunds

While VEAP more closely resembles the Montgomery GI Bill than earlier versions of the GI Bill, it has some provisions that are unique.

Unlike under the Montgomery GI Bill, a veteran can drop out of the VEAP program and receive a refund. The refund includes only the veteran's contribution, not the government's matching funds. The government will not pay interest on a servicemember's contribution.

Refunds are also made to survivors when VEAP-eligible veterans die without using all of their educational benefits.

Veterans who haven't used their entire benefits under VEAP by the tenth anniversary of discharge can receive refunds for their unused contributions to the program. Refunds for unused VEAP benefits should be automatic after the tenth anniversary of discharge.

The nearest VA office can help veterans or their survivors apply for refunds.

Reenrollments

A unique provision of VEAP allows people to drop out of the program and receive refunds, then to sign up for it again.

This affects veterans who qualified for VEAP during an early stint in the military, who leave the armed forces and get refunds of their unused VEAP contributions, and who later return to active duty.

They would be unable to qualify for the Montgomery GI Bill because VEAP was the educational benefit that was on the books when they first joined the military. Consequently, if they rejoin the military, they can rejoin VEAP.

Conversions

For some veterans, VEAP isn't as useful or as generous as the Montgomery GI Bill. Lawmakers have recognized that, and they have been allowing different categories of VEAP participants who are facing discharge to switch to the Montgomery GI Bill.

If your discharge date is approaching, check with a military education office or transition office to find out whether you qualify for one of the conversion programs.

VIETNAM-ERA GI BILL

Although the Vietnam-Era GI Bill has elapsed and no payments are being made to anyone under this program, there are still people who are affected by it.

These are the veterans and the military people who served on active duty during the switch from the Vietnam-Era GI Bill to the Montgomery GI Bill, roughly the period 1984 to 1987 (more precise dates are listed below).

For them, it's possible to convert their eligibility for the Vietnam-Era GI Bill into eligibility for the Montgomery GI Bill, under a process known as "a Chapter 34 to 30 Conversion."

If they qualify, they will receive the same Montgomery GI Bill rates as everyone else, plus a little more. That additional payment is about $200 monthly for full-time educational study.

Eligibility

To make the conversion, Vietnam-era veterans must have been eligible for the Vietnam-Era GI Bill. They also must have benefits remaining, technically, under the educational program. Who has benefits remaining? Everyone who never used the Vietnam-Era GI Bill, plus everyone who used it but for less than the maximum time or for less than the maximum amounts for full-time study.

Typically, veterans of that era were entitled to forty-five months of education under the Vietnam-Era GI Bill. If they received checks for less than forty-five months, or checks that were for less than full-time study for forty-five months, then they have benefits remaining under the Vietnam-Era GI Bill.

Deadlines

Like participants in the Montgomery GI Bill, Vietnam-era veterans who are switching educational programs generally have ten years from the date of their last discharge to use the benefit.

As a rule, VA officials keep the ten-year clock running for any period that a veteran spent off active duty between January 1, 1977, and June 30, 1985.

For veterans who spent two years on active duty and four years in the Selected Reserve, the ten-year clock begins on the date of discharge from active duty or at the end of the four years in the Selected Reserve, whichever is later.

VOCATIONAL REHABILITATION

Disability compensation is often not enough to live on. Despite their handicaps, many disabled veterans want work that challenges them and increases their income.

For those disabled veterans, VA has a special program that helps them prepare for suitable employment or achieve greater independence in daily living. Under this program, the government pays for all school-related expenses, while giving the veteran an allowance. Active-duty personnel may also qualify for some parts of the program.

Eligibility

Although many veterans could benefit from a program of vocational training, this effort is targeted at a specific group of disabled people.

Participants must meet all of these three conditions:

1. They must have a discharge officially rated as "under other than dishonorable conditions" or be awaiting discharge from active duty for a disability.
2. They must be certified by VA officials as needing vocational rehabilitation to overcome a disability that prevents them from holding a job that is consistent with their skills and interests.

3. Their disabilities must meet the official definition for being service-connected, and those disabilities must meet one of the following criteria:

- Be rated by VA officials at 20 percent or greater, if the applicant is on active duty; or.
- Be rated by VA officials at least 10 percent if the applicant is a veteran.

Note that vocational rehabilitation is a VA program for which some people on active duty can qualify.

A form of vocational training is also available to some low-income veterans with disabilities not related to their military service. These are veterans who receive a VA pension.

Details of the Program

Vocational rehabilitation includes government-paid education or training, a subsistence allowance for people already discharged from the military, and counseling and other help.

The government will pay the costs of tuition, fees, books, supplies, and equipment, plus some transportation costs. Also included among fully paid services are tutorial assistance, prosthetic devices, and lip-reading training or signing for the deaf.

Usually, people can participate in vocational rehabilitation for up to forty-eight months. That period can be extended for veterans with severe handicaps to employment.

Vocational rehabilitation pays the bills for the following:

- College-level institutions, trade schools, and business or technical schools.
- On-the-job training and apprenticeship training.
- On-the-farm training.
- Combinations of classroom instruction and on-the-job experience.
- Special rehabilitative facilities.
- Some at-home study.

The subsistence allowance that's a part of vocational training isn't affected by what the government spends on tuition, fees, and other educational expenses. Nor is it affected by disability compensation, military retirement pay, or income from a work-study program.

The amount of subsistence is spelled out in VA charts that set different rates for the number of dependents, the kind of training, and whether the veteran is attending full-time, half-time, or at some other pace.

The amount of the subsistence allowance doesn't change automatically every year to keep up with inflation, like many other VA payments. Here are some examples of the monthly rates in effect in the year 2010:

- Full-time instruction in an institution: veterans with no dependents, about $550; with one dependent, about $680; with two dependents, about $800; for each additional dependent, about $60 more.
- Full-time training on a farm, apprenticeship program, or on-the-job training: veterans with no dependents, about $480; with one dependent, about $580; with two dependents, about $670; for each additional dependent, about $45 more.
- Full-time evaluation or independent living program: veterans with no dependents, about $550; with one dependent, about $680; with two dependents, about $800; for each additional dependent, about $60 more.

The program will pay for up to four years of full-time vocational training, or for an equivalent period of part-time training—for example, eight years of half-time training. Payments will continue for two months after a veteran completes a training program or educational class.

Each program is individually designed and approved by VA officials, based on the needs and circumstances of the disabled veteran.

Normally, the training must be completed within twelve years after discharge from active duty. The start of the twelve-year eligibility period can be delayed if:

- A medical condition made the veteran unable to begin training.
- VA officials failed to notify a veteran of approval for a disability rating, which often sets the groundwork for eligibility for vocational training.

TWELVE

TYING UP LOOSE ENDS WITH THE MILITARY

> **In This Chapter:**
>
> - *Copies of Discharges*
> - *Upgrading Discharges*
> - *Correcting Military Records*
> - *Copies of Medals*

The military can cast a long shadow over a veteran's life. Job skills and personal relationships developed while on active duty can have a decisive impact on veterans and their families decades afterward.

Unpleasant aspects of military service can also persist for decades. The injury that was a nuisance when it happened during military training can deteriorate into a true disability. Or a scrape that resulted in a hasty departure from the armed forces—along with something less than an honorable discharge—can block passage to important benefits.

Fortunately, the Pentagon and the Department of Veterans Affairs recognize the lasting imprint made by the military on the lives of veterans. Officials have created administrative channels that enable veterans to bring their concerns to the right offices or agencies.

As anyone who has explored those channels can tell you, however, they're not quick. And it's not always clear what's important, why certain decisions were made, or what a veteran should do next.

Before you go it alone or hire a lawyer, it's always best to check into the free sources of help available. VA officials may be restricted in the advice they can give, but they are able to offer copies of forms and written information about procedures.

The major veterans organizations also have full-time professionals, called "service officers," who handle these sorts of problems every week. Their help is free and offered equally to members and nonmembers. Many have desks at VA regional offices.

COPIES OF DISCHARGES

Your discharge papers—known to veterans during the last several decades as DD Form 214—are the basic ticket for admission to a full range of veterans benefits, from disability pay to burial in a national cemetery. Duplicate DD Form 214s can be obtained, free of charge, from the federal government.

Eligibility

Everyone who has received a discharge from the military can obtain a copy of his or her personal DD Form 214.

If a veteran is incapacitated or otherwise unable to sign a request, a spouse may request a copy on the veteran's behalf. To prevent unnecessary delays, a spouse should clearly explain why the veteran isn't making the request and include documentation—such as a note from a doctor or an admission form to a nursing home—that supports the explanation. If a widow or widower is requesting a copy, he or she should include a copy of the veteran's death certificate.

Application

If possible, everyone—veterans and family members—requesting a copy of discharge papers should use Standard Form 180, "Request Pertaining to Military Records." That form is available from VA regional offices, veterans organizations, or the government's website at www.archives.gov/veterans.

A safety deposit box at a local bank is a good place to keep discharge papers, but make sure family members have access to it.

The government will also fulfill requests made in a letter, which should be typed or clearly printed and specify exactly what is being sought, such as a DD Form 214 or any other portion of the military member's official record.

The request should include as much of the following information as possible:

- The veteran's legal name.
- Date and place of birth.
- The veteran's Social Security number or service number.
- The veteran's service (e.g., the Army).
- The date the veteran entered the military (or an approximate date).
- The date the veteran left the military (or an approximate date).

The veteran, spouse, widow, or widower should sign the request and make sure it includes a return address. The request, whether made with Standard Form 180 or by letter, should be mailed to: National Personnel Records Center, Military Personnel Records, 9700 Page Boulevard, Saint Louis, MO 63132-5100.

Emergencies

It's possible to obtain copies of a DD Form 214 by making a request over the telephone, but this option is limited to people with genuine emergencies.

Legitimate emergencies are defined on a case-by-case basis. People who feel they have an immediate need for a DD Form 214 should contact the nearest VA regional office. Officials there can explain the procedure for making a telephone request.

UPGRADING DISCHARGES

Because most VA benefits depend on receiving at least a general discharge, the government has created several avenues for veterans who believe they were erroneously given an unfavorable discharge.

Using any one of these options, a veteran can have his or her original discharge canceled and receive a new discharge. This process is commonly called "upgrading" a discharge.

The most direct approach for an upgrade is to file an appeal with a discharge review board. Each military department has one of these boards. The U.S. Department of Homeland Security oversees a board for the Coast Guard, and former members of the Marine Corps use the board operated by the Department of the Navy.

Eligibility

Every veteran who has received a discharge that wasn't rated as honorable can apply for an upgrade.

Details of the Program

Discharge review boards are empowered to have most discharges changed or replaced.

Veterans applying to a board can present documentation on their own behalf or call witnesses. They can appear in person. They have a right to hire an attorney, be represented by an accredited member of a major veterans organization, or be aided by an employee of a state department of veterans affairs.

Veterans are responsible for paying their own way if they choose to appear personally before a board.

To be successful, a veteran must prove that a discharge was illegally or unfairly given. Boards can review discharges in light of current standards. The boards will commonly upgrade an unfavorable discharge from years ago if someone currently discharged would receive an honorable or general discharge for the same problem or infraction.

Normally, the five-member discharge review boards hold hearings in Washington, DC. Occasionally, however, they conduct hearings in selected sites around the country. The boards also sometimes send a single person called a hearing examiner to take testimony from veterans across the country.

The decisions made by the discharge review boards must be approved by the secretary of the appropriate military department.

Discharge review boards cannot change any document in a veteran's military personnel file except discharge papers. Other limitations on the boards' authority are significant:

- They cannot review a discharge ordered by a general court-martial.
- They cannot directly determine eligibility for any VA benefit. (But access to more VA benefits usually comes from an upgraded discharge.)
- They cannot change a discharge to a disability discharge. Nor can they change a disability discharge to something else.
- They cannot revoke any discharge or recall any veteran to active duty.

On this last point, it's important to note that discharge review boards commonly recommend to service secretaries that a veteran be given a chance to return to active duty. That's just a recommendation. The final decision rests with the service secretary.

Application

Requests for a discharge review board hearing to examine a veteran's case must be made within fifteen years after leaving the military.

Applications must be made on DD Form 293, "Application for Review of Discharge from the Armed Forces of the Unites States." It's available at most VA facilities, from service officers for the major veterans groups, and online at www.archives. gov/veterans/military-service-records/correctingrecords.html. Applications should be accompanied by copies of the original discharge and any supporting materials.

When veterans have died or if they are unable to manage their own affairs, then their applications can be made by a spouse, next of kin, or legal representative. Written evidence of the veteran's death, incapacity, relationship to the applicant, or power of attorney should accompany applications made by other people.

Applications should be mailed to the appropriate address for each service:

- *Army:* Army Review Boards Agency, Support Division, St. Louis, 9700 Page Avenue, St. Louis, MO 63132-5200.
- *Navy and Marine Corps:* Naval Council of Personnel Boards, 720 Kennon Street, S.E., Room 309 (NDRB), Washington Navy Yard, DC 20374-5023.
- *Air Force:* Air Force Review Boards Agency, SAF/MRBR, 550-C Street West, Suite 40, Randolph AFB, TX 78150-4742.
- *Coast Guard:* U.S. Coast Guard Commandant (CG-122), 2100 Second Street, S.W., Room 5500, Washington, DC 20593

Fine Points

Congress created the discharge review boards to right discharges that were wrongly given. They weren't created to help people get VA benefits. Historically, the boards have turned a deaf ear to veterans who argued that their discharges should be upgraded just to ensure access to VA programs.

Discharge review boards were set up *solely* to review discharges. Another panel, the military's Board for the Correction of Military Records, discussed next, can also authorize upgrades.

CORRECTING MILITARY RECORDS

Problems that began in the military as minor, sometimes even clerical mistakes on official documents, can linger for years and cause serious consequences.

Congress has created special three-person boards in each military department that have wide-ranging authority to correct any military document, including discharge papers. This review board is called "Board for the Correction of Military Records" in the Army and Air Force. The Navy and Marine Corps call it "Board for the Correction of Naval Records."

Eligibility

Everyone who has served in the military can petition one of these boards to correct a military record. Also eligible are people who are still on active duty or still in the reserves.

Details of the Program

Boards for the correction of records have broad powers that are rare for such administrative operations. By law, they can "correct any military record . . . to correct an error or remove an injustice."

Veterans and military members applying to a board can present documentation on their own behalf. If a board takes up a case, the panel will obtain the person's military records.

Most of the work of the boards is done by studying official records and documentation submitted by people requesting a correction. Hearings are rare, occurring in only a small percentage of cases.

When a board agrees to a hearing, people can be represented by an attorney or an accredited member of a major veterans organization. Veterans can call their own witnesses, but the board has no authority to require anyone to testify.

All hearings are held in Washington, DC. People petitioning the board are responsible for paying their own expenses related to a hearing.

Typically, it takes more than a year between the time an application is filed with a board and the time the board issues a final decision.

To be successful, a veteran must show that a military record is erroneous or unjust. Often, in disciplinary cases, that means showing that a punishment was too severe for the offense committed. Decisions of the boards for the correction of records must be approved by the secretary of the appropriate military department.

These boards have considerable authority to change official documents in ways affecting the benefits available from the military and the Department of Veterans Affairs. In particular, these boards can do the following:

- Place veterans on the retired rolls.
- Change a previous discharge to a disability retirement.
- Reinstate a veteran on active duty.
- Order a promotion.
- Change performance evaluations.
- Credit a veteran with additional active-duty time, with the result of making the veteran eligible for VA benefits.
- Change the date of a discharge to show completion of an enlistment or active-duty obligation.
- Upgrade discharges ordered by a general court-martial.

On this last item, it's important to note that the boards can upgrade discharges—on the basis that a sentence was unfairly severe—but they cannot overturn convictions.

Application

Requests for reviews by a board for the correction of records should be made within three years after a veteran discovers an error or injustice.

The boards have the authority to waive the three-year rule if a veteran has a good reason for failing to file within that time. The trend in recent years has been for the boards to follow the three-year rule closely.

Applications must be made on DD Form 149, "Application for Correction of Military or Naval Record." It's available at most VA facilities, from on-base military legal offices, from service officers for the major veterans groups, and online at www.archives.gov/ veterans/military-service-records/correcting-records.html.

> Correct problems with your military records now. You might not have the time later, when that problem keeps you from getting a vital VA benefit.

If possible, applications should be accompanied by copies of the document that a person wants to change, plus any supporting materials.

A veteran who wants to present his or her case in person before a board must specifically request a hearing when submitting the DD Form 149. The forms have a block for entering those requests.

For veterans who have died or are unable to manage their own affairs, applications can be made by a spouse, parent, next of kin, or legal representative. Written evidence of the veteran's death, incapacity, relationship to the applicant, or power of attorney should accompany applications made by other people.

Applications should be mailed to the appropriate service:

- *Army (Active Duty):* Army Board for Correction of Military Records, 1901 South Bell Street, 2nd Floor, Arlington, VA 22202-4508.
- *Army (All Other):* Army Review Boards Agency, Support Division St. Louis, 9700 Page Avenue, St. Louis, MO 63132-5200.
- *Navy and Marine Corps:* Board for Correction of Naval Records, Navy Annex, Washington, DC 20370-5100.
- *Air Force:* Board for Correction of Air Force Records, SAF/MRBR, 550-C Street West, Suite 40, Randolph AFB, TX 78150-4742.
- *Coast Guard:* Board for Correction of Military Records, 245 Murray Lane, Room 5126, Mail Stop #0900, Washington, DC 20528.

Fine Points

The boards for the correction of records do most of their work with paper. Hearings are rare. This has major consequences for anyone who asks a board to correct something on the official record.

The application and the supporting documentation submitted by a veteran must be enough to persuade the board that an error or injustice has occurred. If a board takes up a case, it will study the pertinent portions of the veteran's personnel file. Again, the paperwork initially submitted with the application must make the veteran's case, clearly and persuasively.

Assistance from a professional who has dealt with boards for the correction of records is invaluable. Service officers from the major veterans organizations can provide assistance free of charge. Civilian attorneys who specialize in military law can also help, although they charge for their services.

A typical problem encountered by "go-it-alone" applicants is that they fail to exhaust other available administrative remedies. This is common for active-duty members and reservists, and for veterans with cases more properly handled by a discharge review board.

COPIES OF MEDALS

Awards and decorations given for military service often become more important—not less—as veterans age and their time in uniform slips farther into the past. Unfortunately, the decorations that veterans originally received on active duty often get misplaced or lost over the years.

Provisions are on the books to provide veterans with copies of the awards and decorations they received on active duty or while members of the reserves.

Eligibility

Anyone who was officially awarded a military decoration can request a copy of that medal at any time. Family members and survivors can make those requests when the veteran is unable to do it.

Details of the Program

If possible, requests should be submitted using Standard Form 180, "Request Pertaining to Military Records," which is obtainable at VA offices, from most major veterans organizations, and at www.archives.gov/veterans.

Written requests are also accepted. Requests should be typed or printed very clearly and contain the following:

- The veteran's name.
- The veteran's Social Security or military service number.
- The veteran's branch of service.
- The veteran's dates of service (or approximate dates).
- The specific medal being sought.

If possible, include a copy of the veteran's discharge papers, known in recent years as DD Form 214.

All requests, whether by the veteran, a family member acting on the veteran's behalf, or a survivor, should be signed.

Applications
Whether the request is made on the appropriate VA form or in a letter, it should be sent to the office maintained by each service for these issues.

- *Army:* U.S. Army Reserve Personnel Center, 9700 Page Boulevard, Saint Louis, MO 63132-5100.
- *Navy, Marine Corps, Coast Guard:* Navy Personnel Command, Liason Office, Room 5409, 9700 Page Avenue, Saint Louis, MO 63132-5100.
- *Air Force:* Headquarters, Air Force Personnel Center, AFPC/DPPPR, 550 C Street West, Suite 12, Randolph AFB, TX 78150-4714.

Fine Points
These procedures were set up for veterans who were awarded medals, misplaced them, and now want the government to replace them. They won't help people who think they should have been given a certain decoration while they were in uniform.

Commercial firms that sell medals often advertise in publications catering to veterans and active-duty military personnel. Sometimes it's quicker to deal with these companies than with the government.

A copy of a medal purchased from a commercial outfit is no less authentic than one given, free, by the government. In fact, the government buys its medals from commercial sources.

When dealing by mail or telephone with a commercial supplier, make sure the medal meets all the formal government specifications and that it's suitable for wear on an active-duty uniform.

THIRTEEN

TAPS

In This Chapter:

- *Burial Allowances*
- *Headstones and Markers*
- *National Cemeteries*
- *Final Honors*

Old soldiers may just "fade away," but the nation's obligation to them and their families doesn't end.

Survivors of veterans may be entitled to ongoing benefits, especially if the veterans were military retirees, if they were drawing VA disability compensation or VA pensions at the time of their death, or if there were children in the household who were underage or disabled. (You may want to reread chapter 9, "Payments to Families," for more about payments to survivors.)

The government also provides financial assistance for the burial of certain kinds of veterans, space in national cemeteries, headstones and markers for burials outside national cemeteries, and occasionally honor guards.

Burial-related benefits are the one category of veterans programs for which the local VA office might not be the best, quickest authority. Instead, the directors of local funeral homes usually have the most up-to-date and comprehensive summaries of benefits, along with the forms necessary to file for various programs.

Of course, survivors can go to the nearest VA office or major veterans group for help in understanding and securing their benefits. It may be easier, though, for them to start with the funeral director handling arrangements for their veteran.

BURIAL ALLOWANCES

The government provides some financial help in paying for the burial expenses of some veterans, but this is a limited benefit that goes only to specific categories of veterans.

The families of most veterans aren't entitled to financial support unless the veteran can meet some eligibility rule, as discussed below.

Eligibility

As happens with many veterans benefits, the rules pertaining to burial allowances were written at different times and apply to different categories of veterans.

In general, some sort of burial allowance is available for the following:

- People who die on active duty.
- Military retirees.
- Veterans who die directly from service-connected injuries.
- Recipients of VA disability compensation.
- Recipients of VA pensions.
- Disabled vets without next of kin or financial resources.
- Veterans who die in VA facilities.

Amount of Benefits

The most generous death benefits go to families of active-duty servicemembers. Survivors receive $100,000 for a death on active duty, inactive duty, or training, or within 120 days after discharge if due to a service-connected disability. This payment is unaffected by any other benefit paid to survivors, such as life insurance.

The families of veterans whose deaths were directly related to some disability caused by their military service could receive, in 2010, a burial allowance of $2,000. According to federal law, those deaths must be "as a result of a service-connected disability." It doesn't count if a veteran with a service-connected disability dies of some other cause.

Recipients of VA disability compensation and VA pensions qualify for a modest burial allowance. In 2010, it was $300.

When veterans die in VA facilities or state-run veterans homes, their survivors are entitled to a $300 burial allowance, plus government-paid transportation of the remains to the community in which the veteran will be buried.

Application

Application forms are available from funeral directors, VA regional offices, and military survivors assistance and casualty assistance offices.

HEADSTONES AND MARKERS

Until the early 1990s, the federal government provided either a free headstone or a marker for a veteran's grave, or the government provided a token payment—usually about $50—that could be used by the family toward the purchase of one. Legal authority for the government to pay that allowance is no longer on the books, but headstones and markers are still being provided by the government.

Eligibility

The rules for free government headstones and markers are broadly written. Those eligible for this benefit include the following:

- Almost all veterans.
- Everyone who dies on active duty.

- Reservists with twenty years of service.
- Spouses of veterans and active-duty people, and dependent children of these people, when buried in national cemetaries.
- Members of the Merchant Marines from December 7, 1941, to December 31, 1946.

The government will replace, at no charge to survivors, any government headstone or marker in a private cemetary that is stolen or damaged.

Spouses and dependent children of veterans and active-duty people are ineligible for government-paid headstones and markers if they are buried anywhere but in a national, federal, or state veterans cemetery.

Two major categories of former servicemembers ineligible for headstones or markers are those discharged "under dishonorable conditions" and those convicted of "subversive activities."

Description

The headstones and markers can be flat bronze, flat granite, flat marble, or upright marble. Also covered are niche markers for cremated remains.

Inscriptions at government expense include the following information:

- Name.
- Years of birth and death.
- Branch of service.
- Military rank.
- War service.
- Religious symbol.
- Awards for valor.
- Purple Heart.

Survivors can include other inscriptions or symbols at their own expense.

Transportation

The government assumes all costs for transporting headstones and markers, and for placing them in national and state cemetaries. For veterans not buried in national or state cemeteries, however, the family may have to pay the costs of placing the headstone or marker on the grave.

Application

Applications for headstones and markers are available from funeral directors, VA regional offices, and military survivors assistance and casualty assistance offices.

NATIONAL CEMETERIES

National cemeteries are special final resting places for the men and women who have served their country in uniform. There are no costs to a veteran's family for burial in a national cemetery or for the maintenance of the plot. The Department of Veterans Affairs has a full-time professional staff that guarantees the finest care for those gravesites. The government has put its full faith and credit behind preserving the national cemeteries, in perpetuity, as dignified resting places for the nation's veterans.

Some national cemeteries are "closed." That means they've used up available land and they're not digging any more gravesites.

Eligibility

Almost everyone who has ever worn a uniform of a U.S. armed service qualifies for burial in a national cemetery, including the following:

- Veterans of active-duty service.
- People who die on active duty.
- Reservists with twenty years of service.
- Reservists who die on inactive duty training while being treated for service-connected medical problems.

- Members of the Merchant Marines from December 7, 1941, to December 31, 1946.
- Certain Filipino veterans of World War II.
- Members of the Reserve Officers Training Corps (under specific circumstances).

Three major categories of former servicemembers usually ineligible for burial in national cemeteries are those discharged "under dishonorable conditions," those convicted of "subversive activities," and those who are sentenced to death or to life sentences by a military, federal, or state court.

The following are also eligible for burial in a national cemetery:

- Spouses and dependent children if the veteran is eligible for burial in a national cemetery.
- Former spouses of veterans who married non-veterans and whose new marriages ended in death or divorce, if they died after January 1, 2000.

Except for this last category, the survivors of other veterans who married nonveterans after the death of the veteran lose the right to burial in a national cemetery.

Spouses and dependent children are buried in the same plot as the veteran. If a family member dies before the veteran, he or she can be buried in a national cemetery if the veteran also plans to be buried in the same plot.

Columbaria

Increasingly, national cemeteries have columbaria for the burial of cremated remains. Everyone eligible for burial in a national cemetery is also eligible for admission to a columbarium.

Arlington

Veterans eligible for burial at Arlington National Cemetery outside Washington, DC, are limited to the following:

- Military retirees.
- People who die on active duty.
- Former POWs.
- Veterans who were honorably discharged before October 1, 1949, with disabilities rated at 30 percent or more.
- Recipients of the Medal of Honor, Distinguished Service Cross, Air Force Cross, Navy Cross, Distinguished Service Medal, Silver Star, or Purple Heart.

Access to the columbarium at Arlington is less limited. Basically, everyone eligible for burial in a national cemetery is eligible for inurnment at Arlington.

Application

Unlike private cemeteries, national cemeteries do not accept reservations for plots. Applications are accepted only after the death of a veteran. Funeral directors know the necessary application procedures.

FINAL HONORS

A 1997 federal law guarantees that at least two members of the military will attend the burial of each veteran in addition to either a bugler or a CD recording of "taps." Normally, other honors, such as flags, honor guards, and special certificates, are also available for the burial of veterans.

Flag

The government will provide a flag to drape the coffin of most veterans during their funerals and at graveside. This includes the following:

- Veterans of any wartime period.
- People who die on active duty.
- Veterans who served at least one enlistment or obligated period of service since January 31, 1955.

- Veterans who were discharged after January 31, 1955, with a disability.

The flag is presented at the gravesite to a next of kin. Provisions exist authorizing it to be given to "a close friend or associate" of the deceased.

Honor Guard

Veterans buried in national cemeteries and private cemeteries don't have any legal right to an honor guard to render services at the grave site.

> Can veterans in your area receive military honors during local burials? If not, maybe it's time to work with a veterans group to establish a local honor guard.

Active-duty installations frequently dispatch riflemen and a trumpeter for the nearby burial of veterans. Honor guards are assigned only when it doesn't conflict with military duties. Veterans groups and schools often provide honor guards.

Presidential Certificates

The survivors of veterans with honorable discharges are entitled to receive a "Presidential Memorial Certificate," a parchment certificate with the veteran's name, an inscription noting the veteran's service to the nation, and the signature of the president.

Application

Funeral directors know the procedures for obtaining flags and presidential certificates. They also know contact points at military installations and veterans groups who may be able to provide honor guards.

VA FACILITIES

ALABAMA
Medical Centers

Birmingham: More than 140 beds, including blind rehabilitation center. Open-heart surgery, geriatrics, hemodialysis, mental health clinic. *(700 S. 19th Street, Zip: 35233. Phone: 205/933-8101)*

Montgomery: About 140 beds. General medicine, surgery, outpatient psychiatry. Intensive care unit, nursing home/domiciliary. *(215 Perry Hill Road, Zip: 36109. Phone: 334/260-4194)*

Tuscaloosa: More than 550 beds, including nursing care and domiciliary. Acute and long-term psychiatry, addictions treatment, rehabilitation medicine, post-traumatic stress. *(3701 Loop Road, East, Zip: 35404. Phone: 205/554-2000)*

Tuskegee: More than 140 beds, plus nursing care/domiciliary. Post-traumatic stress, homeless and chronically mentally ill, geriatric evaluation, female veterans, substance abuse program. *(2400 Hospital Road, Zip: 36083. Phone: 334/727-0550)*

Clinics

Bessemer: *(975 9th Avenue, Zip: 32055. Phone: 205/428-3495)*

Childersburg: *(151 9th Avenue, NW, Zip: 35044. Phone: 256/378-9026)*

Dothan: *(2020 Alexander Drive, Zip: 36301. Phone: 334/673-4166)*

Dothan: Mental health clinic *(3753 Ross Clark Circle, Zip: 36303. Phone: 334/678-1933)*

Ft. Rucker: *(301 Andrews Avenue, Zip: 36362. Phone: 334/727-0550)*

Gadsden: *(206 Rescia Avenue, Zip: 35906. Phone: 256/413-7154)*Guntersville: *(100 Judy Smith Drive, Zip: 35976. Phone: 256/582-4033)*

Huntsville: *(301 Governor's Drive, S.W., Zip: 35801. Phone: 256/535-3100)*

Jasper: *(3400 Highway 78 East, Zip: 35501. Phone: 205/221-7384)*

Madison: *(8075 Madison Boulevard, Zip: 35758. Phone: 256/772-6220)*

Mobile: *(1504 Springhill Avenue, Ziop: 36604. Phone: 251/219-3900)*

Oxford: *(96 Ali Way Creekside South, Zip: 36203. Phone: 256/832-4141)*

Sheffield: *(422 Cox Boulevard, Zip: 35660. Phone: 256/381-9055)*

Selma: *(206 Vaughan Memorial Drive, Zip: 36701. Phone: 334/418-4975)*

Regional Office
Montgomery: *(345 Perry Hill Road, Zip: 36109. Phone: 800/827-1000)*

Vet Centers
Birmingham: *(1500 5th Avenue, S., Zip: 35205. Phone: 205/731-0550)*
Huntsville: *(2939 Johnson Road SW, Zip: 35805. Phone: 205/276-3434)*
Mobile: *(3725 Airport Boulevard, Suite 143, Zip: 36608. Phone: 205/304-0108)*
Montgomery: *(4405 Atlanta Highway, Zip: 36109. Phone: 334/273-7796*

National Cemeteries
Montevallo: *(3133 Highway 119, Zip: 35115. Phone: 205/665-9039)*
Fort Mitchell: *(553 Highway 165, Seale, Zip: 36856. Phone: 334/855-4731)*
Mobile: *(1202 Virginia Street, Zip: 36604. Phone: 805/453-4108)*

ALASKA
Clinics
Anchorage: Outpatient services include general medicine, alcohol and drug treatment, mental health, and pharmacy. Arranges for comprehensive medical care with civilian and military facilities, plus VA hospitals in lower forty-eight states. *(1201 N. Muldoon Road, Zip: 99504. Phone: 907/257-4700)*
Fort Wainwright: Bassett Army Hospital. *(Neeley Road, Zip: 99703. Phone: 907/361-6370)*
Kenai: *(11312 Kenai Spur Highway, Zip: 99669. Phone: 907-395-4100)*
Wasilla: *(865 N. Seward Meridian Parkway, Zip: 99654. Phone: 907-631-3100)*

Regional Office
Anchorage: *(2925 De Barr Road, Zip: 99508. Phone: 800/827-1000)*

Vet Centers
Anchorage: *(4201 Tudor Centre Drive, Zip: 99508. Phone: 907/563-6966)*
Fairbanks: *(540-4th Avenue, Zip: 99701. Phone: 907/456-4238)*
Kenai: *(43335 Kalifornsky Beach Road, Zip: 99669. Phone: 907/260-7640)*
Wasilla: *(851 E. Westpoint Avenue, Suite 111, Zip: 99654. Phone: 907/376-4318)*

National Cemeteries
Fort Richardson: *(P.O. Box 5-498, Bldg. 997, Davis Highway, Zip: 99505. Phone: 907/384-7075)*
Sitka: *(803 Saw Mill Creek Road, Zip: 99835. Phone: 907/384-7075)*

ARIZONA
Medical Centers
Phoenix: About 280 beds, including nursing care unit. Post-traumatic stress, day hospital. *(650 East Indian School Road, Zip: 85012. Phone: 602/277-5551)*
Prescott: More than 230 beds, including nursing care unit and domiciliary. Intensive care unit, pulmonary disease, physical therapy, pharmacy. *(500 Highway 89, Zip: 86313. Phone: 928/445-4860)*
Tucson: More than 283 beds, including nursing care and domiciliary. Cancer, cardiology, neurology, geriatrics, blindness rehabilitation, spinal cord injury. *(3601 S. 6th Avenue, Zip: 85723. Phone: 800/470-8262)*

Clinics
Anthem: *(3618 W. Anthem Way, Building D, Zip: 85086. Phone: 623/551-6092)*
Bellemont: *(Camp Navajo Army Depot, Zip: 86015. Phone: 520/226-1056)*
Buckeye: *(306 E. Monroe, Zip: 85326. Phone: 623/386-4814)*

Casa Grande: *(900 E. Florence Blvd, Zip: 85222. Phone: 520/629-4900)*

Cottonwood: *(203 Candy Lane, Building Zip: 86326. Phone: 928/649-1523)*

Globe: *(5860 S. Hospital Drive, Zip: 85501. Phone: 928/425-0027)*

Green Valley: *(380 W. Hermosa Drive, Zip: 85614. Phone: 520/629-4900)*

Kingman: *(1726 Beverly Avenue, Zip: 86401. Phone: 928/692-0080)*

Lake Havasu City: *(2035 Mesquite, Zip: 86403. Phone: 928/680-0090)*

Mesa: *(6950 E. Williams Field Road, Zip: 85212. Phone: 602/222-6568)*

Payson: *(1106 N. Beeline Highway, Zip: 85541. Phone: 928/472-3148)*

Safford: *(711 South 14th Avenue, Zip: 85546. Phone: 520/629-4900)*

Show Low: *(2450 Show Low Lake Road, Zip: 85901. Phone: 928/532-1069)*

Sun City: *(10147 Grand Ave., Zip: 85351. Phone: 602/222-2630)*Tucson, Northeast: 2945 W. Ina Road, Zip:85741. Phone: 520/792-1450)

Tucson, Southeast: *7395 S. Houghton Road, Zip: 85747. Phone: 520/792-1450)*

Yuma: *(2555 E. Gila Ridge Road, Zip: 85365. Phone: 520/629-4900)*

Regional Office

Phoenix: *(3225 N. Central Avenue, Zip: 85012. Phone: 800/827-1000)*

Vet Centers

Chinle: *(Zip: 86503. Phone: 928/674-3682)*

Hotevilla: *(Zip: 86030. Phone: 928/734-5166)*

Phoenix: *(77 E. Weldon, Zip: 85012. Phone: 602/640-2981)*

Mesa: *(1303 S. Longmore, Zip: 85202. Phone: 480/610-6727)*

Prescott: *(3180 Stillwater Drive, Zip: 86303. Phone: 928/778-3469)*

Tucson: *(3055 N. 1st Avenue, Zip: 85719. Phone: 520/882-0333)*

National Cemeteries

Phoenix: National Memorial Cemetery of Arizona. *(23029 N. Cave Creek Road, Zip: 85024. Phone: 602/379-4615)*

Prescott: VA Medical Center. *(500 Highway 89 North, Zip: 86301. Phone: 602/445-4860)*

ARKANSAS
Medical Centers

Fayetteville: About 70 beds for medical, surgical, and psychiatric care. *(1100 N. College Avenue, Zip: 72703. Phone: 479/443-4301)*

Little Rock: More than 180 beds. Open-heart surgery, post-traumatic stress, geriatrics, rehabilitation medicine, cancer center, neurosurgery, prosthetics, dentistry. *(4300 W. 7th Street, Zip: 72205. Phone: 501/257-1000)*

North Little Rock: Almost 360 beds, including nursing home and domiciliary. Open-heart surgery, geriatrics, respite care, mental health, prosthetics. *(2200 Fort Roots Drive, Zip: 72114. Phone: 501/257-1000)*

Clincs

El Dorado: *(460 W. Oak Street, Zip: 71730. Phone: 870/862-2489)*

Fort Smith: *(1500 Dodson Avenue, Zip: 72917. Phone: 479/709-6850)*

Harrison: *(707 North Main Street, Zip: 72601. Phone: 870/741-3592)*

Hot Springs: *(1401 Malvern Avenue, Zip: 71901. Phone: 501/624-0700)*

Jonesboro: *(1901 Woodsprings Road, Zip: 72401. Phone: 870/972-0063)*

Mena: *(1706 Highway 71 North, Zip: 71953. Phone: 479/394-4800)*

Mountain Home: *(10 Medical Plaza, Zip: 72653. Phone: 870/424-4109)*

Mountain Home: *(405 Buttercup Drive, Zip: 72653. Phone: 870/425-3030)*

Paragould: *(1101 Morgan Street, Zip: 72450. Phone: 870/541-9300)*

Texarkana: *(910 Realtor Avenue, Zip: 71854. Phone: 870/779-2750)*

Regional Office
North Little Rock: *(Bldg. 65, Fort Roots, P.O. Box 1280, Zip: 72115. Phone: 800/827-1000)*

Vet Center
Fayetteville: *(1416 N. College Avenue, Zip: 72703. Phone: 479/582-7152)*
North Little Rock: *(201 W. Broadway, Suite A, Zip: 72114. Phone: 501/324-6395)*

National Cemeteries
Fayetteville: *(700 Government Avenue, Zip: 72701. Phone: 479/444-5051)*
Fort Smith: *(522 Garland Avenue, Zip: 72901. Phone: 501/783-5345)*
Little Rock: *(2523 Confederate Boulevard, Zip: 72206. Phone: 501/324-6401)*

CALIFORNIA
Medical Centers
Fresno: More than 110 beds, including nursing home and domiciliary. Medicine, surgery, psychiatry, rehabilitation, dentistry, extended care, and geriatrics. *(2615 E. Clinton Avenue, Zip: 93703. Phone: 559/225-6100)*
Livermore: More than 100 beds in nursing care unit. Long-term care, respite care, geriatric evaluation, neurology, ophthalmology, hospice, preventative medicine. *(4951 Arroyo Road, Zip: 94550. Phone: 925/477-2560)*
Loma Linda: About 250 beds, including nursing home. Intensive care, alcohol dependency, cardiac catheterization lab, nuclear medicine, electron microscopy, hemodialysis center, sleep disorders, post-traumatic stress. *(11201 Benton Street, Zip: 92357. Phone: 909/825-7084)*

Long Beach: Nearly 300 beds, including nursing home, domiciliary, and spinal cord injury center. Lithotripsy unit, laser center. *(5901 E. 7th Street, Zip: 90822. Phone: 562/826-8000)*
Los Angeles: Nearly 1,000 beds, including nursing home and domiciliary. Geriatrics, spinal cord injury, womens' health, homeless, epilepsy, mental health. *(11301 Wilshire Boulevard, Zip: 90073. Phone: 310/478-3711)*
Menlo Park: Domiciliary, post-traumatic stress, mental health, geriatrics. *(795 Willow Road, Zip: 94025. Phone: 650/493-5000)*
Palo Alto: Nearly 500 beds. Spinal cord injury, blindness rehab center, schizophrenia research center, women's trauma recovery, post-traumatic stress. *(3801 Miranda Avenue, Zip: 94304. Phone: 650/493-5000)*
Sacramento: More than 50 beds. Women's health, geriatrics, long-term care. *(10535 Hospital Way, Zip: 95655. Phone: 916/366-5366)*
San Diego: More than 300 beds, including nursing home and spinal center. Cardiac surgery, AIDS, diabetes, extended care, hospice, geropsychiatry, substance abuse, Alzheimer's, neurology. *(3350 La Jolla Village Drive, Zip: 92161. Phone: 858/552-8585)*
San Francisco: More than 240 beds, including nursing care. AIDS, pacemaker center, post-traumatic stress, open-heart surgery, prosthetics, hemodialysis, orthopedics, angioplasty. *(4150 Clement Street, Zip: 94121. Phone: 415/221-4810)*

Clinics
Anaheim: *(1801 W. Romneya Drive, Zip: 92801. Phone: 714/780-5400)*
Atwater: *(3605 Hospital Road, Zip: 95301. Phone: 209/381-0105)*

Auburn: *(11985 Heritage Oaks Place, Zip: 95603. Phone: 530/889-0872)*

Bakersfield: *(1801 Westwind Drive, Zip: 93301. Phone: 661/632-1800)*

Capitola: *(1350 N. 41st Street, Zip: 95010. Phone: 831/464-5519)*

Chico: *(280 Cohasset Road, Zip: 95926. Phone: 530/879-5000)*

Chula Vista: *(835 Third Avenue, Zip: 91910. Phone: 619/409-1600)*

Commerce: *(5426 E. Olympic Boulevard, Zip: 90040. Phone: 323/725-7557)*

Corona: *(800 Magnola Avenue, Zip: 92879. Phone: 951/817-8820)*

El Centro: *(1600 South Imperial Road, Zip: 92243. Phone: 760/352-1506)*

Escondido: *(815 E. Pennsylvania Avenue, Zip: 92025. Phone: 760/466-7020)*

Eureka: *(714 F Street, Zip: 95501. Phone: 707/442-5335)*

Fairfield: *(103 Bodin Circle, Travis Air Force Base, Zip: 94535. Phone: 707/437-1800)*

Fremond: *(39199 Liberty Street, Zip: 94538. Phone: 510/791-4000)*

French Camp: *(7777 South Freedom Drive, Zip: 95231. Phone: 209/946-3400)*

Gardena: *(1251 Redondo Beach Boulevard, Zip: 90247. Phone: 310/851-4705)*

Laguna Hills: *(25292 McIntyre Street, Zip: 92653. Phone: 949/269-0700)*

Lancaster: *(547 West Lancaster Boulevard, Zip: 93536. Phone: 661/729-8655)*

Long Beach: *(2001 River Avenue, Zip: 90806. Phone: 562/388-8000)*

Los Angeles: *(11301 Wilshire Boulevard, Zip: 90073. Phone: 310/268-3526)*

Los Angeles: *(351 E. Temple, Zip: 90012. Phone: 213/253-2677)*

Lynwood: *(3737 Martin Luther King Boulevard, Zip: 90262. Phone: 310/537-6825)*

Martinez: *(150 Muir Road, Zip: 94553. Phone: 925/372-2000)*

Modesto: *(1524 McHenry Avenue, Zip: 95330. Phone: 209/557-6200)*

Monterey: *(3401 Engineer Lane, Zip: 93950. Phone: 831/883-3800)*

North Hills: *(16111 Plummer Street, Zip: 91343. Phone: 818/891-7711)*

Oakland: *(2221 Martin Luther King Jr. Way, Zip: 94612. Phone: 510/267-7800)*

Oakland: Mental health. *(2505 West 14th Street, Oakland Army Base, Zip: 94626. Phone: 510/587-3400)*

Oceanside: *(1300 Rancho del Oro Road, Zip: 92056. Phone: 760/643-2000)*

Oxnard: *(250 W. Citrus Grove Avenue, Zip: 93030. Phone: 805/983-6384)*

Palm Desert: *(41-990 Cook Street, Zip: 92211. Phone: 951/341-5570)*

Rancho Cucamonga: *(8599 Haven Avenue, Zip: 91730. Phone: 909/946-5348)*

Redding: *(351 Hartnell Avenue, Zip: 96002. Phone: 530/226-7555)*

Sacramento: Mental health. *(10633 Grissom Road, Zip: 95655. Phone: 916/366-5420)*

Sacramento: *(5401 Arnold Avenue, Zip: 95652. Phone: 916/561-7800)*

Sacramento: *(5342 Dudley Boulevard, Zip: 95652. Phone: 916/561-7400)*

San Bruno: *(1001 Sneath Lane, Zip: 94066. Phone: 650/615-6000)*

San Diego: *(8810 Rio San Diego Drive, Zip: 92108. Phone: 619/400-5000)*

San Francisco: *(401 Third Street, Zip: 94107. Phone: 415/551-7300)*

San Gabriel: *(420 W. Las Tunas Drive, Zip: 91776. Phone: 626/289-5973)*

San Jose: *(80 Great Oaks Boulevard, Zip: 95119. Phone: 408/363-3011)*

San Lois Obispo: *(1288 Morro Street, Zip: 93401. Phone: 805/543-01233)*

Santa Ana: *(2740 S. Bristol Street, Zip: 92704. Phone: 714/825-3500)*

Santa Barbara: *(4440 Calle Real, Zip: 93110. Phone: 805/683-1491)*

Santa Fe Springs: *(10210 Orr & Day Road, Zip: 90670. Phone: 562/864-5565)*

Santa Maria: *(1550 East Main Street, Zip: 93454. Phone: 805/354-6000)*

Santa Rosa: *(3841 Brickway Boulevard, Zip: 95404. Phone: 707/569-2300)*

Seaside: *(3401 Engineering Lane, Zip: 93955. Phone: 831/883-3800)*

Sonora: *(19747 Greenley Road, Zip: 95370. Phone: 209/588-2600)*

Stockton: *(500 West Hospital Road, Zip: 95231. Phone: 209/946-3400)*

Sun City: *(28125 Bradley Road, Zip: 92586. Phone: 951/672-1931)*

Susanville: *(110 Bella Way, Zip: 96130. Phone: 775/328-1453)*

Tulare: *(1050 N. Cherry Street, Zip: 93274. Phone: 559/684-8703)*

Ukiah: *(630 Kings Court, Zip: 95482. Phone: 707/468-7700)*

Vallejo: *(201 Walnut Avenue, Zip: 94592. Phone: 707/562-8200)*

Ventura: *(120 N. Ashwood Avenue, Zip: 93003. Phone: 805/658-5800)*

Victorville: *(12138 Industrial Boulevard, Zip: 92395. Phone: 760/951-2599)*

Regional Offices

Los Angeles: Serving counties of Inyo, Kern, Los Angeles, Orange, San Bernardino, San Luis Obispo, Santa Barbara, and Ventura. *(Federal Building, 11000 Wilshire Boulevard, Zip: 90024. Phone: 800/827-1000)*

Oakland: Serving remaining counties in California, except for Alpine, Lassen, Modoc, and Mono. *(1301 Clay Street, Room 1300, North, Zip: 94612. Phone: 800/827-1000)*

San Diego: Serving counties of Imperial, Riverside, and San Diego. *(8810 Rio San Diego Drive, Zip: 92108. Phone: 800/827-1000)*

Counties of Alpine, Lassen, Modoc, and Mono are served by the regional office in Reno, Nevada.

Vet Centers

Anaheim: *(859 S. Harbor Boulevard, Zip: 92805. Phone: 714/776-0161)*

Colton: *(11325 E. Cooley Drive, Zip: 92324. Phone: 909/801-5762)*

Chico: *(280 Cohasset Road, Zip: 95926. Phone: 530/899-8549)*

Concord: *(1899 Clayton Road, Zip: 94520. Phone: 925/680-4526)*

Corona: *(800 Magnolia Avenue, Zip: 92879. Phone: 951/734-0525)*

Culver City: *(5730 Uplander Way, Zip: 90230. Phone: 310/641-0326)*

East Los Angeles: *(5400 E. Olympic Boulevard, Zip: 90022. Phone: 323-728-9966)*

Eureka: *(2830 G Street, Zip: 95501. Phone: 707/444-8271)*

Fresno: *(3636 N. 1st Street, Zip: 93726. Phone: 559/4878-5660)*

Gardena: *(1045 W. Redondo Beach Boulevard, Zip: 90247. Phone: 310/767-1221)*

Modesto: *(1219 N. Carpenter Road, Zip: 95351. Phone: 209/527-5961)*

Oakland: *(1504 Franklin Street, Zip: 94612. Phone: 510/763-3904)*

Redwood City: *(2946 Broadway Street, Zip: 94062. Phone: 650/299-0672)*

Rohnert Park: *(6225 State Farm Drive, Zip: 94928. Phone: 707/586-3295)*

Sacramento: *(1111 Howe Avenue, Zip: 95825. Phone: 916/566-7430)*

San Diego: *(2790 Truxton Road, Zip: 92103. Phone: 858/642-1500)*

San Francisco: *(505 Polk Street, Zip: 94102. Phone: 415/441-5051)*

San Jose: *(278 N. Second Street, Zip: 95112. Phone: 408/993-0729)*

San Marcos: *(1 Civic Center Drive, Zip: 92069. Phone: 760/744-6914)*

Santa Cruz: *(1350 41st Avenue, Zip: 95010. Phone: 831-464-4575)*
Sepulveda: *(9737 Haskell Avenue, Zip: 91343. Phone: 818/892-9227)*
Temecula: *(40935 County Center Drive, Zip: 92591. Phone: 951-296-5608)*
Ventura: *(790 E. Santa Clara, Zip: 93001. Phone: 805/585-1860)*
Victorville: *(15095 Amargosa, Zip: 92394. Phone: 760/955-9703)*

National Cemeteries
Bakersfield: *(30338 E. Bear Mountain Boulevard, Zip: 93301. Phone: 866-632-1845)*
Fort Rosencrans/Point Loma: *(Point Loma, San Diego, Zip: 92106. Phone: 619/553-2084)*
Golden Gate: *(1300 Sneath Lane, San Bruno, Zip: 94006. Phone: 650/761-1646)*
Los Angeles: *(950 S. Sepulveda Boulevard, Zip: 90049. Phone: 310/268-3257)*
Riverside: *(22495 Van Buren Boulevard, Zip: 92518. Phone: 909/653-8417)*
Sacramento: *(5810 Midway Drive, Zip: 95620. Phone: 707/693-2460)*
San Francisco: *(1 Lincoln Boulevard, Presidio of San Francisco, Zip: 94129. Phone: 650/761-1646)*
San Joaquin Valley: *(32053 W. McCabe Road, Gustine, Zip: 95322. Phone: 209/854-6259)*

COLORADO
Medical Centers
Denver: Nearly 250 beds, including nursing unit and domiciliary. Sleep laboratory, AIDS, prosthetics, geriatrics. *(1055 Clermont Street, Zip: 80220. Phone: 303/399-8020)*
Grand Junction: More than 60 beds, including nursing home and domiciliary. Intensive care unit, surgery, inpatient psychiatry, substance abuse. *(2121 North Avenue, Zip: 81501. Phone: 970/242-0731)*

Clinics
Alamosa: *(622 Del Sol Drive, Zip: 81101. Phone: 719/587-6800)*
Aurora: *(13001 East 17th Place, Zip: 80045. Phone: 303/724-0190)*
Burlington: *(1177 Rose Avenue, Zip: 80807. Phone: 719/346-5239)*
Colorado Springs: *(25 North Spruce, Zip: 80905. Phone: 719/327-5660)*
Craig: *(551 Tucker Street, Zip: 81625. Phone: 970/824-9721)*
Durango: *(400 S. Camino Del Rio, Zip: 81301. Phone: 970/247-2214)*
Fort Collins: *(2509 Research Boulevard, Zip: 80526. Phone: 970/224-1550)*
Greeley: *(2001 70th Avenue, Zip: 80631. Phone: 970/313-0027)*
La Junta: *(1100 Carson Avenue, Zip: 81050. Phone: 719/383-5195)*
Lakewood: *(155 Van Gordon Street, Zip: 80225. Phone: 303/914-2680)*
Lamar: *(201 Kendall Drive, Zip: 81052. Phone: 719/336-5972)*
Montrose: *(4 Hillcrest Plaza Way, Zip: 81401. Phone: 970/249-7791)*
Pueblo: *(4112 Outlook Boulevard, Zip: 81008. Phone: 719/553-1000)*
Salida: *(920 Rush Drive, Zip: 81201. Phone: 719/539-8666)*

Regional Office
Denver: *(155 Van Gordon Street, Zip: 80228. Phone: 800/827-1000)*

Vet Centers
Boulder: *(2336 Canyon Boulevard, Zip: 80302. Phone: 303/440-7306)*
Colorado Springs: *(602 N. Nevada Avenue, Zip: 80903. Phone: 719/471-9992)*
Denver: *(7465 E. First Avenue, Zip: 80230. Phone: 303/326-0645)*

Grand Junction: *(2472 F. Road, Zip: 81505. Phone: 970/245-4156)*
Fort Collins: *(1100 Poudre River Drive [Lower Level], Zip: 80524. Phone: 970/221-5176)*
Pueblo: *(909 N. Elizabeth Street, Zip: 81003. Phone: 719/543-8343)*

National Cemeteries
Fort Logan: *(4400 W. Kenyan Avenue, Denver, Zip: 80236. Phone: 303/761-0117)*
Fort Lyon: *(15700 County Road, Zip: 81504. Phone: 303/761-0117)*

CONNECTICUT
Medical Centers
Newington: Outpatient services. *(555 Willard Avenue, Zip: 06111. Phone: 860/666-6951)*
West Haven: More than 200 beds, including nursing home and domiciliary. Blindness rehabilitation, cardiac arrhythmia center, comprehensive cancer, respite, stroke, post-traumatic stress, epilepsy, open-heart surgery. *(950 Campbell Avenue, Zip: 06516. Phone: 203/932-5711)*

Clinics
Danbury: *(7 Germantown Road, Zip: 06810. Phone: 203/798-8422)*
New London: *(4 Shaw's Cove, Zip: 06320. Phone: 860/437-3611)*
Stamford: *(1275 Summer Street, Zip: 06905. Phone: 203/465-5292)*
Waterbury: *(95 Scovill Street, Zip: 06706. Phone: 203/465-5292)*
Windham: *(96 Mansfield Street, Zip: 06226. Phone: 860/450-7583)*
Winsted: *(115 Spencer Street, Zip: 06098. Phone: 860/738-6985)*

Regional Office
Hartford: *(450 Main Street, Zip: 06103. Phone: 800/827-1000)*

Vet Centers
Rocky Hill: *(25 Elm Street, Zip: 06067. Phone: 860/563-8800)*
Norwich: *(2 Cliff Street, Zip: 06360. Phone: 860/887-1755)*
West Haven: *(141 Captain Thomas Boulevard, Zip: 06516. Phone: 203/932-9899)*
Wethersfield: *(30 Jordan Lane, Zip: 06109. Phone: 860/563-2320)*

DELAWARE
Medical Center
Wilmington: About 120 beds, including nursing home and domiciliary. Hemodialysis, respiratory care, cardiopulmonary, rehabilitation medicine, geriatric evaluation, substance abuse. *(1601 Kirkwood Highway, Zip: 19805. Phone: 302/994-2511)*

Clinics
Dover: *(1198 Governor Avenue, Zip: 19901. Phone: 302/994-2511)*
Georgetown: *(15 Georgetown Plaza, Zip: 19947. Phone: 302/904-2511)*

Regional Office
Wilmington: *(1601 Kirkwood Highway, Zip: 19805. Phone: 800/827-1000)*

Vet Center
Wilmington: *(VAMROC Bldg. 2, 1601 Kirkwood Highway, Zip: 19805. Phone: 302/994-1660)*

DISTRICT OF COLUMBIA
Medical Center
Washington: More than 320 beds, including nursing home and domiciliary. Open-heart surgery, war-related injury center, hemodialysis, pain clinic, sleep lab, Persian Gulf illnesses. *(50 Irving Street, N.W., Zip: 20422. Phone: 202/745-8000)*

Clinic
Southeast: *(820 Chesapeake Street, S.E., Zip: 20032. Phone: 202/745-8685)*

Regional Office
Washington: *(1120 Vermont Avenue, N.W., Zip: 20421. Phone: 800/827-1000)*

Vet Center
Washington: *(1250 Taylor Street, NW, Zip: 20011. Phone: 202/726-5212)*

FLORIDA
Medical Centers
Bay Pines: More than 650 beds, including nursing home and domiciliary. Cardiac care, visual, womens' program, bariatric surgery, spinal cord injury, sexual trauma, and mental health. *(10000 Bay Pines Boulevard, N., Zip: 33744. Phone: 727/398-6661)*

Gainesville: Nearly 250 beds, including nursing home and domiciliary. Geriatric research lab, post-traumatic stress. *(1601 S.W. Archer Road, Zip: 32608. Phone: 352/376-1611)*

Lake City: Nearly 90 beds, including nursing home and domiciliary. Vietnam veterans outreach program. Acute psychiatry, recreational therapy, female veterans program, noninvasive cardiology, speech therapy. *(619 S. Marion Street, Zip: 32025. Phone: 386/755-3016)*

Miami: More than 400 beds, including nursing home and domiciliary. Geriatric care, inpatient psychiatry, rehabilitation, eye, cancer, oral surgery, open-heart surgery. *(1201 N.W. 16th Street, Zip: 33125. Phone: 305/575-7000)*

Orlando: Under construction and scheduled to open in 2012. Nearly 200 beds, including nursing home and domiciliary. Full range of inpatient and outpatient services. *(5201 Raymond Street, Zip: 32803. Phone: 407/629-1599)*

Tampa: More than 550 beds, including nursing home and domiciliary. Polytrauma center, emergency department, pain center, intensive care, spinal cord injury, traumatic brain injury, eye clinic, magnetic resonance imaging, hemodialysis, open-heart surgery, homeless vets, orthopedic surgery. *(13000 Bruce B. Downs Boulevard, Zip: 33612. Phone: 813/972-2000)*

West Palm Beach: More than 250 beds, including nursing home and domiciliary. Medical, surgical, and mental health care, with adult day health care, dialysis, noninvasive cardiology, eye clinic. *(7305 N. Military Trail, Zip: 33410. Phone: 561/422-8262)*

Clinics
Boca Raton: *(901 Meadows Road, Zip: 33431. Phone: 561/416-8995)*

Bradenton: *(5520 State Road 64, Zip: 34208. Phone: 941/721-0649)*

Brooksville: *(14540 Cortez Boulevard, Zip: 34613. Phone: 352/597-8287)*

Broward: *(9800 West Commercial Boulevard, Zip: 33351. Phone: 954/745-5500)*

Coral Springs: *(9900 West Sample Road, Zip: 33065. Phone: 954/575-4940)*

Daytona Beach: *(551 National Health Care Drive, Zip: 32114. Phone: 386/323-7500)*

Deerfield Beach: *(2100 S.W. 10th Street, Zip: 33442. Phone: 954/570-5572)*

Delray Beach: *(4800 Linton Boulevard, Zip: 33445. Phone: 561/495-1973)*

Eglin AFB: *(100 Veterans Way, Zip: 32542. Phone: 850/609-2600)*

Fort Myers: *(3033 Winkler Extension, Zip: 33916. Phone: 239/939-3939)*

Fort Pierce: *(727 North U.S. 1, Zip: 34950. Phone: 772/595-5150)*

Hollywood: *(3702 Washington Street, Zip: 33021. Phone: 954/986-1811)*

Hollywood: *(7369 W. Sheridan Street, Zip: 33024. Phone: 954/894-1668)*

Homestead: *(950 Krome Avenue, Zip: 33030. Phone: 305/248-0874)*

Jacksonville: *(1833 Boulevard, Zip: 32206. Phone: 904/232-2751)*

Key Largo: *(105662 Overseas Highway, Zip: 33037. Phone: 305/451-0164)*

Key West: *(1300 Douglas Circle, Zip: 33040. Phone: 305/293-4609)*

Kissimmee: *(2285 North Central Avenue, Zip: 34741. Phone: 407/518-5004)*

Lakeland: *(4237 South Pipkin Road, Zip: 33811. Phone: 863/701-2470)*

Lecanto: *(2804 W. Marc Knighton Court, Zip: 34461. Phone: 352/746-8000)*

Leesburg: *(711 W. Main Street, Zip: 34748. Phone: 352/435-4000)*

Mariana: *(4970 Highway 90, Zip: 32446. Phone: 850/718-5620)*

Miami: *(1492 West Flagler Street, Zip: 33135. Phone: 305/541-5864*

Naples: *(2685 Horseshoe Drive, Zip: 34101. Phone: 239/659-9188)*

New Port Richey: *(9912 Little Road, Zip: 34654. Phone: 727/869-4100)*

Ocala: *(1515 Silver Springs Boulevard, Zip: 34470. Phone: 352/369-3320)*

Okeechobee: *(1201 N. Parrot Avenue, Zip: 34972. Phone: 863/824-3232)*

Orange City: *(2583 South Volusia Avenue, Zip: 32763. Phone: 386/456-2080)*

Palm Harbor: *(US Highway 19 North, Zip: 35209. Phone: 727/734-5276)*

Panama City: *(101 Vernon Avenue, Zip: 32407. Phone: 850-636-7000)*

Panama City: *(4408 Delwood Lane, Zip: 32408. Phone: 850/636-7000)*

Panama City: *(6703 West Highway 98, Zip: 32407, Phone: 850/636-*

Pensacola: *(312 Kenmore Road, Zip: 32503. Phone: 850/476-1100)*

Pensacola: *(790 Veterans Way, Zip: 32507. Phone: 850/912-2000)*

Port Charlotte: *(4161 Tamiami Trail, Zip: 33952. Phone: 941/941/235-2710)*

Port St. Lucie: *(126 SW Chambers Court, Zip: 34986. Phone: 772/878-7876)*

Sanford: *(1403 Medical Plaza Drive, Zip: 32771. Phone: 407/323-5999)*

Sarasota: *(5682 Bee Ridge Road, Zip: 34233. Phone: 941/371-3349)*

Sebring: *(3760 US Highway 27 South, Zip: 33870. Phone: 863/471-6227)*

St. Augustine: *(1955 U.S. 1 South, Zip: 32086. Phone: 904/829-0814)*

Saint Petersburg: *(840 Dr. Martin Luther King Street North Zip: 33705. Phone: 727/322-502-1700)*

Stuart: *(3501 S.E. Willoughby Boulevard, Zip: 34997. Phone: 772/288-0304)*

Sunrise: *(9800 W. Commercial Street, Zip: 33351. Phone: 954/475-5500)*

Tallahassee: *(1607 St. James Court, Zip: 32308. Phone: 850/878-0191)*

Villages: *(1950 Laurel Manor Drive, Zip: 32162. Phone: 352/205-8900)*

Vero Beach: *(372 17th Street, Zip: 32960. Phone: 772/299-4623)*

Viera: *(2900 Veterans Way, Zip: 32940. Phone: 321/637-3788)*

Zephyrhills: *(6937 Medical View Lane, Zip: 33541. Phone: 813/780-2550)*

Regional Office

Saint Petersburg: *(9500 Bay Pines Boulevard, Zip: 33708. Phone: 800/827-1000)*

Benefits Offices

Fort Lauderdale: *(299 East Broward Boulevard, Room 324, Zip: 33301)*

Jacksonville: *(7825 Baymeadows Way, Suite 120-B, Zip: 32256)*
Miami: *(Federal Building, 51 S.W. 1st Avenue, Room 120, Zip: 33130)*
Oakland Park: *(5599 N. Dixie Highway, Zip: 33334)*
Pensacola: *(312 Kenmore Road, Room 1-G-250, Zip: 32503)*

Vet Centers
Clearwater: *(29298 US Highway 19N, Zip: 3761. Phone: 727/549-3600)*
Fort Lauderdale: *(713 N.E. 3rd Avenue, Zip: 33304. Phone: 954/356-7926)*
Fort Myers: *(4110 Center Pointe Drive, Zip: 33916. Phone: 239/479-4401)*
Gainesville: *(105 NW 75th Street, Zip: 32607. Phone: 352/331-1408)*
Jacksonville: *(300 E. State Street, Zip: 32202. Phone: 904/232-3621)*
Miami: *(2700 S.W. 3rd Avenue, Suite 1-A, Zip: 33129. Phone: 305/859-8387)*
Jupitor: *(2074 W. Indiantown Road, Zip: 33458. Phone: 561/422-1220)*
Melbourne: *(2098 Sarno Road, Zip: 32935. Phone: 321/254-3410)*
Miami: *(8280 NW 27th Street, Zip: 33122. Phone: 305/859-8387)*
Orlando: *(5575 S. Semoran Boulevard, Zip: 32822. Phone: 407/857-2800)*
Palm Beach: *(2311-10th Avenue, Zip: 33461. Phone: 561/585-0441)*
Pensacola *(4501 Twin Oaks Drive, Zip: 32506. Phone: 850/456-5886)*
Sarasota: *(4801 Swift Road, Zip: 34231. Phone: 941/927-8285)*
St. Petersburg: *(6798 Crosswinds Drive Zip: 33710, Phone: 727/549-3633)*
Tallahassee: *(548 Bradford Road, Zip: 32303. Phone: 850/942-8810)*
Tampa: *(3637 W. Waters Avenue, Zip: 33614. Phone: 813/228-2621)*

National Cemeteries
Barrancas: Pensacola Naval Air Station. *(80 Hovey Road, Zip: 32508. Phone: 850/452-3357)*
Bay Pines: *(10000 Bay Pine Boulevard North, Zip: 33504. Phone: 727/398-9426)*
Bushnell: *(6502 S.W. 102nd Avenue, Zip: 33513. Phone: 352/793-7740)*
Jackson: *(4083 Lannie Road, Zip: 32218. Phone: 904/766-5222Saint Augustine:* (104 Marine Street, Zip: 32084. Phone: 352/793-7740)

GEORGIA
Medical Centers
Augusta: Regional facility with about 450 beds for spinal cord injury, post-traumatic stress, long-term psychiatry, hemodialysis, open-heart surgery. Sleep, speech, and stroke rehabilitation. Nursing home and domiciliary. *(1 Freedom Way, Zip: 30904. Phone: 706/733-0188)*
Decatur: About 400 beds, including nursing home and domiciliary. Open-heart surgery, geriatrics, AIDS, Alzheimer's, prosthetics, psychiatric, alcohol and drug treatment. *(1670 Clairmont Road, Zip: 30033. Phone: 404/321-6111)*
Dublin: Nearly 350 beds, including domiciliary and nursing home. Cardiology, intensive care, optometry, respiratory care, rehabilitation medicine, long-term psychiatric. *(1826 Veterans Boulevard, Zip: 31021. Phone: 478/272-1210)*

Clinics
Albany: *(526 West Broad Avenue, Zip: 31701. Phone: 229/446-9000)*
Athens: *(9249 Highway 29, Zip: 30601. Phone: 706/227-4534)*
Columbus: *(1310 13th Street, Zip: 31906. Phone: 706/257-7200)*

Decatur: *(755 Commerce Drive, Zip: 30030. Phone: 404/417-5200))*
East Point: *(1513 Cleveland Avenue, Zip: 30344. Phone: 404/321-6111)*
Kathleen: *(2370 S. Houston Lake Road, Zip: 31047. Phone: 478/224-1309)*
Lawrenceville: *(1970 Riverside Parkway, Zip: 30043. Phone: 404/417-1750)*
Macon: *(5398 Thomaston Road, Zip: 31220. Phone: 478/476-8868)*
Newnan: *(39A Oak Hill Court, Zip: 30265. Phone: 404/329-2222)*
Oakwood: *(3931 Munday Mill Road, Zip: 30566. Phone: 404/728-8212)*
Rome: *(30 Chateau Drive SE, Zip: 30161. Phone: 706/235-6581)*
Savannah: *(325 W. Montgomery Crossroads, Zip: 31406. Phone: 912/920-0214)*
Smyrna: *(562 Concord Road, Zip: 30082. Phone: 404/417-1760)*
St. Marys: *(205 Lake Shore Point, Zip: 31558. Phone: 912-510-3420)*
Stockbridge: *(175 Medical Boulevard, Zip: 30281. Phone: 404/329-2222)*
Valdosta: *(2841 N. Patterson Street, Zip: 31602. Phone: 229/293-0132)*

Regional Office
Decatur: *(1700 Clairmont Road, Zip: 30033. Phone: 800/827-1000)*

Vet Centers
Atlanta: *(1440 Dutch Valley Place, Zip: 30324. Phone: 404/347-7264)*
Lawrenceville: *(930 River Center Place, Zip: 30043. Phone: 404-728-4195)*
Macon: *(750 Riverside Drive, Zip: 31201. Phone: 478/477-3813)*
Mariette: *(40 Dodd Street, Zip: 30060. Phone: 404/327-4954)*
Savannah: *(321 Commercial Drive, Zip: 31406. Phone: 912/961-5800)*

National Cemeteries
Canton: *(2025 Mt. Carmel Church Lane, Zip: 866/236-8159)*
Marietta: *(500 Washington Avenue, Zip: 30060. Phone: 334/855-4731)*

HAWAII
Medical Center
Honolulu: Nearly 100 beds, including nursing home and domiciliary. Clinic-based home care, substance abuse rehabilitation, post-traumatic stress. *(459 Patterson Road, Zip: 96819. Phone: 808/433-0100)*

Clinics
Hilo: *(1285 Waianuenue Avenue, Suite 211, Zip: 96720. Phone: 808/935-3781)*
Honolulu: *(3375 Koapaka Street, Zip: 96819. Phone: 808/566-1546)*
Kaui: *(3-3367 Kuhio Highway, Zip: 96766. Phone: 808/246-0497)*
Kona: *(75-377 Hualalai Road, Zip: 96740. Phone: 808/329-0774)*
Maui: *(203 Ho'ohana Street, Suite 303, Zip: 96732. Phone: 808/871-2454)*

Regional Office
Honolulu: *(459 Patterson Road, Zip: 96819. Phone: 800/827-1000)*

Vet Centers
Hilo: *(126 Pu'uhonu Way, Zip: 96720. Phone: 808/969-3833)*
Honolulu: *(1680 Kapiolani Boulevard, Zip: 96814. Phone: 808/973-8387)*
Kailua-Kona: *(73-497 Kamanu Street, Zip: 96740. Phone: 808/329-0574)*
Lihue: *(3-3367 Kuhio Highway, Zip: 96766. Phone: 808/246-1163)*
Wailuku: *(35 Lunaliho Street, Zip: 96793. Phone: 808/242-8557)*

National Cemetery

Honolulu: National Memorial Cemetery of the Pacific. *(2177 Puowaina Drive, Zip: 96813. Phone: 808/532-3720)*

IDAHO

Medical Center

Boise: Nearly 80 beds, plus nursing home and domiciliary. Intensive care unit, speech pathology, hemodialysis, mental health clinic, respiratory care. *(500 W. Fort Street, Zip: 83702. Phone: 208/422-1000)*

Clinics

Caldwell: *(120 E. Pine Street, Zip: 83605. Phone: 208/454-4820)*
Coeur d'Alene: *(2177 N. Ironwood Drive, Zip: 83805. Phone: 208/454-4820*
Lewiston: *(1630 23rd Avenue, Zip: 83501. Phone: 208/746-7784)*
Pocatello: *(444 Hospital Way, Zip: 83201. Phone: 208/232-6214)*
Salmon: *(111 Lillian Street, Zip: 83467. Phone: 208/756-8515)*
Twin Falls: *(260 Second Avenue East, Zip: 83301. Phone: 208/732-0947)*

Regional Office

Boise: *(805 W. Franklin Street, Zip: 83702. Phone: 800/827-1000)*

Vet Centers

Boise: *(2424 Bank Drive, Zip: 83705. Phone: 208/342-3612)*
Pocatello: *(1800 Garret Way, Zip: 83201. Phone: 208/232-0316)*

ILLINOIS

Medical Centers

Chicago/Westside: More than 200 beds. Post-traumatic stress, drug and alcohol dependency, Alzheimer's, geriatrics. *(820 S. Damen Avenue, Zip: 60612. Phone: 312/569-8387)*

Danville: More than 400 beds, including nursing care beds and domiciliary. Long-term psychiatric care, alcohol treatment, mental health, visual impairment services, rehabilitation services. Regional signage program. *(1900 E. Main Street, Zip: 61832. Phone: 217/554-3000)*
Hines: Nearly 500 acute-care hospital beds, including nursing home and domiciliary. Heart and kidney transplants, spinal cord injury, magnetic resonance imaging, comprehensive rehabilitation center, adult day care center. *(5000 South 5th Avenue, Zip: 60141. Phone: 708/202-8387)*
Marion: More than 100 beds, plus nursing care unit. Respite care, geriatric evaluation, general dentistry, women's health, cardiology, nuclear medicine, kinesiotherapy, urology, psychiatry. *(2401 W. Main Street, Zip: 62959. Phone: 618/997-5311)*
North Chicago: Nearly 500 beds, including nursing care unit and domiciliary. Stress disorder unit, geriatric evaluation, psychiatric day treatment. Independent-living program, respite care. *(3001 Green Bay Road, Zip: 60064. Phone: 847/688-1900)*

Clinics

Aurora: *(1700 N. Landmark Road, Zip: 60506. Phone: 630/859-2504)*
Belleville: *(75 W. Main Street, Zip: 62223. Phone: 314/286-6988)*
Chicago: *(7731 S. Halsted Street, Zip: 60620. Phone: 773/962-3700)*
Chicago: *(211 E. Ontario, Zip: 60611. Phone: 312/569-8387)*
Chicago Heights: *(30 E. 15th Street, Zip: 60411. Phone: 708/756-5454)*
Decatur: *(3035 E. Mound Road, Zip: 62526. Phone: 217/875-2670)*

Effingham: *(1901 South 4th Street, Zip: 62401. Phone: 217/347-7600)*

Elgin: *(450 W. Dundee Road, Zip: 60120. Phone: 847/742-5920)*

Evanston: *(107-109 Clyde Street, Zip: 60202. Phone: 847/869-6315)*

Freeport: *(1301 Kiwanis Drive, Zip: 61032. Phone: 815/235-4881)*

Galesburg: *(387 East Grove, Zip: 61401. Phone: 309/343-0311)*

Joliet: *(2000 Glenwood Avenue, Zip: 60435. Phone: 815/744-0492)*

LaSalle: *(2970 Chartes Street, Zip: 61301. Phone: 815/223-9678)*

Manteno: *(1 Veterans Drive, Zip: 60950. Phone: 815/468-1027)*

Mattoon: *(501 Lake Land Boulevard, Zip: 61938 . Phone: 217/258-3370)*

McHenry: *(620 S. Route 31, Zip: 60050. Phone: 815/759-2306)*

Mount Vernon: *(1 Doctors Park Road, Zip: 62864. Phone: 618/246-2910)*

Oak Lawn: *(4700 W. 95th Street, Zip: 60453. Phone: 708/499-3675)*

Oak Park: *(149 S. Oak Park Avenue, Zip: 60302. Phone: 708/386-3008)*

Peoria: *(411 Martin Luther King Jr. Drive, Zip: 61605. Phone: 309/497-0790)*

Quincy: *(721 Broadway, Zip: 62301. Phone: 217/224-3366)*

Rockford: *(4940 E. State Street, Zip: 61108. Phone: 815/227-0081)*

Springfield: *(700 North 7th Street, Zip: 62701. Phone: 217/522-9730)*

Regional Office

Chicago: *(536 S. Clark Street, Zip: 60605. Phone: 800/827-1000)*

Vet Centers

Chicago: *(7731 S. Halsted Street, Zip: 60620. Phone: 773/962-3740)*

Chicago Heights: *(1600 S. Halsted Street, Zip: 60411. Phone: 708/754-0340)*

East Saint Louis: *(1265 N. 89th Street, Zip: 62203. Phone: 618/397-6602)*

Evanston: *(565 Howard Street, Zip: 60202. Phone: 847/332-1019)*

Moline: *(1529 46th Avenue, Zip: 61265. Phone: 309/762-6954)*

Oak Park: *(155 S. Oak Park Avenue, Zip: 60302. Phone: 708/338-3225)*

Peoria: *(3310 N. Prospect Road, Zip: 61603. Phone: 309/671-7300)*

Springfield: *(624 S. 4th Street, Zip: 62702. Phone: 217/492-4955)*

National Cemeteries

Alton: *(600 Pearl Street, Zip: 62003. Phone: 314/263-8720)*

Danville: *(1900 E. Main Street, Zip: 61832. Phone: 217/554-4550)*

Elwood: Abraham Lincoln National Cemetery. *(20953 W. Hoff Road, Zip: 60421. Phone: 815/423-9958)*

Mound City: *(P.O. Box 128, Zip: 62963. Phone: 314/260-8720)*

Quincy: *(36th & Maine Streets, Zip: 62301. Phone: 309/782-2094)*

Rock Island: *(Rock Island Arsenal, Zip: 61299. Phone: 309/782-2094)*

Springfield: *(5063 Camp Butler Road, Zip: 62707. Phone: 217/492-4070)*

INDIANA

Medical Centers

Fort Wayne: About 30 beds, with nursing care unit. Primary care, surgery, and mental health. Specializes in hospital-based home care, cancer treatment, gerontology, and optometry. *(2121 Lake Avenue, Zip: 46805. Phone: 260/426-5431)*

Indianapolis: More than 200 beds, including nursing care and domiciliary. Acute medical, surgical, neurological, and nursing home care. Inpatient psychiatric care, kidney transplants, intensive care, orthopedic services. *(1481 W. 10th Street, Zip: 46202. Phone: 317/554-0000)*

Marion: More than 240 beds, plus nursing care unit. AIDS, combat veterans treatment program, geri-

atric evaluation, halfway house,
oral surgery, podiatry, pulmonary
function, rehabilitation medicine,
respite care. *(1700 E. 38th Street,
Zip: 46953. Phone: 765/674-3321)*

Clinics

Bloomington: *(455 South Landmark
Avenue, Zip: 47403. Phone:
812/336-5723)*
Crown Point: *(9330 S. Broadway, Zip:
46307. Phone: 219/662-5000)*
Evansville: *(500 E. Walnut, Zip:
47713. Phone: 812/465-6202)*
Goshen: *(2014 Lincolnway East, Zip:
46526. Phone: 574/534-6108)*
Greendale: *(1600 Flossie Drive, Zip:
47025. Phone: 812/539-2313)*
Muncie: *(3500 W. Purdue Avenue, Zip:
47304. Phone: 765/284-6822)*
New Albany: *(811 Northgate Boule-
vard, Zip: 47150. Phone: 502/287-
4100)*
Richmond: *(4351 South A Street, Zip:
47374. Phone: 765/973-6915)*
Scottsburg: *(279 N. Gardner Street,
Zip:47170. Phone: 812/752-8375)*
South Bend: *(5735 S. Ironwood Road,
Zip: 46614, Phone: 574/299-4847)*
Terre Haute: *(110 W. Honeycreek
Parkway Zip: 47802, Phone:
812/232-2890)*
Vincennes: *(1813 Willow Street, Zip:
47591. Phone: 812/882-0894)*
West Lafayette: *(3851 N. River Road,
Zip: 47906. Phone: 765/464-2280)*

Regional Office

Indianapolis: *(575 N. Pennsylvania
Street, Zip: 46204. Phone:
800/827-1000)*

Vet Centers

Evansville: *(311 N. Weinbach Avenue,
Zip: 47711. Phone: 612/473-5993)*
Fort Wayne: *(528 W. Berry Street, Zip:
46802. Phone: 260/460-1456)*

Indianapolis: *(3833 N. Meridian
Street, Zip: 46208. Phone:
317/927-1600)*
Merillville: *(6505 Broadway Avenue,
Zip: 46410. Phone: 219/736-5633)*
National Cemeteries
Crown Hill: *(700 W. 38th Street, Indi-
anapolis, Zip: 46208. Phone:
317/925-8231)*
Marion: *(1700 E. 38th Street, Zip:
46952. Phone: 765/674-0284)*
New Albany: *(1943 Ekin Avenue, Zip:
47150. Phone: 502/893-3852)*

IOWA

Medical Centers

Des Moines: About 200 beds, including nursing home and domiciliary.
Basic medical, surgical, psychiatric, and rehabilitative care.
Low-vision clinic, home health
unit, dental care. *(3600 30th
Street, Zip: 50310. Phone:
515/699-5999)*
Iowa City: Nearly 100 beds. Extended
care, rehabilitation, geriatrics.
*(601 Highway 6 West, Zip: 52246.
Phone: 319/338-0581)*
Knoxville: Ambulatory care, inpatient
psychiatry. Special programs for
mental health, including substance abuse, Alzheimer's. *(1515
W. Pleasant Street, Zip: 50138.
Phone: 641/842-3101)*

Clinics

Bettendorf: *(2979 Victoria Drive, Zip:
52722. Phone: 563-8528)*
Dubuque: *(250 Mercy Drive, Zip:
52001. Phone: 563/589-8899)*
Fort Dodge: *(2419 2nd Avenue, Zip:
50501. Phone: 515/576-2235)*
Mason City: *(520 S. Pierce, Zip: 50401.
Phone: 641/421-8077)*
Shenandoah: *(512 S. Fremont Street,
Zip: 51104. Phone: 712/246-0092)*
Sioux City: *(1551 Indian Hills Drive,
Zip: 51104. Phone: 712/258-4700)*

Spirit Lake: *(1310 Lake Street, Zip: 51360. Phone: 712/336-6400)*
Waterloo: *(1015 S. Hackett Road, Zip: 50701. Phone: 319/235-1230)*

Regional Office
Des Moines: *(210 Walnut Street, Zip: 50309. Phone: 800/827-1000)*

Vet Centers
Cedar Rapids: *(1642 42nd Street, N.E., Zip: 52402. Phone: 319/378-0016)*
Des Moines: *(2600 Martin Luther King Parkway, Zip: 50310. Phone: 515/284-4929)*
Sioux City: *(1551 Indian Hills Drive, Zip: 51104, Phone: 712/255-3808)*

National Cemetery
Keokuk: *(1701 J Street, Zip: 52632. Phone: 309/782-2094)*

KANSAS
Medical Centers
Leavenworth: Nearly 240 beds, including nursing care unit and domiciliary. Geriatrics, acute medical, surgical, and psychiatric programs. Intensive-care unit. *(4101 S. 4th Street, Zip: 66048. Phone: 913/682-2000)*
Topeka: More than 230 beds, including nursing care. Intensive care, post-traumatic stress, alcohol and drug treatment, biofeedback, respiratory care, inpatient rehabilitation. *(2200 S.W. Gage Boulevard, Zip: 66622. Phone: 785/350-3111)*
Wichita: More than 80 beds, including nursing care and domiciliary. Primary care and advanced care in medicine, surgery, and psychiatry. Women's clinic, mental hygiene, visual impairment services, ambulatory surgery. *(5500 E. Kellogg, Zip: 67218. Phone: 316/651-3666)*

Clinics
Chanute: *(629 South Plummer, Zip: 66720. Phone: 620/431-4000)*
Emporia: *(919 W. 12th Avenue, Zip: 66801. Phone: 800/574-8387)*
Dodge City: *(300 Custer, Zip: 67801. Phone: 620/225-7146)*
Ft. Scott: *(902 Horton Street, Zip: 66701. Phone: 620/223-8655)*
Garnett: *(421 South Maple, Zip: 66032. Phone: 785-448-3131)*
Hays: *(207-B East Seventh, Zip: 67601. Phone: 785/625-3550)*
Holton: *(1110 Columbine Drive, Zip: 66436. Phone: 800/574-8387)*
Hutchinson: *(1625 E. 30th Avenue, Zip: 67502. Phone: 888/878-6881)*
Junction City: *(715 Southwind Drive, Zip: 66441. Phone: 800/574-8387)*
Kansas City: *(21 N. 12th Street, Zip: 66102. Phone: 913/758-2228)*
Lawrence: *(2200 Harvard Road, Zip: 66049. Phone: 800/574-8387)*
Liberal: *(2 Rock Island Road, Suite 200, Zip: 67901. Phone: 620/626-5574)*
Paola: *(510 S. Hospital Drive, Zip: 66071. Phone: 816/922-2160)*
Parsons: *(1907 Harding Drive, Zip: 67357. Phone: 316/423-3858)*
Russell: *(200 S. Main Street, Zip: 67665. Phone: 785/483-3131)*
Salina: *(1410 East Iron, Zip: 67401. Phone: 785/826-1580)*
Seneca: *(1600 Community Drive, Zip: 66538. Phone: 800/574-8387)*

Regional Office
Wichita: *(5500 E. Kellogg, Zip: 67211. Phone: 800/827-1000)*

Vet Center
Manhattan: *(205 S. 4th Street, Zip: 66502. Phone: 785-587-8257)*
Wichita: *(251 N. Water Street, Zip: 67202. Phone: 316/685-2221)*

National Cemeteries

Fort Leavenworth: *(Zip: 66027. Phone: 913/758-4105)*
Fort Scott: *(P.O. Box 917, Zip: 66701. Phone: 316/223-2840)*
Leavenworth: *(P.O. Box 1694, Zip: 66048. Phone: 913/758-4105)*

KENTUCKY

Medical Centers

Lexington: Nearly 200 beds, including nursing care and domiciliary. Intensive-care units, cardiac labs, ventilator-dependent unit, electronmicroscopy, geriatric evaluation, pulmonary function lab, hemodialysis. *(1101 Veterans Drive, Zip: 40502. Phone: 859/233-4511)*
Louisville: More than 100 beds. Diabetics, cancer, hypertension, shock, laser therapy, orthopedics, geriatric evaluation, rehabilitation medicine, nuclear medicine, day treatment center. *(800 Zorn Avenue, Zip: 40206. Phone: 502/895-3401)*

Clinics

Bellvue: *(103 Landmark Drive, Zip: 41073. Phone: 859/392-3840)*
Berea: *(209 Pauline Drive, Zip: 40403. Phone: 859/986-1259)*
Bowling Green: *(1110 Wilkinson Trace Circle, Zip: 42103. Phone: 270/796-3590)*
Carrolton: *(309 Eleventh Street, Zip: 41008. Phone: 502/732-7146)*
Clarkson: *(619 W. Main Street, Zip: 42726. Phone: 866/653-8283)*
Florence: *(7711 Ewing, Zip: 41042. Phone: 859/282-4480)*
Ft. Campbell: *(Desert Storm Avenue, Zip: 42223. Phone: 270/798-4118)*
Ft. Knox: *(851 Ireland Loop, Zip: 40121. Phone: 502/624-9396)*
Hanson: *(926 Veterans Drive, Zip: 42413. Phone: 270/322-8019)*
Hazard: *(210 Black Gold Boulevard, Zip: 41701. Phone: 606/436-2350)*

Hopkinsville: *(1102 S. Virginia Drive, Zip: 42240. Phone: 270/885-2106)*
Louisville: *(4010 Dupont Circle, Zip: 40207. Phone: 502/287-6986)*
Louisville: *(3430- Newburg Road, Zip: 40218. Phone: 502/287-6223)*
Louisville: *(3934 North Dixie Highway, Zip: 40216. Phone: 502/287-6000)*
Louisville: *(1101 Grade Lane, Zip: 40213. Phone: 502/413-4635)*
Mayfield: *(1253 Paris Road, Zip: 42066. Phone: 270/247-2455)*
Morehead: *(333 Beacon Hill Drive, Zip: 40351. Phone: 606/684-03004)*
Owensboro: *(3400 New Hartford Road, Zip: 42303. Phone: 270/684-5034)*
Pacaducah: *(2620 Perkins Creek Drive, Zip: 42001. Phone: 270/444-8465)*
Prestonsburg: *(5230 Ky. Route 321, Zip: 41653. Phone: 606/886-1970)*
Somerset: *(104 Hardin Lane, Zip: 42503. Phone: 606/676-0786)*

Regional Office

Louisville: *(545 S. Third Street, Zip: 40202. Phone: 800/827-1000)*

Vet Centers

Lexington: *(301 E. Vine Street, Zip: 40503. Phone: 859/253-0717)*
Louisville: *(1347 S. 3rd Street, Zip: 40208. Phone: 502/634-1916)*

National Cemeteries

Camp Nelson: *(6980 Danville Road, Nicholasville, Zip: 40356. Phone: 859/885-5727)*
Cave Hill: *(701 Baxter Road, Louisville, Zip: 40204. Phone: 502/893-3852)*
Danville: *(277 N. 1st. Street, Zip: 40442. Phone: 859/885-5727)*
Lebanon: *(20 Highway 208, Zip: 40033. Phone: 502/692-3390)*
Lexington: *(833 W. Main Street, Zip: 40508. Phone: 859/885-5727)*

Mill Springs: *(9044 West Highway 80, Nancy, Zip: 42544. Phone: 859/885-5727)*
Zachary Taylor: *(4701 Brownsboro Road, Louisville, Zip: 40207. Phone: 502/893-3852)*

LOUISIANA
Medical Centers
Alexandria: More than 250 beds, including nursing home and domiciliary. Adult day care, alcohol and drug treatment, long-term psychiatric services. *(2495 Shreveport Highway, Zip: 71360. Phone: 318/473-0010)*
New Orleans: VA medical center in New Orleans destroyed by Hurricane Katrina in August 2005. Replacement facility with more than 250 beds expected by 2014.
Shreveport: More than 250 beds. Primary, specialty, surgury, and psychiatric care. Visual impairment team, readjustment counseling, respite care, ambulatory surgery, drug dependence, cardiac catheterization, nuclear medicine, neurology, mental hygiene. *(510 E. Stoner Avenue, Zip: 71101. Phone: 318/221-8411)*

Clinics
Baton Rouge: *(79809 Essen Park Avenue, Zip: 70809. Phone: 225/761-3400)*
Hammond: *(1331 South Morrison Avenue, Zip: 70403. Phone: 985/902-5026*
Houma: *(1750 Martin Luther King Boulevard, Zip: 70360. Phone: 985/851-0188)*
Jennings: *(1907 Johnson Street, Zip: 70546. Phone: 337/824-1000)*
Lafayette: *(2100 Jefferson Street, Zip: 70501. Phone: 337/261-0734)*
Monroe: *(250 De Siard Plaza Drive, Zip: 71203. Phone: 318/343-6100)*

Reserve: *(247 Veterans Boulevard, Zip: 70084. Phone: 504/565-4705)*
Slidell: *(340 Gateway Drive, Zip: 70461. Phone: 800/935-8387)*

Regional Office
New Orleans: *(701 Loyola Avenue, Zip: 70113. Phone: 800/827-1000)*

Vet Centers
Baton Rouge: *(5207 Essen Lane, Zip: 70809. Phone: 225/757-0045)*
Kenner: *(2200 Veterans Memorial Boulevard, Zip:70062. Phone: 504/565-4977)*
Shreveport: *(2800 Youree Drive, Zip: 71104. Phone: 318/861-1776)*

National Cemeteries
Alexandria: *(209 Shamrock Avenue, Pineville, Zip: 71360. Phone: 601/445-4981)*
Baton Rouge: *(220 N. 19th Street, Zip: 70806. Phone: 225/654-3767)*
Port Hudson: *(20978 Port Hickey Road, Zachary, Zip: 70791. Phone: 225/654-3767)*

MAINE
Medical Center
Togus: More than 130 beds, including nursing home and domiciliary. Medical, surgical, and psychiatric care. Post-traumatic stress, substance abuse, day treatment. *(1 VA Center, Zip: 04330. Phone: 207/623-8411)*

Clinics
Bangor: *(304 Hancock Street, Zip: 04401. Phone: 207/561-3600)*
Calais: *(50 Union Street, Zip: 04619. Phone: 207/204-3700)*
Caribou: *(163 Van Buren Road, Zip: 04736. Phone: 207/493-3800)*
Lincoln: *(99 River Road, Zip: 04457. Phone: 207/403-2000)*
Rumford: *(431 Franklin Street, Zip: 04276. Phone: 207/369-3200)*

Saco: *(655 Main Street, Zip: 04072. Phone: 207/294-3100)*

Regional Office
Togus: *(1 VA Center, Zip: 04330. Phone: 800/827-1000)*

Vet Centers
Bangor: *(368 Harlow Street, Zip: 04401. Phone: 207/947-3391)*
Caribou: *(456 York Street, Zip: 04619. Phone: 207/496-3900)*
Lewiston: *(29 Westminster Street, Zip: 04240. Phone: 207/783-0068)*
Portland: *(475 Stevens Avenue, Zip: 04103. Phone: 207/780-3584)*
Springvale: *(628 Main Street, Zip: 04083. Phone: 207/490-1513)*

National Cemetery
Togus: *(VA Medical Center, Zip: 04330. Phone: 508/563-7113)*

MARYLAND
Medical Centers
Baltimore: More than 200 beds, including nursing unit and domiciliary. Comprehensive geriatrics, cancer treatment, AIDS, infectious diseases, post-traumatic stress, substance abuse, psychiatry, neurosurgery, acute rehabilitation. *(10 N. Greene Street, Zip: 21201. Phone: 410/605-7000)*
Loch Raven: Inpatient rehabilitation center. Hospice and nursing care, Alzheimer's. *(3900 Loch Raven Boulevard, Zip: 21218. Phone: 410/605-7000).*
Perry Point: More than 500 beds, plus nursing care unit. Geriatric evaluation, inpatient psychiatric, rehabilitation, respite care, substance abuse, geriatric. *(Zip: 21902. Phone: 410/642-2411)*

Clinics
Baltimore: *(3900 Loch Raven Boulevard, Zip: 21218. Phone: 410/605-7000)*
Cambridge: *(830 Chesapeake Drive, Zip: 21613. Phone: 410/228-6243)*
Charlotte Hall: *(29431 Charlotte Hall Road, Zip: 20622. Phone: 301/884-7102)*
Cumberland: *(200 Glenn Street, Zip: 21502. Phone: 301/724-0061)*
Fort Howard: *(9600 North Point Road, Zip: 21052. Phone: 410/477-1800)*
Glen Burnie: *(808 Landmark Drive, Zip: 21061. Phone: 410/590-4140)*
Greenbelt: *(7525 Greenway Center Drive, Zip: 20770. Phone: 301/345-2463)*
Hagerstown: *(1101 Opal Court, Zip: 21742. Phone: 301/665-1462)*
Pocomoke: *(101 Market Street, Zip: 21851. Phone: 410/957-6718)*

Regional Office
Baltimore: Serving all counties except Montgomery and Prince Georges, which are served by the regional office in Washington, DC *(31 Hopkins Plaza Federal Building, Zip: 21201. Phone: 800/827-1000)*

Vet Centers
Baltimore: *(1777 Reistertown Road, Zip: 21208. Phone: 410/764-9400)*
Cambridge: *(830 Chesapeake Drive, Zip: 21613. Phone: 410/228-6305)*
Elkton: *(103 Chesapeake Boulevard, Zip: 21921. Phone: 410/392-4485)*
Silver Spring: *(1015 Spring Street, Zip: 20910. Phone: 301/589-1073)*

National Cemeteries
Annapolis: *(800 West Street, Zip: 21401. Phone: 410/644-9696)*
Baltimore: *(5501 Frederick Avenue, Zip: 21228. Phone: 410/644-9696)*
Loudoun Park: *(3445 Frederick Avenue, Baltimore, Zip: 21228. Phone: 410/644-1563)*

MASSACHUSETTS
Medical Centers
Bedford: More than 500 beds, including nursing unit and domiciliary. Emphasis on psychiatry, geriatrics, alcohol and drug treatment, Alzheimer's, geriatric dentistry. *(200 Springs Road, Zip: 01730. Phone: 781/687-2000)*

Brockton: More than 400 beds, plus nursing home and domiciliary. Regional center for spinal cord injury. Also mental health, inpatient psychiatric, women's health, respite care. *(940 Belmont Street, Zip: 02301. Phone: 508/583-4500)*

Jamaica Plan: More than 430 beds, including nursing home and domiciliary. Outpatient care, including ambulatory surgery, eye center, mental heath, post-traumatic stress disorder, and women's health. *(150 S. Huntington Avenue, Zip: 02130. Phone: 617/232-9500)*

Northampton: Nearly 100 beds. Primary medical care, post-traumatic stress, mental health, substance abuse. *(421 N. Main Street, Zip: 01053. Phone: 413/584-4040)*

West Roxbury: More than 400 beds and twenty-four hour emergency room. Regional center for inpatient and specialty care. Cardiac center, rehabilitation, cancer surgery, orthopedics, plastic surgery. *(1400 VFW Parkway, Zip: 02132. Phone: 617/323-7700)*

Clinics
Boston: *(251 Causeway Street, Zip: 02114. Phone: 617/248-1000)*

Dorchester: *(895 Blue Hill Avenue, Zip: 02121. Phone: 617/822-7146)*

Fitchburg: *(275 Nichols Road, Zip: 01420. Phone: 978/342-9781)*

Framingham: *(61 Lincoln Street, Zip: 01702. Phone: 508/628-0205)*

Gloucester: *(298 Washington Street, Zip: 01930. Phone: 978/282-0676)*

Greenfield: *(143 Munson Street, Zip: 01301. Phone: 413/773-8428)*

Haverhill: *(108 Merrimac Street, Zip: 01830. Phone: 978/372-5207)*

Hyannis: *(233 Stevens Street, Zip: 02601. Phone: 508/771-3190)*

Lowell: *(130 Marshal Road, Zip: 01852. Phone: 978/671-9000)*

Lynn: *(225 Boston Road, Zip: 01904. Phone: 781/595-9818)*

Martha's Vineyard: *(Hospital Road, Zip: 02557. Phone: 508/693-0410)*

Nantucket: *(57 Prospect Street, Zip: 02554. Phone: 508/825-8195)*

New Bedford: *(175 Elm Street, Zip: 02740. Phone: 508/994-0217)*

Pittsfield: *(73 Eagle Street, Zip: 01201. Phone: 413/443-4857)*

Quincy: *(114 Whitwell Street, Zip: 02169. Phone: 617/376-2010)*

Springfield: *(25 Bond Street, Zip: 01104. Phone: 413/731-6000)*

Worcester: *(605 Lincoln Street, Zip: 01605. Phone: 508/856-0104)*

Regional Office
Boston: Serving all communities except the towns of Fall River and New Bedford, and counties of Barnstable, Dukes, Nantucket, Bristol, and part of Plymouth, which are served by the regional office in Providence, Rhode Island. *(JFK Federal Building, Zip: 02114. Phone: 800/827-1000)*

Vet Centers
Boston: *(665 Beacon Street, Zip: 02215. Phone: 617/424-0665)*

Brockton: *(1041 Pearl Street, Zip: 02401. Phone: 508/580-2730)*

Hyannis: *(474 West Main Street, Zip: 02601. Phone: 508/778-0124)*

Lowell: *(10 George Street, Zip: 01852. Phone: 978/453-1151)*

New Bedford: *(73 Huttleston Avenue, Zip: 02719. Phone: 508/999-6920)*

Springfield: *(1985 Main Street, Zip: 01103. Phone: 413/737-5167)*

Worcester: *(691 Grafton Street, Zip: 01605. Phone: 508/753-7902)*

National Cemetery
Bourne: *(Zip: 02532. Phone: 508/563-7113)*

MICHIGAN
Medical Centers
Ann Arbor: About 150 beds, including nursing units and domiciliary. Intensive care, neurosurgery, audiology, cancer, and diabetes. *(2215 Fuller Road, Zip: 48105. Phone: 734/769-7100)*

Battle Creek: More than 330 beds, including nursing unit and domiciliary. Primary care, extended care, psychiatric. Dementia unit, substance abuse, mental health clinic, post-traumatic stress programs. *(5500 Armstrong Road, Zip: 49037. Phone: 269/966-5600)*

Detroit: More than 250 beds, including nursing home and domiciliary. General medicine, surgery, and psychiatry. Women's center, POW program, cancer center. *(4646 John R. Street, Zip: 48201. Phone: 313/576-1000)*

Iron Mountain: More than 50 beds, including nursing home and domiciliary. Primary care, extended care, rehabilitation, womens' programs, mental health. *(325 East H Street, Zip: 49801. Phone: 906/774-3300)*

Saginaw: More than 100 beds, including nursing care and domiciliary. Primary care, inpatient, and surgery. *(1500 Weiss Street, Zip: 48602. Phone: 989/497-2500)*

Clinics
Benton Harbor: *(115 Main Street, Zip: 49022. Phone: 269/934-9123)*

Flint: *(3267 Beecher Road, Zip: 48532. Phone: 810/720-2913)*

Gaylord: *(806 S. Otsego, Zip: 49735. Phone: 989/732-7525)*

Grand Rapids: *(3019 Coit Street, N.E., Zip: 49505. Phone: 616/365-9575)*

Hancock: *(787 Market Street, Zip: 49930. Phone: 906/482-7762)*

Ironwood: *(629 W. Cloverland Drive, Zip: 49938. Phone: 906/932-0032)*

Kincheloe: *(16523 S. Watertower Drive, Zip: 49788. Phone: 906/495-3030)*

Lansing: *(2025 S. Washington Avenue, Zip: 48910. Phone: 517/267-3925)*

Marquette: *(1414 W. Fair Avenue, Zip: 49855. Phone: 906/226-4618)*

Manistique: *(813 East Lakeshore Drive, Zip: 49854. Phone: 906/341-3420)*

Menominee: *(1101 10th Avenue, Zip: 49858. Phone: 906/863-1286)*

Michigan Center: *(4328 Page Avenue, Zip: 49254. Phone: 517-764-3609)*

Muskegon: *(165 E. Apple Avenue, Zip: 49442. Phone: 231/725-4105)*

Oscoda: *(5671 Skeel Avenue, Zip: 48750. Phone: 989/747-0026)*

Pontiac: *(1701 Baldwin Avenue, Zip: 48340. Phone: 248/409-0585)*

Sault Saint Marie: *(2864 Ashmun Road, Zip: 49783. Phone: 906/253-9564)*

Traverse City: *(3271 Racquet Club Drive, Zip: 49684. Phone: 231/932-9720)*

Yale: *(7470 Brockway Drive, Phone: 810/387-3211)*

Regional Office
Detroit: *(McNamara Federal Building, 477 Michigan Avenue, Zip: 48226. Phone: 800/827-1000)*

Vet Centers
Dearborn: *(2881 Monroe Street, Zip: 48124. Phone: 313/277-1428)*

Detroit: *(4161 Cass Avenue, Zip: 48201. Phone: 313/831-6509)*

Escanaba: *(3500 Ludington Street, Zip: 49829. Phone: 906/233-0244)*

Grand Rapids: *(205 Bretib Road, S.E., Zip: 49507. Phone: 616/285-5795)*

Saginaw: *(4048 Bay Road, Zip: 48603.*
Phone: 989/321-4650)
National Cemetery
Fort Custer: *(15501 Dickman Road,*
Augusta, Zip: 49012. Phone:
616/731-4164)
Great Lakes: *(4200 Belford Road, Zip:*
48442. Phone: 866/348-8603)

MINNESOTA
Medical Centers
Minneapolis: Nearly 200 beds, including nursing care and domiciliary.
Primary care, medicine, surgery,
rehabilitation, and short-term psychiatric. HIV clinic, amputation
care, substance abuse, dentistry,
adult day care. *(1 Veterans Drive,*
Zip: 55417. Phone: 612/725-2000)
Saint Cloud: Nearly 400 beds, including domiciliary and nursing care
unit. Primary care, acute psychiatric care, residential and inpatient substance abuse, vocational
rehabilitation, adult day care.
(4801 Veterans Drive, Zip: 56303.
Phone: 320/252-1670)

Clinics
Bemidji: *(705 5th Street, Zip: 56601.*
Phone: 218/755-6360)
Brainerd: *(722 NW 7th Street, Zip:*
56401. Phone: 218/855-1115)
Fergus Falls: *(1821 N. Park Street,*
Zip: 56537. Phone: 218/739-1400)
Gaylord: *(315 4th Street, Zip: 55334)*
Hibbing: *(1101 East 37th Street, Zip:*
55746. Phone: 218/263-9698)
Maplewood: *(2785 White Bear Avenue,*
Zip: 55109. Phone: 651/290-3040)
Montevideo: *(1025 North 13th Street,*
Zip: 56265. Phone: 320/269-2222)
Rochester: *(1617 Skyline Drive, Zip:*
55902. Phone: 507/252-0885)
St. James: *(1101 Moultin and Parsons*
Drive, Zip: 56081. Phone: 507/375-
3391)

Regional Office
Saint Paul: Serving all communities
except counties of Becker, Bel-
trami, Clay, Clearwater, Kittson,
Lake of the Woods, Mahnomen,
Marshall, Norman, Otter Tail,
Pennington, Polk, Red Lake,
Roseau, and Wilkin, which are
served by the regional office in
Fargo, North Dakota. *(Federal*
Building, 1 Federal Drive, Fort
Snelling, Zip: 55111. Phone:
800/827-1000)

Vet Centers
Brooklyn Park: *(701 78th Avenue,*
North, Zip: 55445. Phone:
763/503-2220)
Duluth: *(405 E. Superior Street, Zip:*
55802. Phone: 218/722-8654)
Saint Paul: *(550 County Road, Zip:*
55112. Phone: 651/644-4022)

National Cemetery
Fort Snelling: *(7601 34th Avenue, S.,*
Minneapolis, Zip: 55450. Phone:
612/726-1127)

MISSISSIPPI
Medical Centers
Biloxi: More than 200 beds, including
nursing unit and domiciliary. Inpatient and outpatient care in medicine, surgery, and psychiatry. Neurology, cancer, dentistry, geriatrics,
extended care, rehabilitation. *(400*
Veterans Avenue, Zip: 39531.
Phone: 228/523-5000)
Jackson: More than 250 beds, including nursing unit and domiciliary.
Inpatient and outpatient care, including cancer, spinal cord injury,
post-traumatic stress, and substance abuse. *(1500 E. Woodrow*
Wilson Drive, Zip: 39216. Phone:
601/362-4471)

Clinics
Byhalia: *(12 East Brunswick Street,*
Zip: 38611. Phone: 662/838-2163)

Columbus: *(824 Alabama Street, Zip: 39702. Phone: 662/244-0391)*
Greenville: *(1502 S. Colorado Street, Zip: 38703. Phone: 662/332-9872)*
Hattiesburg: *(231 Methodist Boulevard, Zip: 39401. Phone: 601/296-3530)*
Houlka: *(106 Walker Street, Zip: 38850. Phone: 662/568-3316)*
Kosciusko: *(332 Highway 12W, Zip: 39039. Phone: 662/289-1800)*
Meadville: *(595 Main Street East, Zip: 39653. Phone: 601/384-3650)*
Natchez: *(46 Sgt. Prentiss Drive, Zip: 39120. Phone: 601/442-7141)*
Smithville: *(63420 Highway 25N, Zip: 38870. Phone: 662/651-4637)*

Regional Office
Jackson: *(1600 E. Woodrow Wilson Avenue, Zip: 39216. Phone: 800/827-1000)*

Vet Centers
Biloxi: *(288 Veterans Avenue, Zip: 39531. Phone: 228/388-9938)*
Jackson: *(1755 Lelia Drive, Zip: 39216. Phone: 601/965-5727)*

National Cemeteries
Biloxi: *(400 Veterans Avenue, Zip: 39535. Phone: 228/388-6668)*
Corinth: *(1551 Horton Street, Zip: 38834. Phone: 901/386-8311)*
Natchez: *(41 Cemetery Road, Zip: 39120. Phone: 601/445-4981)*

MISSOURI
Medical Centers
Columbia: More than 100 beds, including nursing unit and domiciliary. General medicine and surgury. Intensive care, coronary care units. Neurosurgery, open-heart surgery, substance abuse, hospital-based home care. *(800 Hospital Drive, Zip: 65201. Phone: 573/814-6000)*

Kansas City: More than 150 beds, including nursing unit and domiciliary. Primary care, medicine, surgery, psychiatry, plus regional eye center. homeless veterans program, cardiac care. *(4801 Linwood Boulevard, Zip: 64128. Phone: 816/861-4700)*
Poplar Bluff: More than 50 beds, including nursing unit and domiciliary. Primary care, diabetes, hypertension, optometry, dermatology, rheumatology, podiatry, female veterans, post-traumatic stress, Persian Gulf illnesses. *(1500 N. Westwood Boulevard, Zip: 63901. Phone: 573/686-4151)*
Saint Louis: More than 300 beds in two units, Jefferson Barracks and John Cochran divisions. Nursing unit and domiciliary. Organ transplants, spinal cord injury, prosthetics, psychiatry, drug and alcohol dependence. *(John Cochran Division: 915 N. Grand Boulevard, Zip: 63106. Phone: 314/652-4100. Jefferson Barracks Division: Zip: 63125. Phone: 314/652-4100)*

Clinics
Belton: *(17140 Bel-Ray Place, Zip: 64021. Phone: 816/922-2161)*
Branson: *(5571 Gretna Road, Zip: 65616. Phone: 417/243-2300)*
Camdenton: *(246 E Highway 54, Zip: 65020. Phone: 573/317-1150)*
Cameron: *(1111 Euclid Drive, Zip: 64429. Phone: 816/922-2500)*
Cape Girardeau: *(2420 Veterans Memorial Drive, Zip: 63701. Phone: 573/339-0909)*
Farmington: *(1580 W. Columbia Street, Zip: 63640. Phone: 573/760-1365)*
Ft. Leonard Wood: *(126 Missouri Avenue, Zip: 65473. Phone: 573/329-8305)*

Kirksville: *(1108 East Patterson, Zip: 63501. Phone: 660/627-8387)*
Jefferson City: *(2707 W. Edgewood, Zip: 65109. Phone: 573/635-0233)*
Mexico: *(One Veterans Drive, Zip: 65265. Phone: 573/581-9630)*
Mt. Vernon: *(600 N. Main, Zip: 65712. Phone: 417/466-4000)*
Nevada: *(322 South Prewitt, Zip: 64772. Phone: 317/448-8905)*
Paola: *(501 S. Hospital Drive, Zip: 66071. Phone: 913/294-4765)*
Salem: *(Highway 72 North, Zip: 65560. Phone: 573/729-6626)*
Saint Charles: *(7 Jason Court, Zip: 63304. Phone: 314/286-6988)*
St. James: *(620 N. Jefferson, Zip: 65559. Phone: 573/265-0448)*
St. Joseph: *(1314 North 36th Street, Zip: 64506. Phone: 800/952-8387)*
St. Louis: *(10600 Lewis and Clark Boulevard, Zip: 63136. Phone: 314/286-6988)*
Warrensburg: *(1300 Veterans Drive, Zip: 64093. Phone: 660/747-3864)*
West Plains: *(1211 Missouri Avenue, Zip: 65775. Phone: 417/257-2454)*

Regional Office

Saint Louis: *(400 S. 18th Street, Zip: 63103. Phone: 800/827-1000)*

Vet Centers

Kansas City: *(301 Armour Road, Zip: 64111. Phone: 816/753-1866)*
Saint Louis: *(2345 Pine Street, Zip: 63103. Phone: 314/231-1260)*

National Cemeteries

Jefferson Barracks: *(2900 Sheridan Road, Zip: 63125. Phone: 314/260-8720)*
Jefferson City: *(1024 E. McCarty Street, Zip: 65101. Phone: 314/260-8691)*
Springfield: *(1702 E. Seminole Street, Zip: 65804. Phone: 417/881-9499)*

MONTANA
Medical Centers

Fort Harrison: About 80 beds, including nursing unit and domiciliary. Acute care, surgery, inpatient and outpatient psychiatry, sleep lab, pain management, eye care, telemedicine. *(3687 Veterans Drive, Zip: 59636. Phone: 406/442-6410)*

Clinic

Anaconda: *(118 East 7th Street, Zip: 59711. Phone: 406/563-6090)*
Billings: *(1775 Spring Creek Lane, Zip: 59102. Phone: 406/373-5000)*
Bozeman: *(300 N. Wilson, Zip: 59715. Phone: 406/582-3500)*
Cut Bank: *(519 East Main Street, Zip: 59427. Phone: 406/873-5670)*
Glasgow: *(640 3rd Avenue South, Zip: 59230. Phone: 406/228-4101)*
Great Falls: *(1417-9th Street South, Zip: 59405. Phone: 406/761-3200)*
Havre: *(130 13th Street, Zip: 59501. Phone: 406/265-4304)*
Kalispell: *(31 Three Mile Drive, Zip: 59901. Phone: 406/758-2700)*
Lewistown: *(629 NE Main Street, Zip: 59457. Phone: 406/535-4790)*
Miles City: *(210 S. Winchester, Zip: 59301. Phone: 406/874-4790)*
Missoula: *(2687 Palmer Street, Zip: 59808. Phone: 406/829-5400)*

Regional Office

Fort Harrison: *(William Street, Zip: 59636. Phone: 800/827-1000)*

Vet Centers

Billings: *(2795 Enterprise Avenue, Zip: 59102. Phone: 406/657-6071)*
Missoula: *(500 N. Higgins Avenue, Zip: 59802. Phone: 406/721-4918)*

NEBRASKA

Medical Centers

Grand Island: About 60 beds, plus nursing care unit. Geriatrics, extended care, rehabilitation, respite care. *(2201 N. Broadwell Avenue, Zip: 68803. Phone: 308/382-3660)*

Lincoln: Outpatient primary care. *(600 South 70th Street, Zip: 68510. Phone: 402/489-3802)*

Omaha: More than 100 beds including nursing unit and domiciliary. Inpatient medical, surgial, and psychiatric care. *(4101 Woolworth Avenue, Zip: 68105. Phone: 402/346-8800)*

Clinics

Alliance: *(524 Box Butte Avenue, Zip: 69301. Phone: 605/745-2000)*

Bellevue: *(2501 Capehart Road, Zip: 68113. Phone: 402/591-4500)*

Grand Island: *(2201 N. Broadwell Avenue, Zip: 68803. Phone: 308/382-3660)*

Holdrege: *(1118 Burlington Street, Zip: 68949. Phone: 308/995-3760)*

Lincoln: *(600 South 70th Street, Zip: 68510. Phone: 402/489-3802)*

Norfolk: *(710 S. 13th Street, Zip: 68701. Phone: 402/370-4570)*

North Platte: *(600 East Francis, Zip: 69101. Phone: 308/532-6906)*

Rushville: *(300 E. 8th Street, Zip: 69343. Phone: 605/745-2000)*

Scottsbluff: *(1720 E. Portal Place, Zip: 69361. Phone: 308/220-3930)*

Sidney: *(1116 10th Avenue, Zip: 69162. Phone: 308/254-5544)*

Regional Office

Lincoln: *(5631 S. 48th Street, Zip: 68516. Phone: 800/827-1000)*

Vet Centers

Lincoln: *(3119 O Street, Zip: 68510. Phone: 800/228-6838)*

Omaha: *(2428 Cuming Street, Zip: 68131. Phone: 402/346-6735)*

National Cemetery

Fort McPherson: *(12004 South Spur 56 A, Maxwell, Zip: 69151. Phone: 308/582-4433)*

NEVADA

Medical Centers

Las Vegas: New facility under construction and scheduled to open late in 2011.

Reno: More than 110 beds, including nursing unit and domiciliary. General medicine, surgery and psychiatric services. Alzheimer's, Parkinson's, diabetes, cardiology. *(1000 Locust Street, Zip: 89502. Phone: 702/786-7200)*

Clinics

Elko: *(762 14th Street, Zip: 89801. Phone: 775/753-2014)*

Ely: *(6 Steptoe Circle, Zip: 89301. Phone: 775/289-3612)*

Fallon: *(345 West A Street, Zip: 89406. Phone: 775/428-6161)*

Henderson: *(2930 N. Greenvalley Parkway, Zip: 89014. Phone: 702/636-6363)*

Las Vegas: *(916 West Owens Avenue, Zip: 89106. Phone: 702/636-6380)*

Las Vegas: *(630 S. Rancho Lane, Zip: 89106. Phone: 702/636-6355)*

Las Vegas: *(2410 Fire Mesa, Zip: 89129. Phone: 702/636-6320)*

Las Vegas: *(3880 S. Jones Boulevard, Zip: 89103. Phone: 702/636-6390)*

Minden: *(925 Ironwood Drive, Zip: 89423, Zip: Phone: 888/838-6256)*

Pahrump: *(2100 E. Calvada Boulevard, Zip: 89048. Phone: 775/727-7535)*

Regional Office

Reno: Serves all communities in Nevada plus California counties of Alpine, Lassen, Modoc, and Mono. *(1201 Terminal Way, Zip: 89520. Phone: 800/827-1000)*

Vet Centers

Las Vegas: *(1919 S. Jones Boulevard, Zip: 89146. Phone: 702/251-7873)*
Reno: *(1155 W. 4th Street, Zip: 89503. Phone: 775/323-1294)*

NEW HAMPSHIRE
Medical Center

Manchester: More than 110 beds, including nursing unit and domiciliary. Primary care, plus medical, surgical, and extended care. Hospital-based home care, adult day care, respite care, hospice. *(718 Smyth Road, Zip: 03104. Phone: 603/624-4366)*

Clinics

Conway: *(7 Greenwood Avenue, Zip: 03818. Phone: 603/447-3500)*
Littleton: *(600 St. Johnsbury Road, Zip: 03561. Phone: 603/444-9328)*
Portsmouth: *(302 Newmarket Street, Zip: 03803. Phone: 603/624-4366)*
Somersworth: *(200 Route 108, Zip: 03878. Phone: 603/624-4366)*
Tilton: *(139 Winter Street, Zip: 03276. Phone: 603/624-4366)*

Regional Office

Manchester: *(Cotton Federal Building, 275 Chestnut Street, Zip: 03101. Phone: 800/827-1000)*

Vet Center

Berline: *(515 Main Street, Zip: 03581. Phone: 603/752-2571)*
Manchester: *(103 Liberty Street, Zip: 03104. Phone: 603/668-7060)*

NEW JERSEY
Medical Centers

East Orange: More than 200 beds. Medical, surgical, and psychiatric programs. *(385 Tremont Avenue, Zip: 07018. Phone: 973/676-1000)*
Lyons: Nearly 650 beds, including nursing unit and domiciliary. Primary care, plus long-term care and rehabilitation. *(151 Knollcrott Road, Zip: 07939. Phone: 908/647-0180)*

Clinics

Brick: *(970 Route 70, Zip: 08724. Phone: 732/206-8900)*
Cape May: *(1 Monroe Avenue, Zip: 08204. Phone: 609/898-8700)*
Elizabeth: *(654 E. Jersey Street, Zip: 07206. Phone: 908/994-0120)*
Fort Dix: *(8th & Alabama, Zip: 08640. Phone: 609/562-2999)*
Fort Monmouth: *(1075 Stephenson Avenue, Zip: 07703. Phone: 732/532-4500)*
Hackensack: *(385 Prospect Avenue, Zip: 07601. Phone: 201/487-1390)*
Jersey City: *(115 Christopher Columbus Drive, Zip: 07302. Phone: 201/435-3055)*
Morristown: *(340 West Hanover Avenue, Zip: 07960. Phone: 973/539-9791)*
New Brunswick: *(317 George Street, Zip: 08901. Phone: 732/729-0646)*
Newark: *(20 Washington Place, Zip: 07102. Phone: 973/645-1441)*
Paterson: *(275 Getty Avenue, St. Joseph's Hospital & Medical Center, Zip: 07503. Phone: 973/247-1666)*
Sewel: *(211 County House Road, Zip: 08080. Phone: 856/401-7665)*
Trenton: *(171 Jersey Street, Zip: 08611. Phone: 609/989-2355)*
Ventnor: *(6601 Ventnor Avenue, Zip: 08406. Phone: 609/823-3122)*
Vineland: *(New Jersey Vets Home, Northwest Boulevard, Zip: 08360. Phone: 856/692-1588)*
Vineland: *(1051 West Sherman Avenue, Zip: 08360. Phone: 856/692-2881)*

Regional Office
Newark: *(20 Washington Place, Zip: 07102. Phone: 800/827-1000)*

Vet Centers
Bloomfield: *(2 Broad Street, Zip: 07003. Phone: 973/748-0980)*
Ewing: *(934 Parkway Avenue, Zip: 08618. Phone: 609/882-5744)*
Lakewood: *(1255 Route 70, Zip: 08701. Phone: 908/607-6364)*
Secaucus: *(110 Meadowlands Parkway, Zip: 07094. Phone: 201/223-7787)*
Ventnor: *(6601 Ventnor Avenue, Zip: 08406. Phone: 609/487-8387)*

National Cemeteries
Beverly: *(R.D. #1, Bridgeboro Road, Zip: 08010. Phone: 609/877-5460)*
Finn's Point: *(RFD #3, Fort Mott Road, Salem, Zip: 08079. Phone: 609/871-4691)*

NEW MEXICO
Medical Center
Albuquerque: More than 300 beds, including nursing home and domiciliary. Primary care and major specialties. Provides services to entire state through rural health program. Spinal cord injury unit, heart surgery, magnetic imaging. *(1501 San Pedro Drive, S.E., Zip: 87108. Phone: 505/265-1711)*

Clinics
Alamagordo: *(1410 Aspen, Zip: 88310. Phone: 505/437-7000)*
Artesia: *(1700 W. Main Street, Zip: 88210. Phone: 505/746-3531)*
Durango: *(1970 E. 3rd Avenue, Zip: 81301. Phone: 970/247-2214)*
Espanola: *(620 Coronado Street, Zip: 87532. Phone: 505/747-7395)*
Farmington: *(1001 W. Broadway, Zip: 87401. Phone: 505/326-4383)*
Gallup: *(320 Highway 564, Zip: 87301. Phone: 505/722-7234)*

Las Vegas: *(1235 8th Street, Zip: 87701. Phone: 505/425-6788)*
Raton: *(1275 S. 2nd Street, Zip: 87740. Phone: 575/445-2921)*
Sante Fe: *(2213 Brothers Road, Zip: 87505. Phone: 505/986-8645.*
Silver City: *(1302 32nd Street, Zip: 88061. Phone: 505/538-2921)*
Truth Or Consequences: *(1960 North Date Street, Zip: 87901. Phone: 505/894-7662)*

Regional Office
Albuquerque: *(Danis Chavez Federal Building, 500 Gold Avenue, S.W., Zip: 87102. Phone: 800/827-1000)*

Vet Centers
Albuquerque: *(1600 Mountain Road, N.W., Zip: 87104. Phone: 505/346-6562)*
Farmington: *(4251 E. Main Street, Zip: 87402. Phone: 505/327-9684)*
Lakewood: *(1255 Route 70, Zip: 08701. Phone: 908/607-6364)*
Las Cruces: *(230 S. Water Street, Zip: 88001. Phone: 575/523-9826)*
Santa Fe: *(2209 Brothers Road, Zip: 87505. Phone: 505/988-6562)*

National Cemeteries
Fort Bayard: *(P.O. Box 189, Zip: 88036. Phone: 915/564-0201)*
Santa Fe: *(501 N. Guadalupe Street, Zip: 87501. Phone: 505/988-6400)*

NEW YORK
Medical Centers
Albany: Nearly 300 beds, including nursing home and domiciliary. Medicine, surgery, mental health, and rehabilitation. Home-based primary care, alcohol rehabilitation, post-traumatic stress, psychiatry, hemodialysis, state-of-the-art cancer treatment, eye institute. *(113 Holland Avenue, Zip: 12208. Phone: 518/626-5000)*

Batavia: More than 100 beds, with nursing unit. Referral center for cancer and cardiology. Intensive-care unit, rehabilitative services, geriatric evaluation. *(222 Richmond Avenue, Zip: 14020. Phone: 585/297-1000)*

Bath: More than 400 beds, including nursing home and domiciliary. Primary care, outpatient services, vocational rehabilitation. *(76 Veterans Avenue, Zip: 14810. Phone: 607/664-4000)*

Bronx: More than 200 beds, including nursing home and domiciliary. Spinal cord, alcohol and drug dependency, schizophrenia and Alzheimer's, kidney dialysis, prosthetics, pain management. *(130 W. Kingsbridge Road, Zip: 10468. Phone: 718/584-9000)*

Brooklyn: Nearly 300 beds, including nursing home and domiciliary. Medicine, surgery, psychiatry. Cancer center, cardiology, substance abuse. *(800 Poly Place, Zip: 11209. Phone: 718/836-6600)*

Buffalo: Nearly 220 beds, including nursing home and domiciliary. Regional cancer center. Open-heart surgery, heart transplant, pacemaker, drug and alcohol treatment, post-traumatic stress, hemodialysis, geriatrics, neurodiagnostics. *(3495 Bailey Avenue, Zip: 14215. Phone: 716/834-9200)*

Canandaigua: More than 200 beds, including nursing home and domiciliary. Emphasis on long-term care and mental health. Geriatrics, substance abuse, outpatient post-traumatic stress, vocational rehabilitation. *(400 Fort Hill Avenue, Zip: 14424. Phone: 585/394-2000)*

Castle Point: About 100 beds, with nursing unit. Primary care, medicine, surgery, mental health. Outpatient spinal cord injury, rehabili-tation. *(Route 9-D, Zip: 12511. Phone: 845/831-2000)*

Montrose: Nearly 300 beds, including nursing home and domiciliary. Intensive-care unit. Geriatrics, eye center, dentistry, podiatry, womens health. *(2094 Albany Post Road, Zip: 10548. Phone: 914/737-4400)*

New York City: Nearly 300 beds, including nursing home and domiciliary. Inpatient AIDS, advanced care for cardiology and neurosurgery. *(423 E. 23rd Street, Zip: 10010. Phone: 212/686-7500)*

Northport: More than 330 beds, including nursing home and domiciliary. Medical, surgical, psychiatric, and rehabilitative care. Neurosurgery, dialysis, prosthetic sensory aids, radiation therapy, respite care, eye center, women veterans. *(79 Middleville Road, Long Island, Zip: 11768. Phone: 631/261-4400)*

Syracuse: About 150 beds, including nursing home and domiciliary. Laser treatments, cardiac catheterization, respiratory care, lithotripsy, women veterans, audiology, speech pathology, nuclear medicine, computerized axial tomography. *(800 Irving Avenue, Zip: 13210. Phone: 315/425-4400)*

Clinics

Auburn: *(17 Lansing Street, Zip: 13021. Phone: 315/255-7002)*

Bainbridge: *(109 North Main Street, Zip: 13733. Phone: 607/967-8590)*

Binghamton: *(425 Robinson Street, Zip: 13901. Phone: 607/772-9100)*

Bronx: *(953 Southern Boulevard, Zip: 10459. Phone: 718/741-4900)*

Brooklyn: *(40th Flatbush Avenue Extension, Zip: 11201. Phone: 718/439-4300)*

Carmel: *(1875 Route 6, Zip: 10512. Phone: 845/228-5291)*

Carthage: *(3 Bridge Street, Zip: 13619. Phone: 315/493-4180)*

Catskill: *(159 Jefferson Heights, Zip: 12414. Phone: 518/943-7515)*

Clifton Park: *(1673 Route 9, Zip: 12065. Phone: 518/383-8508)*

Cortland: *(1104 Commons Avenue, Zip: 13045. Phone: 607/662-1517)*

Dunkirk: *(166 East 4th Street, Zip: 14048. Phone: 716/366-2122)*

Elizabethtown: *(277 Park Street, Zip: 12932. Phone: 518/873-3295)*

Elmira: *(200 Madison Avenue, Zip: 14901. Phone: 877/845-3247)*

Fonda: *(2623 State Highway 30A, Zip: 12068. Phone: 518/853-1247)*

Glens Falls: *(84 Broad Street, Zip: 12801. Phone: 518/798-6066)*

Goshen: *(30 Hartfield Lane, Zip: 10924. Phone: 845/294-6927)*

Ithaca: *(10 Arrowwood Drive, Zip: 14850. Phone: 607/274-4680)*

Jamestown: *(608 W. 3rd Street, Zip: 14701. Phone: 716/338-1511)*

Kingston: *(63 Hurley Avenue, Zip: 12401. Phone: 845/331-8322)*

Lackawanna: *(227 Ridge Road, Zip: 14218. Phone: 716/822-5944)*

Lockport: *(5883 Snyder Drive, Zip: 14094. Phone: 716/438-3890)*

Malone: *(3372 State Route 11, Zip: 12953. Phone: 518/483-1529)*

Massena: *(1 Hospital Drive, Zip: 13662. Phone: 315/769-4253)*

Monticello: *(60 Jefferson Street, Zip: 12701. Phone: 845/791-4936)*

New York: *(345 N. Main Street, Zip: 10970. Phone: 845/634-8942)*

New York: *(437 West 16th Street, Zip: 10011. Phone: 212/462-4461)*

New York: *(55 W. 125th Street, 11th Floor, Zip: 10027. Phone: 212/828-5265)*

Niagara Falls: *(2201 Pine Avenue, Zip: 14301. Phone: 800/223-4810)*

Olean: *(465 North Union Street, Zip: 14760. Phone: 716/375-7709)*

Oswego: *(105 County Route 45-A, Zip: 13126. Phone: 315/343-0925)*

Patchogue: *(4 Phyllis Drive, Zip: 11772. Phone: 631/475-6610)*

Pine Plains: *(2881 Church Street, Zip: 12567. Phone: 518/398-9240)*

Plainview: *(1425 Old Country Road, Zip: 11803. Phone: 516/572-8567)*

Plattsburgh: *(80 Sharon Sharron Avenue, Zip: 12901. Phone: 518/561-6247)*

Port Jervis: *(150 Pike Street, Zip: 12771. Phone: 845/856-5396)*

Poughkeepsie: *(488 Freedom Plains Road, Zip: 12603. Phone: 845/452-5151)*

Rochester: *(465 Westfall Road, Zip: 14620. Phone: 585/463-2600)*

Rome: *(125 Brookley Road, Zip: 13441. Phone: 315/334-7100)*

Schenectady: *(1322 Gerling Street, Zip: 12308. Phone: 518/346-3334)*

Springville: *(27 Franklin Street, Zip: 14141. Phone: 716/592-7400)*

Staten Island: *(1150 South Avenue, Zip: 10314. Phone: 718/761-2973)*

Sunnyside: *(41-03 Queens Boulevard, Zip: 11104. Phone: 718/741-4800)*

Troy: *(295 River Street, Zip: 12180. Phone: 518/274-7707)*

Warsaw: *(400 North Main Street, Zip: 14569. Phone: 585/786-2233)*

Wellsville: *(3458 Riverside Drive, Zip: 14895. Phone: 585/596-4111)*

Westhampton: *(150 Old Riverhead Road, Zip: 11978. Phone: 631/898-0599)*

White Plains: *(23 S. Broadway, Zip: 10601. Phone: 914/421-1951)*

Yonkers: *(124 New Main Street, Zip: 10705. Phone: 914/375-8055)*

Regional Offices

Buffalo: *(Federal Building, 111 W. Huron Street, Zip: 14202. Phone: 800/827-1000)*

New York City: Serving counties of Albany, Bronx, Clinton, Columbia, Delaware, Dutchess, Essex, Franklin, Fulton, Greene, Hamilton, Kings, Montgomery, Nassau,

New York, Orange, Otsego, Put-
nam, Queens, Rensselaer, Richmond, Rockland, Saratoga, Schenectady, Schoharie, Suffolk,
Sullivan, Ulster, Warren, Washington, and Westchester. *(245 W.
Houston Street, Zip: 10014. Phone:
800/827-1000)*

Vet Centers
Albany: *(17 Computer Drive West, Zip:
12205. Phone: 518/626-5130)*
Babylon: *(116 W. Main Street, Zip:
11702. Phone: 631/661-3930)*
Binghamptom: *(53 Chenango Street,
Zip: 13901. Phone: 607/722-2393)*
Bronx: *(2471 Morris Avenue, Zip:
10468. Phone: 718/367-3500)*
Brooklyn: *(25 Chapel Street, Zip:
11201. Phone: 718/624-2765)*
Buffalo: *(2372 Sweet Home Road, Zip:
14228. Phone: 716/862-7350)*
Middletown: *(726 East Main Street,
Zip: 10940. Phone: 845/342-9917)*
New York: *(32 Broadway, Zip: 10004.
Phone: 212/742-9591)*
New York: *(2279 3rd Avenue, Zip:
10035. Phone: 212/426-2200)*
Plainview: *(1425 Old Country Road,
Zip: 11803. Phone: 516/572-8455)*
Rochester: *(1867 Mt. Hope Avenue,
Zip: 14620. Phone: 585/232-5040)*
Staten Island: *(150 Richmond Terrace,
Zip: 10301. Phone: 718/816-4499)*
Syracuse: *(716 E. Washington Street,
Zip: 13210. Phone: 315/478-7127)*
White Plains: *(300 Hamilton Avenue,
Zip: 10601. Phone: 914/682-6250)*
Woodhaven: *(75-10B 91st Avenue, Zip:
11421. Phone: 718/296-2871)*

National Cemeteries
Bath: *(VA Medical Center, Zip: 14810.
Phone: 607/664-4853)*
Calverton: *(210 Princeton Boulevard,
Zip: 11933. Phone: 631/727-5410)*
Cypress Hills: *(625 Jamaica Avenue,
Brooklyn, Zip: 11208. Phone:
631/454-4949)*

Long Island: *(2040 Wellwood Avenue
Farmingdale, Zip: 11735. Phone:
631/454-4949)*
Saratoga: *(200 Duell Road, Zip:
12871. Phone: 518/581-9128)*
Woodlawn: *(1825 Davis Street,
Elmira, Zip: 14901. Phone:
607/664-4853)*

NORTH CAROLINA
Medical Centers
Asheville: More than 250 beds, including nursing home and domiciliary.
Open-heart surgery, speech pathology, psychiatry, alcohol treatment.
*(1100 Tunnel Road, Zip: 28805.
Phone: 828/298-7911)*
Durham: More than 250 beds, including nursing home and domiciliary.
Inpatient care in medicine, surgery, and psychiatry. Primary outpatient care, home-based primary,
mental health. *(508 Fulton Street,
Zip: 27705. Phone: 919/286-0411)*
Fayetteville: More than 150 beds, including nursing home and domiciliary. Acute medical, surgical, and
psychiatric care. Primary outpatient care. *(2300 Ramsey Street,
Zip: 28301. Phone: 910/488-2120)*
Salisbury: Nearly 500 beds. Medicine,
surgery, and psychiatry, including
cardiology, rehabilitation, and extended care. *(1601 Brenner Avenue, Zip: 28144. Phone: 704/638-
9000)*

Clinics
Charlotte: *(8601 University East
Drive, Zip: 28213. Phone: 704/597-
3500*
Durham: (1824 Hillandale Road, Zip:
27705. Phone: 919/383-6107)
Franklin: (647 Wayah Street, Zip:
28734. Phone: 828/369-1781)
Greenville: (800 Moye Boulevard, Zip:
27858. Phone: 252/830-2149)
Hamlet: (100 Jefferson Street, Zip:
28345. Phone: 910/582-3536)

Hickory: (1170 Fairgrove Church Road, Zip: 28601. Phone: 828/431-5600)
Jacksonville: (1021 Harget Street, Zip: 28450. Phone: 910/219-1339)
Morehead City: (5420 Highway 70, Zip: 28557. Phone: 252/240-2349)
Raleigh: (3305 Sungate Boulevard, Zip: 27610. Phone: 919/212-0129)
Wilmington: (1606 Physicians Drive, Zip: 28401. Phone: 910/362-8811)
Winston-Salem: (190 Kimel Park Drive, Zip: 27103. Phone: 336/768-3296)

Regional Office

Winston-Salem: *(251 N. Main Street, Zip: 27155. Phone: 800/827-1000)*

Vet Centers

Charlotte: *(2114 Ben Craig Drive, Zip: 28262. Phone: 704/549-8025)*
Fayetteville: *(4140 Ramsey Street, Zip: 28311. Phone: 910/488-6252)*
Greensboro: *(2009 S. Elm-Eugene Street, Zip: 27406. Phone: 336/333-5366)*
Greenville: *(1021 WH Smith Boulevard, Zip: 27834. Phone: 252/355-7920)*
Raleigh: *(1649 Old Louisburg Road, Zip: 27604. Phone: 919/856-4616*

National Cemeteries

New Bern: *(1711 National Avenue, Zip: 28560. Phone: 252/637-2912)*
Raleigh: *(501 Rock Quarry Road, Zip: 27610. Phone: 704/636-2661)*
Salisbury: *(202 Government Road, Zip: 28144. Phone: 704/636-2661)*
Wilmington: *(2011 Market Street, Zip: 28403. Phone: 910/815-4877)*

NORTH DAKOTA
Medical Center

Fargo: More than 100 beds, including nursing home and domiciliary. Inpatient and outpatient primary and specialty care. Cardiology, cancer, Gulf War illnesses, neurology, infectious diseases. *(2101 N. Elm Street, Zip: 58102. Phone: 701/232-3241)*

Clinics

Bismark: *(2700 State Street, Zip: 58503. Phone: 701/221-9152)*
Dickinson: *(33-9th Street, Zip: 58601. Phone: 701/483-6017)*
Grafton: *(W. 6th Street, Zip: 58237. Phone: 701/352-4059)*
Jamestown: *(419 Fifth Street NE, Zip: 58401. Phone: 701/952-4787)*
Minot: *(10 Missile Avenue, Zip: 58705. Phone: 701/727-9800)*
Williston: *(3 Fourth Street East, Zip: 58801. Phone: 701/577-9838)*

Regional Office

Fargo: *(2101 N. Elm Street, Zip: 58102. Phone: 800/827-1000)*

Vet Centers

Bismark: *(1684 Capital Way, Zip: 58501. Phone: 701/244-9751)*
Fargo: *(3310 Fletcher Drive, Zip: 58103. Phone: 701/237-0942)*
Minot: *(1400 20th Avenue, Zip: 58701. Phone: 701/852-0177)*

OHIO
Medical Centers

Chillicothe: About 300 beds, including nursing unit and domiciliary. Specialty in mental health, including neuropsychiatry. Post-traumatic stress, substance abuse. *(17273 State Route 104, Zip: 45601. Phone: 740/773-1141)*
Cincinnati: More than 250 beds, including nursing unit and domiciliary. General medicine, surgery, mental health. Cardiology, infectious diseases, vascular surgery, neuro-oncology, Vietnam-era readjustment. *(3200 Vine Street, Zip: 45220. Phone: 513/861-3100)*

Cleveland: More than 600 beds, including nursing unit and domiciliary. Acute and chronic psychiatry, cardiac surgery, spinal cord injury, geriatrics, post-traumatic stress, electrical stimulation center. *(10701 East Boulevard, Zip: 44106. Phone: 216/791-3800)*

Dayton: About 500 beds, including nursing unit and domiciliary. Medicine, surgery, psychiatry. Homeless veterans, dentistry, rehabilitation. *(4100 W. 3rd Street, Zip: 45428. Phone: 937/268-6511)*

Clinics

Akron: *(55 Waterloo, Zip: 44319. Phone: 330/724-7715)*
Ashtabula: *(1230 Lake Avenue, Zip: 44004. Phone: 866/463-0912)*
Athens: *(510 W. Union Street, Zip: 45701. Phone: 740/593-7314)*
Cambridge: *(2146 Southgate Parkway, Zip: 43727. Phone: 740/432-1963)*
Canton: *(733 Market Avenue South, Zip: 44702. Phone: 330/489-4600)*
Cincinnati: *(4355 Ferguson Drive, Zip: 45245. Phone: 513/943-3680)*
Cleveland: *(4242 Lorain Avenue, Zip: 44113. Phone: 216/939-0699)*
Grove City: *(1955 Ohio Avenue, Zip: 43123. Phone: 614/257-5800)*
Hamilton: *(1755-C South Erie Highway, Zip: 45011. Phone: 513/870-9444)*
Lancaster: *(1550 Sheridan Drive, Zip: 43130. Phone: 740/653-6145)*
Lima: *(1303 Bellefontaine Avenue, Zip: 45804. Phone: 419/222-5788)*
Lorain: *(205 W. 20th Street, Zip: 44052. Phone: 440/244-3833)*
Mansfield: *(1456 Park Avenue, W., Zip: 44906. Phone: 419/529-4602)*
Marietta: *(418 Colegate Drive, Zip: 45750. Phone: 740/568-0412)*
Marion: *(1203 Delaware Avenue, Zip: 43302. Phone: 740/223-8089)*

Middletown: *(675 N. University Boulevard, Zip: 45042. Phone: 513/423-8387)*
New Philadelphia: *(1260 Monroe Avenue, Zip: 44663. Phone: 330/602-5339)*
Newark: *(1912 Tamarck Road, Zip: 43055. Phone: 740/788-8329)*
Painesville: *(7 West Jackson Street, Zip: 44077. Phone: 440/357-6740)*
Portsmouth: *(820 Gallia Street, Zip: 45622. Phone: 740/353-3236)*
Ravenna: *(6751 N. Chestnut Street, Zip: 44266. Phone: 330/296-3641)*
Sandusky: *(3416 Columbus Avenue, Zip: 44870. Phone: 419/625-7350)*
Springfield: *(512 S. Burnett Road, Zip: 45505. Phone: 937/328-3385)*
St. Clairsville: *(107 Plaza Drive, Zip: 43950. Phone: 740/695-9321)*
Toledo: *(3333 Glendale Avenue, Zip: 43614. Phone: 419/259-2000)*
Warren: *(1400 Tod Avenue, N.W., Zip: 44485. Phone: 330/392-0311)*
Youngstown: *(2031 Belmont, Zip: 44505. Phone: 330/740-9200)*
Zanesville: *(2800 Maple Avenue, Zip: 43701. Phone: 740/453-7725)*

Regional Office

Cleveland: *(1240 E. 9th Street, Zip: 44199. Phone: 800/827-1000)*

Vet Centers

Cincinnati: *(801-B West 8th Street, Zip: 45203. Phone: 513/763-3500)*
Cleveland Heights: *(2022 Lee Road, Zip: 44118. Phone: 216/932-8471)*
Columbus: *(30 Spruce Street, Zip: 43215. Phone: 614/257-5550)*
Dayton: *(1 Elizabeth Place, Zip: 45408. Phone: 937/461-9150)*
Parma: *(5700 Pearl Road, Zip: 44129. Phone: 440/845-5023)*
Toledo: *(1565 S. Byrne Road, Zip: 43614. Phone: 419/213-7533)*

National Cemeteries

Dayton: *(4100 W. 3rd Street, Zip: 45428. Phone: 937/262-2115)*

Rittman: Ohio Western Reserve. *(10175 Rawiga Road, Zip: 44270. Phone: 330/335-3069)*

OKLAHOMA
Medical Centers

Muskogee: Nearly 100 beds. General medicine and surgery. Internal medicine, rehabilitation, speech pathology, geriatrics, psychiatry, hospice, substance abuse, ex-POWs. *(1011 Honor Heights Drive, Zip: 74401. Phone: 918/577-3000)*

Oklahoma City: More than 200 beds. General medicine, surgery, mental health. Open-heart surgery, cardiac catheterization, hemodialysis, gastroenterology, audiology and speech, laser eye surgery, quantitative fluorescence imaging. *(921 N.E. 13th Street, Zip: 73104. Phone: 405/270-1000)*

Clinics

Altus: *(201 S. Park Lane, Zip: 73521. Phone: 580/482-9020)*

Ardmore: *(2002 12th Avenue NW, Zip: 73401. Phone: 580/226-4580)*

Enid: *(915 E. Garriott, Zip: 73701. Phone: 580/242-5100)*

Fort Sill: *(4303 Pittman, Zip: 73503. Phone: 580/585-5600)*

Harshorne: *(1429 Pennsylvania Avenue, Zip: 74547. Phone: 888/878-1598)*

Jay: *(1569 N. Main Street, Zip: 74346. Phone: 918/253-1900)*

Konawa: *(527 W. 3rd Street, Zip: 74849. Phone: 580/925-3286)*

Oklahoma City: *(2915 Pine Ridge Road, Zip: 73120. Phone: 405/752-6500)*

Ponca City: *(1009 W. Ferguson Avenue, Zip: 74631. Phone: 580/363-0052)*

Stillwater: *(1815 W. 6th Street, Zip: 74074. Phone: 405/743-7300)*

Tulsa: *(9322 East 41st Street, Zip: 74145. Phone: 918/628-2500)*

Vinita: *(269 S. 7th Street, Zip: 74301. Phone: 918/713-5400)*

Wichita Falls: *(1800 7th Street, Zip: 76301. Phone: 940/723-2373)*

Regional Office

Muskogee: *(125 S. Main Street, Zip: 74401. Phone: 800/827-1000)*

Vet Centers

Lawton: *(1016 SW "C" Avenue, Zip: 73501. Phone: 580/585-5885)*

Oklahoma City: *(1024 NW 47th Street, Zip: 73118. Phone: 405/270-5184)*

Tulsa: *(1408 S. Harvard, Zip: 74112. Phone: 918/748-5105)*

National Cemeteries

Fort Gibson: *(1423 Cemetery Road, Zip: 74434. Phone: 918/478-2334)*

Fort Sill: *(2648 N.E. Jake Dunn Road, Zip: 73538. Phone: 580/492-3200)*

OREGON
Medical Centers

Portland: Nearly 225 beds, plus nursing care unit and domiciliary. Organ transplants, cardiology, cardiac surgery, ophthalmology, sleep apnea, Alzheimer's, geriatric evaluation. *(3710 S.W. U.S. Veterans Hospital Road, Zip: 97239. Phone: 503/220-8262)*

Roseburg: More than 140 beds, including nursing unit and domiciliary. General medicine, surgery, mental health. Substance abuse, vocational rehabilitation. *(913 N.W. Garden Valley Boulevard, Zip: 97470. Phone: 541/440-1000)*

White City: About 600 nursing and domiciliary beds. Inpatient care for physical rehabilitation, mental health, substance abuse. *(8495 Crater Lake Highway, Zip: 97503. Phone: 541/826-2111)*

Clinics

Bandon: *(1010 1st Street, S. E., Zip: 97411. Phone: 541/347-4736)*
Bend: *(2115 NE Wyatt Court, Zip: 97701. Phone: 503/220-8262)*
Brookings: *(555-5th Street, Zip: 97415. Phone: 541/412-1152)*
Burns: *(271 N Egan Avenue, Zip: 97720. Phone: 541-573-3339)*
Eugene: *(100 River Avenue, Zip: 97404. Phone: 541/607-0897)*
Hillsboro: *(1925 Amber Glen Parkway, Zip: 97006. Phone: 503/906-5000)*
Klamath Falls: *(2819 Dahlia Street, Zip: 97601. Phone: 541/273-6206)*
La Grande: *(202 12st Street, Zip: 97850. Phone: 541/963-0627)*
Portland: *(10535 NE Glisan Street, Zip: 97220. Phone: 503/220-8262)*
Salem: *(1660 Oak Street SE, Zip: 97301. Phone: 503/220-8262*
Warrenton: *(91400 Rilea Neacoxie Street, Zip: 97146. Phone: 503/220-8262)*
White City: *(8495 Crater Lake Highway, Zip: 97503. Phone: 541/826-2111)*

Domiciliary

White City: Over 750 beds; only independent domiciliary in VA system. *(8495 Crater Lake Highway, Zip: 97503. Phone: 541/826-2111)*

Vet Centers

Eugene: *(1255 Pearl Street, Zip: 97401. Phone: 541/465-6918)*
Grants Pass: *(211 S.E. 10th Street, Zip: 97526. Phone: 541/479-6912)*
Portland: *(8383 N.E. Sandy Boulevard, Zip: 97220. Phone: 503/273-5370)*
Salem: *(12645 Portland Road NE, Zip: 97301. Phone: 503/362-9911)*

National Cemeteries

Eagle Point: *(2763 Riley Road, Zip: 97524. Phone: 541/826-2511)*

Roseburg: *(913 N.W. Garden Valley Boulevard, Zip: 97470. Phone: 541/826-2511)*
Williamette: *(11800 S.E. Mount Scott Boulevard, Portland, Zip: 97266. Phone: 503/273-5250)*

PENNSYLVANIA

Medical Centers

Altoona: Nearly 70 beds, including nursing unit and domiciliary. General medicine, inpatient care, long-term care. *(2907 Pleasant Valley Boulevard, Zip: 16602. Phone: 814/943-8164)*
Butler: More than 100 beds, including nursing unit and domiciliary. Specializes in extended care, rehabilitation, inpatient substance abuse, respite care, hospice, adult day care. *(325 New Castle Road, Zip: 16001. Phone: 724/287-4781)*
Coatesville: Nearly 500 beds, including nursing unit and domiciliary. Primary care in medicine and geriatrics. Specializes in neuropsychiatry, post-traumatic stress, extended care, substance abuse, inpatient Alzheimer's. *(1400 Black Horse Road, Zip: 19320. Phone: 610/384-7711)*
Erie: Nearly 80 beds, including nursing unit and domiciliary. General medicine, surgery, psychiatry. *(135 E. 38th Street, Zip: 16504. Phone: 814/868-8661)*
Lebanon: Nearly 250 beds, including nursing unit and domiciliary. General medicine, surgery, psychiatry, long-term care. *(1700 S. Lincoln Avenue, Zip: 17042. Phone: 717/272-6621)*
Philadelphia: More than 350 beds, including nursing unit and domiciliary. General medicine, surgery, mental health. Parkinson's, sleep clinic, rehabilitation, and long-term care. *(University & Woodland*

*Avenues, Zip: 19104. Phone:
215/823-5800)*
Pittsburgh *(Delafield Road)*: Nearly
350 nursing beds. Specializes in
geriatric care, including primary
care, adult day care, hospice. *(Delafield Road, Zip: 15215. Phone:
866/482-7488)*
Pittsburgh *(Highland Drive)*: More
than 200 beds, including domiciliary. General medicine. Specializes
in psychiatry and long-term care.
Ex-POW center. *(7180 Highland
Drive, Zip: 15206. Phone: 866/482-
7488)*
Pittsburgh *(University Drive)*: More
than 140 beds. General medicine,
surgery, neurology. *(University
Drive, Zip: 15240. Phone: 866/482-
7488)*
Wilkes-Barre: Nearly 200 beds, including nursing unit and domiciliary. Medicine, surgery, psychiatry.
Rehabilitation, cancer, dentistry,
geriatrics, long-term care, dementia, inpatient substance abuse.
*(1111 E. End Boulevard, Zip:
18711. Phone: 877-928-2621)*

Clinics
Allentown: *(3110 Hamilton Boule-
vard, Zip: 18103. Phone: 610/776-
4304)*
Bangor: *(701 Slate Belt Boulevard,
Zip: 18013. Phone: 610/599-0127)*
Berwick: *(301 W. Third Street, Zip:
18603. Phone: 570/759-0351)*
Bradford: *(23 Kennedy Street, Zip:
16701. Phone: 814/368-3019)*
Camp Hill: *(25 N. 32nd Street, Zip:
17011. Phone: 717/730-9782)*
DuBois: *(190 West Park Avenue, Zip:
15801. Phone: 814/375-6817)*
Ellwood City: *(304 Evans Drive, Zip:
16117. Phone: 724/285-2203)*
Foxburg: *(855 Route 58, Zip: 16036.
Phone: 724/659-5601)*
Frackville: *(10 East Spruce Street,
Zip: 17931. Phone: 570/874-4289)*

Franklin: *(464 Allegheny Boulevard,
Zip: 16323. Phone: 866/962-3260)*
Greensburg: *(Route 30, Zip: 15601.
Phone: 724/837-5200)*
Hermitage: *(295 N. Kerrwood Drive,
Zip: 16148. Phone: 724/346-1569)*
Horsham: *(433 Caredean Drive, Zip:
19044. Phone: 215/823-6050)*
Johnstown: *(1425 Scalp Avenue, Zip:
15904. Phone: 814/266-8696)*
Kittanning: *(1 Nolte Drive, Zip: 16201.
Phone: 724/543-8711)*
Lancaster: *(1861 Charter Lane, Zip:
17605. Phone: 717/290-6900)*
Meadville: *(18955 Park Avenue Plaza,
Zip: 16335. Phone: 866-962-3210)*
Monaca: *(90 Wagner Road, Zip: 15061.
Phone: 724/216-0326)*
New Castle: *(1000 S. Mercer Street,
Zip: 16101. Phone: 724/285-2203)*
Philadelphia: *(214 North 4th Street,
Zip: 19106. Phone: 215/923-2600)*
Pottsville: *(700 Schuylkill Manor
Road, Zip: 17901. Phone: 570/621-
4115)*
Reading: *(145 N. 6th Street, Zip:
19601. Phone: 610/208-4717)*
Sayre: *(1537 Elmira, Zip: 18840.
Phone: 570/888-6803)*
Schuylkill: *(6 South Greenview Road,
Zip: 17972. Phone: 570/621-4115)*
Spring City: *(11 Independence Drive,
Zip: 19475. Phone: 610/948-0981)*
Springfield: *(194 W. Sproul Road, Zip:
19064. Phone: 610/543-3246)*
State College: *(3048 Enterprise Drive,
Zip: 16801. Phone: 814/867-5415)*
Tobyhanna: *(Bldg. 220, Tobyhanna
Army Depot, Zip: 18466. Phone:
570/615-8341)*
Uniontown: *(404 W. Main Street, Zip:
15401. Phone: 724/439-4990)*
Warren: *(3 Farm Colony Drive, Zip:
16365. Phone: 866/682-3250)*
Washington: *(100 Ridge Road, Zip:
15301. Phone: 724/250-7790)*
Wilkes-Barre: *(1111 East End Boule-
vard, Zip: 18711. Phone: 570/924-
3521)*

Williamsport: *(1705 Warren Avenue, Zip: 17701. Phone: 570/322-4791)*
York: *(1797 Third Avenue, Zip: 17402. Phone: 717/854-2481)*

Regional Offices

Philadelphia: Serves counties of Adams, Berks, Bradford, Bucks, Cameron, Carbon, Centre, Chester, Clinton, Columbia, Cumberland, Dauphin, Delaware, Franklin, Juniata, Lackawanna, Lancaster, Lebanon, Lehigh, Luzerne, Lycoming, Mifflin, Monroe, Montgomery, Montour, Northampton, Northumberland, Perry, Philadelphia, Pike, Potter, Schuylkill, Snyder, Sullivan, Susquehanna, Tioga, Union, Wayne, Wyoming, and York. *(5000 Wissahickon Avenue, Zip: 19101. Phone: 800/827-1000)*
Pittsburgh: Serves rest of Pennsylvania and the West Virginia counties of Brooke, Hancock, Marshall, and Ohio. *(1000 Liberty Avenue, Zip: 15222. Phone: 800/827-1000)*

Vet Centers

Bristol: *(2 Canal's End Plaza, Zip: 19007. Phone: 215/823-4590)*
Erie: *(1001 State Street, Zip: 16501. Phone: 814/453-7955)*
Dubois: *(100 Meadow Lane, Zip: 15801. Phone: 814/372-2095)*
Harrisburg: *(1500 North Second Street, Zip: 17102. Phone: 717/782-3954)*
McKeesport: *(2001 Lincoln Way, Zip: 15131. Phone: 412/678-7704)*
Norristown: *(314 E. Johnson Highway, Zip: 19401. Phone: 215-823-5800)*
Philadelphia: *(801 Arch Street, Zip: 19107. Phone: 215/627-0238)*
Philadelphia: *(101 E. Olney Avenue, Zip: 19120. Phone: 215/924-4670)*
Pittsburgh: *(2500 Baldwick Road, Zip: 15205. Phone: 412/920-1765)*

Scranton: *(1002 Pittston Avenue, Zip: 18505. Phone: 570/344-2676)*
Williamsport: *(49 E. Fourth Street, Zip: 17701. Phone: 570/327-5281)*

National Cemeteries

Bridgeville - Cemetery of the Alleghenies: 1158 Morgan Road, Zip: 15017. Phone: 724/746-4363)
Indiantown Gap: (Annville, Zip: 17003. Phone: 717/865-5254)
Newtown - Washington Crossing: (830 Highland Road, Zip: 18940. Phone: 215/504-5610)
Philadelphia: (Haines Street & Limekiln Pike, Zip: 19138. Phone: 215/504-5610)

THE PHILIPPINES
Clinic, Regional Office

Manila: Outpatient clinic and VA regional center for U.S. veterans and Filipinos who qualify under U.S. law. General medicine, minor surgery, psychiatry, radiology, pharmacy, diabetic clinic, prosthetics, orthopedic rehabilitation. *(2201 Roxas Boulevard, From U.S.: 011-632-833-4566)*

PUERTO RICO
Medical Center

San Juan: Nearly 500 beds, including nursing unit and domiciliary. General medicine, surgery, mental health. Inpatient blind rehabilitation, spinal cord injury, nuclear medicine. *(10 Casia Street, Zip: 00921. Phone: 787/641-7582)*

Clinics

Arecibo: *(Victor Rojas II, Zip: 00612 Phone: 787/816-1818)*
Guayama: *(FISA Building, Zip: 00784, Phone: 787/866-8766)*
Mayaguez: *(Avenue Hostos 345, Zip: 00689. Phone: 785/834-6900)*
Ponce: *(Paseo Del Veterano, #1010, Zip: 00716. Phone: 787/812-3030)*

Regional Office

San Juan: *(150 Carlos Charden Avenue, Hato Rey, Zip: 00918. Phone: 800/827-1000)*

Vet Centers

Arecibo: *(52 Gonzalo Marin Street, Zip: 00612. Phone: 787/879-4510)*
Ponce: *(35 Mayor Street, Zip: 00731. Phone: 787/841-3260)*
San Juan: *(Condomino Medical Center Plaza, Zip: 00921. Phone: 787/749-4409)*

National Cemetery

Bayamon: *(Avenue Cementerio Nacional #50, Zip: 00960. Phone: 787/798-7620)*

RHODE ISLAND
Medical Center

Providence: Nearly 100 beds. Primary care, surgery, mental health. *(830 Chalkston Avenue, Zip: 02908. Phone: 401/273-7100)*

Clinic

Middletown: *(One Corporate Place, Zip: 02842. Phone: 401/847-6239)*

Regional Office

Providence: *(380 Westminster Mall, Zip: 02903. Phone: 800/827-1000)*

Vet Center

Warwick: *(2038 Warwick Avenue, Zip: 02889. Phone: 401/739-0167)*

SOUTH CAROLINA
Medical Centers

Charleston: More than 100 beds, including nursing unit and domiciliary. General medicine, surgery, inpatient mental health. Major center for open-heart surgery. *(109 Bee Street, Zip: 29401. Phone: 843/577-5011)*
Columbia: More than 200 beds, including nursing unit and domicil-

iary. General medicine, surgery, mental health, extended care, *(6439 Garners Ferry Road, Zip: 29209. Phone: 803/776-4000)*

Clinics

Aiken: *(951 Millbrook Avenue, Zip: 29803. Phone: 803/643-9016)*
Anderson: *(1702 E. Greenville Street, Zip: 29621. Phone: 864/224-5450)*
Beaufort: *(1 Pinckney Road, Zip: 29902. Phone: 843/770-0444)*
Florence: *(1822 Sally Hill Farms Boulevard, Zip: 29505. Phone: 843/292-8383)*
Greenville: *(3510 Augusta Road, Zip: 29605. Phone: 864/299-1600)*
Myrtle Beach: *(3381 Phillis Boulevard, Zip: 29577. Phone: 843/477-0177)*
North Charleston: *(9237 University Boulevard, Zip: 29406. Phone: 843/789-6400)*
Orangeburg: *(1767 Villagepark Drive, Zip: 29118. Phone: 803/536-1335)*
Rock Hill: *(205 Piedmont Boulevard, Zip: 29730. Phone: 803/366-4848)*
Sumter: *(407 North Salem Avenue, Zip: 29150. Phone: 803/938-9901)*

Regional Office

Columbia: *(1801 Assembly Street, Zip: 29201. Phone: 800/827-1000)*

Vet Centers

Charleston: *(5603-A Rivers Avenue, Zip: 29406. Phone: 843/789-7000)*
Columbia: *(11710-A Richland Street, Zip: 29201. Phone: 803/765-9944)*
Greenville: *(14 Lavinia Street, Zip: 29601. Phone: 864/271-2711)*

National Cemeteries

Beaufort: *(1601 Boundary Street, Zip: 29902. Phone: 843/524-3925)*
Florence: *(803 E. National Cemetery Road, Zip: 29501. Phone: 843/669-8783)*

Fort Jackson: *(4170 Percival Road, Zip: 29229. Phone: 803/699-2246)*

SOUTH DAKOTA
Medical Centers

Fort Meade: About 100 beds, plus nursing care and domiciliary. Intensive care, rehabilitation therapy, mobile CAT scan, pulmonary function lab. *(113 Comanche Road, Zip: 57741. Phone: 605/347-2511)*

Hot Springs: About 100 beds, plus domiciliary unit. Audiology and speech pathology, dentistry, cardiac stress testing, mobile imaging scanners, mental health clinic. *(500 N. 5th Street, Zip: 57747. Phone: 605/745-2000)*

Sioux Falls: More than 100 beds, including nursing unit and domiciliary. Medicine, surgery, mental health. Rehabilitation, extended care. *(2501 W. 22nd Street, Zip: 57117. Phone: 605/336-3230)*

Clinics

Aberdeen: *(917 29th Street, Zip: 57401. Phone: 605/622-2640)*

Eagle Butte: *(15 Main Street, Zip: 57625, 605/976-2644)*

McLaughlin: *(302-A Sale Barn Road, Zip: 57642. Phone: 605/823-4574)*

Mission: *(153 Main Street, Zip: 57555. Phone: 605/856-2295*

Pierre: *(1601 North Harrison, Zip: 57501. Phone: 605/945-1710)*

Rapid City: *(3625 5th Street, Zip: 57701. Phone: 605/718-1095)*

Wagner: *(400 W. Highway 46-50, Zip: 57380. Phone: 605/384-2340)*

Watertown: *(917 29th Street SE, Zip: 57201. Phone: 605/884-2420)*

Winner: *(1436 E. 10th Street, Zip: 57580. Phone: 605/842-2443)*

Regional Office

Sioux Falls: *(2501 W. 22nd Street, Zip: 57117. Phone: 800/827-1000)*

Vet Center

Martin: *(105 E. Highway 18, Zip: 57551. Phone: 605/685-1300)*

Rapid City: *(621 Sixth Street, Zip: 57701. Phone: 605/348-0077)*

Sioux Falls: *(601 S. Cliff Avenue, Zip: 57104. Phone: 605/330-4552)*

National Cemeteries

Black Hills: *(20901 Pleasant Valley Drive, Sturgis, Zip: 57785. Phone: 605/347-7299)*

Fort Meade: *(Old Stone Road, Zip: 57785. Phone: 605/347-3830)*

Hot Springs: VA Medical Center. *(Zip: 57747. Phone: 605/347-3830)*

TENNESSEE
Medical Centers

Memphis: More than 250 beds. Medicine, surgery, mental health. Spinal cord injury, cardiology, womens health, neurology. *(1030 Jefferson Avenue, Zip: 38104. Phone: 901/523-8990)*

Mountain Home: More than 500 beds, including nursing unit and domiciliary. General medicine, surgery, extended care. *(Sidney & Lamont Streets, Zip: 37684. Phone: 423/926-1171)*

Murfreesboro: More than 230 beds, including nursing unit and domiciliary. Specializes in geriatrics, extended care, psychiatry. Transplant center. *(3400 Lebanon Road, Zip: 37129. Phone: 615/867-6000)*

Nashville: About 250 beds including nursing unit and domiciliary. General medicine, surgery, major specialties. *(1310 24th Avenue, S., Zip: 37212. Phone: 615/327-4751)*

Clinics

Chattanooga: *(150 Debra Road, Zip: 37411. Phone: 423/983-6500)*

Clarksville: *(1832 Memorial Street, Zip: 37043. Phone: 931/645-3552)*

Cookeville: *(851 S. Willow Avenue, Zip: 38501. Phone: 931/284-4060)*
Covington: *(3461 Austin Peay Highway, Zip: 38127. Phone: 901/261-4500)*
Dover: *(1021 Spring Street, Zip: 37204. Phone: 931-232-5329)*
Knoxville: *(9031 Cross Park Drive, Zip: 37923. Phone: 865/545-4592)*
McMinnville: *(1014 S. Chancery Street, Zip: 931/474-7700)*
Meharry: *(1818 Albion Street. Phone: 615/329-4818)*
Memphis: *(1056 East Raines Road, Zip: 38116. Phone: 901/271-4900)*
Morristown: *(925 E. Morris Boulevard, Zip: 37813. Phone: 423/586-9100)*
Nashville: *(1919 Charlotte Avenue. Phone: 615/873-8000)*
Vine Hill: *(601 Benton Avenue, Zip: 37204. Phone: 615/292-9770)*
Tullahoma: *(225 First Street, Zip: 37389. Phone: 931/454-6134)*

Regional Office
Nashville: *(110 9th Avenue, S., Zip: 37203. Phone: 800/827-1000)*
Vet Centers
Chattanooga: *(951 Eastgate Loop Road, Zip: 37419. Phone: 423/855-6570)*
Johnson City: *(1615-A Market Street, Zip: 37604. Phone: 423/928-8387)*
Knoxville: *(2817 E. Magnolia Avenue, Zip: 37914. Phone: 865/545-4680)*
Memphis: *(1835 Union, Zip: 38104. Phone: 901/544-0173)*
Nashville: *(1420 Donelson Pike, Zip: 37217. Phone: 615/366-1220)*

National Cemeteries
Chattanooga: *(1200 Bailey Avenue, Zip: 37404. Phone: 423/855-6590)*
Knoxville: *(939 Tyson Street, Zip: 37917. Phone: 423/855-6590)*
Memphis: *(3568 Townes Avenue, Zip: 38122. Phone: 901/386-8311)*

Mountain Home: *(Zip: 37684. Phone: 423/461-7935)*
Nashville: *(1420 Gallatin Road, S., Madison, Zip: 37115. Phone: 615/736-2839)*

TEXAS
Medical Centers
Amarillo: About 200 beds, including nursing unit and domiciliary. Primary and specialty care, plus extended care. *(6010 Amarillo Boulevard, W., Zip: 79106. Phone: 806/355-9703)*
Big Spring: About 80 beds, including nursing unit and domiciliary. Primary care, surgery, mental health. Dentistry, eye clinic, substance abuse, rehabilitation. *(300 Veterans Boulevard, Zip: 79720. Phone: 432/263-7361)*
Bonham: More than 360 beds, including nursing unit and domiciliary. Primary and geriatric care, plus rehabilitation. *(1201 E. 9th, Zip: 75418. Phone: 903/583-2111)*
Dallas: More than 500 beds, including nursing unit and domiciliary. Medicine, surgery, psychiatric. Inpatient psychiatry, spinal cord injury center, rehabilitation, women's center, geriatric, cardiology. *(4500 S. Lancaster Road, Zip: 75216. Phone: 214/742-8387)*
Houston: More than 500 beds, including nursing unit and domiciliary. Primary care, surgery, cardiology, nuclear medicine, spinal cord injury, long-term care. *(2002 Holcombe Boulevard, Zip: 77030. Phone: 713/791-1414)*
Kerrville: Almost 200 beds, including nursing care unit. Long-term rehabilitation and extended care. Intensive care, substance abuse, psychiatry, ambulatory care, post-traumatic stress. *(3600 Memorial Boulevard, Zip: 78028. Phone: 210/896-2020)*

San Antonio: About 200 beds. Medicine, surgery, mental health. Spinal cord injury, geriatrics. *(7400 Merton Minter Boulevard, Zip: 78229. Phone: 210/617-5300)*

Temple: More than 670 beds, including nursing unit and domiciliary. Medicine, surgery, mental health, rehabilitation. *(1901 Veterans Memorial Drive, Zip: 76504. Phone: 254/778-4811)*

Waco: Inpatient psychiatric, post traumatic stress. *(4800 Memorial Drive, Zip: 76711. Phone: 254/752-6581)*

Clinics

Abilene: *(4225 Woods Place, Zip: 79602. Phone: 432/263-7361)*

Austin: *(2901 Montopolis Drive, Zip: 78741. Phone: 512/389-1010)*

Beaumont: *(3420 Veterans Circle, Zip: 77707. Phone: 409/981-8550)*

Beeville: *(302 S. Hillside Drive, Zip: 78102. Phone: 361/358-9912)*

Bridgeport: *(812 Woodrow Wilson Ray Circle, Zip: 76426. Phone: 940/683-2297*

Brownwood: *(2600 Memorial Park Drive, Zip: 76801. Phone: 325/641-0568)*

Cedar Park: *(701 Whitestone Boulevard, Zip: 78613. Phone: 512/260-1368)*

Childress: *(1001 Highway 83 North, Zip: 79201. Phone: 940/937-3636)*

Cedar Park: *(701 Whitestone Boulevard, Zip: 78613. Phone: 512/260-1368)*

College Station: *(1651 Rock Prairie Road, Zip: 77845. Phone: 979/680-0361)*

Conroe: *(800 Riverwood Court, Zip: 77304. Phone: 936/522-4000)*

Corpus Christi: *(5283 Old Brownsville Road, Zip: 78405. Phone: 361/806-5600)*

Denton: *(2223 Colorado Boulevard, Zip: 76205. Phone: 800/310-5001)*

Fort Stockton: *(501 N. Main Street, Zip: 79735. Phone: 432/263-7361)*

Fort Worth: *(300 W. Rosedale Street, Zip: 76104. Phone: 817/335-2202)*

Fort Worth: *(855 Montomery Street, Zip: 76107. Phone: 817/735-2228)*

Galveston: *(3828 Avenue N, Zip: 77550. Phone: 409/761-3200)*

Granbury: *(2006 Fall Creek Highway, Zip: 76049. Phone: 817/326-3440)*

Greenville: *(4006 Wellington Road, Zip: 75407. Phone: 903/450-4788)*

Harlingen: *(2106 Treasure Hills Boulevard, Zip: 78550. Phone: 956/366-4500)*

La Grange: *(890 E. Travis Street, Zip: 78945. Phone: 979/968-5878)*

Laredo: *(6551 Star Court, Zip: 78041. Phone: 956/523-7850)*

Longview: *(1205 E. Marshal Avenue, Zip: 75601. Phone: 903/247-8262)*

Lubbock: *(6104 Avenue Q, South Drive, Zip: 79412. Phone: 806/472-3400)*

Lufkin: *(12206 N. John Redditt Drive, Zip: 75904. Phone: 936/637-4300)*

McAllen: *(2101 S. Row Boulevard, Zip: 78503. Phone: 956/618-7100)*

New Braufels: *(189 E. Austin, Zip: 78130. Phone: 830/629-3614)*

Odessa: *(4271 N. Tanglewood, Zip: 79762. Phone: 432/263-7361)*

Palestine: *(2000 South Loop 256, Zip: 75801. Phone: 903/723-9006)*

Paris: *(635 Stone Avenue, Zip: 75460. Phone: 903/785-9900)*

San Angelo: *(2018 Pulliam, Zip: 76905. Phone: 432/263-7361)*

San Antonio: *(5788 Eckert Road, Zip: 78240. Phone: 210/699-2100)*

San Antonio: *(8410 Data Point, Zip: 78299. Phone: 210/949-8900)*

San Antonio: *(1831 S. General McMullen, Zip: 78226. Phone: 210/434-1400)*

San Antonio: *(2455 NE Loop 410, Zip: 78217. Phone: 210/599-6000)*

San Antonio: *(14100 Nacogdoches, Zip: 78217. Phone: 210/653-8989)*

San Antonio: *(4243 E. Southcross, Zip: 78222. Phone: 210/304-3500)*
Sherman: *(3811 US 75N, Zip: 75090. Phone: 903/487-0477)*
Stamford: *(Highway 6 East, Zip: 79553. Phone: 432/263-7361)*
Stratford: *(1220 Purnell Street, Zip: 79084. Phone: 806/396-2852)*
Tyler: *(3414 Golden Road, Zip: 75701. Phone: 903/593-3050)*
Victoria: *(1502 E. Airline Drive, Zip: 77901. Phone: 361/582-7700)*
Wichita Falls: *(1800 7th Street, Zip: 76301. Phone: 940/723-2373)*

Regional Offices

Bowie County: Served by regional office in Little Rock, Arkansas.
Houston: Serving counties of Angelina, Aransas, Atacosa, Austin, Bandera, Bee, Bexar, Blanco, Brazoria, Brewster, Brooks, Caldwell, Calhoun, Cameron, Chambers, Colorado, Comaal, Crockett, De-Witt, Dimitt, Duval, Edwards, Fort Bend, Frio, Galveston, Gillespie, Goliad, Gonzales, Grimes, Guadalupe, Hardin, Harris, Hays, Hidalgo, Houston, Jackson, Jasper, Jefferson, Jim Hogg, Jim Wells, Karnes, Kendall, Kenedy, Kerr, Kimble, Kinney, Kleberg, LaSalle, Lavaca, Liberty, Live Oak, McCulloch, McMullen, Mason, Matagorda, Maverick, Medina, Menard, Montgomery, Nacogdoches, Newton, Nueces, Orange, Pecos, Polk, Real, Refugio, Sabine, San Augustine, San Jacinto, San Patrico, Schleicher, Shelby, Starr, Sutton, Terrell, Trinity, Tyler, Uvalde, Val Verde, Victoria, Walker, Waller, Washington, Webb, Wharton, Willacy, Wilson, Zapata, Zavala. *(6900 Ameda Drive, Zip: 77030. Phone: 800/827-1000)*
Waco: Serves counties not listed above. *(1 Veterans Plaza, Zip: 76799. Phone: 800/827-1000)*

Vet Centers

Amarillo: *(3414 Olsen Boulevard, Zip: 79109. Phone: 806/354-9779)*
Austin: *(2015 S.I.H., Zip: 78741. Phone: 512/416-1314)*
Corpus Christi: *(4646 Corona, Zip: 78411. Phone: 361/854-9961)*
Dallas: *(10501 N. Central Expressway, Zip: 75231. Phone: 214/361-5896)*
El Paso: *(1155 Westmoreland, Zip: 79925. Phone: 915/772-0013)*
Fort Worth: *(1305 W. Magnolia, Suite B, Zip: 76104. Phone: 817/921-9095)*
Harris County: *(14300 Cornerstone Village Drive, Zip: 77014. Phone: 713/578-4002)*
Houston: *(299 Richmond Avenue, Zip: 77098. Phone: 713/523-0884)*
Houston: *(701 N. Post Oak Road, Zip: 77024. Phone: 713/682-2288)*
Killeen Heights: *(302 Millers Crossing, Zip: 76548. Phone:254/953-7100)*
Laredo: *(6020 McPherson Road, Zip: 68041. Phone: 956/723-4680)*
Lubbock: *(3208 34th Street, Zip: 79410. Phone: 806/792-9782)*
McAllen: *(801 W. Nolana Loop, Zip: 78504. Phone: 956/631-2147)*
Midland: *(2817 W. Loop 250N, Zip: 79705. Phone: 432/697-8222)*
San Antonio: *(231 W. Cypress Street, Zip: 78212. Phone: 210/472-4025)*

National Cemeteries

Dallas-Fort Worth: *(2000 Mountain Creek Parkway, Zip: 75211. Phone: 214/467-3374)*
Fort Bliss: *(5200 Fred Wilson Road, Zip: 79906. Phone: 915/564-0201)*
Fort Sam Houston: *(1520 Harry Wurzbach Road, San Antonio, Zip: 78209. Phone: 210/820-3891)*
Houston: *(10410 Veterans Memorial Drive, Zip: 77038. Phone: 281/447-8686)*
Kerrville: *(3600 Memorial Boulevard, Zip: 78028. Phone: 210/820-3891)*

San Antonio: *(517 Paso Hondo Street, Zip: 78202. Phone: 210/820-3891)*

UTAH
Medical Center
Salt Lake City: More than 120 beds, plus nursing care unit. Medical, surgical, and psychiatric care. Cardiology, cancer, prosthetics. *(500 Foothill Drive, Zip: 84148. Phone: 801/582-1565)*

Clinics
Fountain Green: *(300 W. 300 Street, Zip: 84632. Phone: 435/623-3129)*
Nephi: *(48 West 1500 North, Zip: 84648. Phone: 435/623-3129)*
Ogden: *(982 Chambers Street, Zip: 84403. Phone: 801/479-4105)*
Orem: *(740 W. 800 North, Zip: 84057. Phone: 801/235-0953)*
Roosevelt: *(210 West 300 North, Zip: 84066. Phone: 435/725-2082)*
South Ogden: *(982 Chambers Street, Zip: 84403. Phone: 801/479-4105)*
St. George: *(1067 East Tabernacle, Zip: 84770. Phone: 435/634-7608)*

Regional Office
Salt Lake City: *(550 Foothill Drive, Zip: 84158. Phone: 800/827-1000)*

Vet Centers
Provo: *(1807 N. 1120 West, Zip: 84604. Phone: 801/377-1117)*
Salt Lake City: *(1354 E. 3300 South, Zip: 84106. Phone: 801/584-1294)*

VERMONT
Medical Center
White River Junction: About 60 beds, plus nursing care. Medicine, surgery, mental health. Major medical specialties, post-traumatic stress center *(215 N. Main Street, Zip: 05009. Phone: 802/295-9363)*

Clinics
Bennington: *(186 North Street Zip: 05201. Phone: 802/447-6913)*
Colchester: *(162 Hegeman Drive, Zip: 05446. Phone: 802/655-1356)*
Rutland: *(215 Stratton Road, Zip: 05701. Phone: 802/770-6713)*

Regional Office
White River Junction: *(N. Hartland Road, Zip: 05009. Phone: 800/827-1000)*

Vet Centers
Gorham: *(515 Main Street, Zip: 03581. Phone: 603/752-2571)*
Burlington: *(359 Dorset Street, Zip: 05403. Phone: 802/862-1806)*
White River Junction: *(222 Holiday Drive, Zip: 05001. Phone: 802/295-2908)*

VIRGINIA
Medical Centers
Hampton: Nearly 500 beds, including nursing unit and domiciliary. Long-term spinal cord injury, hospice, program for homeless and chronically mentally ill veterans. *(100 Emancipation Drive, Zip: 23667. Phone: 757/722-9961)*
Richmond: More than 400 beds, including nursing unit and domiciliary. Heart transplant, comprehensive cancer treatment, spinal cord injury, prosthetics, geriatrics. *(1201 Broad Rock Boulevard, Zip: 23249. Phone: 804/675-5000)*
Salem: Nearly 300 beds, including nursing unit and domiciliary. Acute and chronic psychiatry, cardiac catheterization, geriatrics, post-traumatic stress, respite care, sleep apnea, substance abuse. *(1970 Roanoke Boulevard, Zip: 24153. Phone: 540/982-2463)*

Clinics

Alexandria: *(6940 S. Kings Highway, Zip: 22301. Phone: 703/313-0694)*

Charlottesville: *(650 Peter Jefferson Parkway, Zip: 22911. Phone: 434/293-3890)*

Danville: *(705 Piney Forrest Road, Zip: 24540. Phone: 434/710-4210)*

Fredericksburg: *(1960 Jefferson Davis Highway, Zip: 22401. Phone: 540/370-4468)*

Harrisonburg: *(847 Cantrell Avenue, Zip: 22802. Phone: 540/442-1773)*

Hillsville: *(702 Pine Street, Zip: 24343. Phone: 276/779-4220)*

Lynchburg: *(1600 Lakeside Drive, Zip: 24501. Phone: 434/316-5000)*

Martinsville: *(315 Hospital Way, Zip: 24112. Phone: 276/632-5929)*

Saltville: *(308 W. Main Street, Zip: 23470. Phone: 276/496-4433)*

Stephens City: *(106 Hyde Court, Zip: 22655. Phone: 540/869-0600)*

Tazewell: *(123 Ben Bolt Avenue, Zip: 24641. Phone: 276/988-2526)*

Virginia Beach: *(244 Clearfield Avenue, Zip: 23462. Phone: 757/726-6070)*

Regional Offices

Roanoke: *(210 Franklin Road, S.W., Zip: 24011. Phone: 800/827-1000)*

Northern Virginia: Counties of Arlington and Fairfax, plus cities of Alexandria, Fairfax, and Falls Church are served by regional office in Washington, D.C.

Vet Centers

Alexandria: *(86940 S. Kings Highway, Zip: 22310. Phone: 703/360-8633)*

Norfolk: *(1711 Church Street, Zip: 23504. Phone: 757/623-7584)*

Richmond: *(4902 Fitzhugh Avenue, Zip: 23230. Phone: 804/353-8958)*

Roanoke: *(350 Albemarle Avenue, S.W., Zip: 24016. Phone: 540/342-9726)*

Virginia Beach: *(324 S. Port Circle, Zip: 23452. Phone: 757-248-3665)*

National Cemeteries

Alexandria: *(1450 Wilkes Street, Zip: 22314. Phone: 703/690-2217)*

Balls Bluff: *(Leesburg, Zip: 22075. Phone: 540/825-0027)*

City Point: *(10th Avenue and Davis Street, Hopewell, Zip: 23860. Phone: 804/795-2031)*

Cold Harbor: *(Route 156 North, Mechanicsville, Zip: 23111. Phone: 804/795-2031)*

Culpeper: *(305 U.S. Avenue, Zip: 22701. Phone: 540/825-0027)*

Danville: *(721 Lee Street, Zip: 24541. Phone: 704/636-2661)*

Fort Harrison: *(8620 Varina Road, Richmond, Zip: 23231. Phone: 804/795-2031)*

Glendale: *(8301 Willis Church Road, Richmond, Zip: 23231. Phone: 804/795-2031)*

Hampton: *(Cemetery Road & Marshall Avenue, Zip: 23667. Phone: 757/723-7104)*

Quantico: *(18425 Joplin Road, Triangle, Zip: 22172. Phone: 703/690-2217)*

Richmond: *(1701 Williamsburg Road, Zip: 23231. Phone: 804/795-2031)*

Seven Pines: *(400 E. Williamsburg Road, Sandston, Zip: 23150. Phone: 804/795-2031)*

Staunton: *(901 Richmond Avenue, Zip: 24401. Phone: 540/825-0027)*

Winchester: *(401 National Avenue, Zip: 22601. Phone: 540/825-0027)*

VIRGIN ISLANDS

Clinics and Vet Centers

St. Croix: *(Rural Route 02, Village Mall, Zip: 00850. Phone: 340/778-5553)*

St. Thomas: *(50 Estates Thomas, Zip: 00802. Phone: 340/774-6674)*

Vet Centers

St. Croix: *(Rural Route 02, Village Mall, Zip: 00850. Phone: 340/778-5553)*

St. Thomas: *(9800 Buchaneer Mall, Zip: 00802. Phone: 340/774-6674)*

WASHINGTON
Medical Centers

Seattle: More than 500 beds, including nursing unit and domiciliary. Spinal cord center, bone marrow transplant, blindness rehabilitation, prosthetics, geriatrics, open-heart surgery, dialysis, neurology, substance abuse, psychiatry. *(1660 S. Columbian Way, Zip: 98108. Phone: 206/762-1010)*

Spokane: More than 80 beds, including nursing unit and domiciliary. General medicine and surgery, with specialties in rehabilitation. Hospice and respite care. *(4815 N. Assembly Street, Zip: 99205. Phone: 509/434-7000)*

Tacoma: About 20 beds. Services for blindness, post-traumatic stress, drug and alcohol treatment, psychiatry, vocational rehabilitation. *(9600 Veterans Drive, S.W., American Lake, Zip: 98493. Phone: 253/582-8440)*

Walla Walla: Nearly 60 beds, including nursing unit and domiciliary. Primary care, hospice, and respite care. *(77 Wainwright Drive, Zip: 99362. Phone: 509/525-5200)*

Clinics

Bellevue: *(13033 Bel-Red Road, Zip: 98005. Phone: 425/214-1055)*

Bremerton: *(925 Adele Avenue, Zip: 98312. Phone: 360/782-0129)*

Federal Way: *(34617 11th Place South, Zip: 98003. Phone: 253/336-4142)*

Port Angeles: *(1005 Georgianna Street, Zip: 98362. Phone: 360/565-9330)*

Richland: *(825 Jadwin Avenue, Zip: 99352. Phone: 509/946-1020)*

Seattle: *(12360 Lake City Way NE, Zip: 98125. Phone: 206/384-4382)*

Wenatchee: *(2530 Chester-Kimm Road, Zip: 98801. Phone: 509/663-7615)*

Yakima: *(717 Fruitvale Boulevard, Zip: 98902. Phone: 509/966-0199)*

Regional Office

Seattle: *(Federal Building, 915 2nd Avenue, Zip: 98174. Phone: 800/827-1000)*

Benefits Office

Fort Lewis: *(Walter Hall, Room 700, P.O. Box 331153, Zip: 98433. Phone: 253/967-7106)*

Vet Centers

Bellingham: *(3800 Byron Avenue, Zip: 98226. Phone: 360/733-9226)*

Everett: *(3311 Wetmore Avenue, Zip: 98201. Phone: 425/252-9701)*

Seattle: *(2030 Ninth Avenue, Zip: 98121. Phone: 206/553-2706)*

Spokane: *(100 N. Mullan Road, Zip: 99206. Phone: 509/444-8387)*

Tacoma: *(4916 Center Street, Zip: 98409. Phone: 253/565-7038)*

Yakima: *(2119 W. Lincoln Avenue, Zip: 98902. Phone: 509/457-2736)*

National Cemetery

Tahoma: *(18600 S.E. 240th Street, Kent, Zip: 98042. Phone: 425/413-9614)*

WEST VIRGINIA
Medical Centers

Beckley: More than 80 beds, plus nursing care unit. General medicine, surgery, mental health. Rehabilitation, prosthetics, spinal cord injury, urology, eye center, cardiology, and cancer treatment. *(200 Veterans Avenue, Zip: 25801. Phone: 304/255-2121)*

Clarksburg: About 100 beds, including nursing unit and domiciliary. General medicine, surgery, mental health. Intensive-care unit, hemodialysis, cancer, psychiatry, post-traumatic stress, substance abuse. *(1 Medical Center Drive, Zip: 26301. Phone: 304/623-3461)*

Huntington: About 80 beds. Primary care, including surgery, rehabilitation,geriatrics, cardiology. *(1540 Spring Valley Drive, Zip: 25704. Phone: 304/429-6741)*

Martinsburg: About 550 beds, including nursing unit and domiciliary. Brain injuries, intensive care, women's outpatient program, post-traumatic stress, substance abuse, homeless program. *(510 Butler Avenue, Zip: 25405. Phone: 304/263-0811)*

Clinics

Charleston: *(104 Alex Lane, Zip: 25304. Phone: 304/926-6001)*

Franklin: *(314 Pine Street, Zip: 36807. Phone: 304/358-2355)*

Logan: *(513 Dingess Street, Zip: 25601. Phone: 304/752-8355)*

Morgantown: *(40 Commerce Drive, Zip: 26501. Phone: 304/292-7535)*

Parkersburg: *(2311 Ohio Avenue, Zip: 26101. Phone: 304/422-5114)*

Parsons: *(206 Spruce Street, Zip: 26287. Phone: 304/478-2219)*

Petersburg: *(Route 55 West, Zip: 26847. Phone: 304/257-5817)*

Sutton: *(93 Skidmore Lane, Zip: 26602. Phone: 304/765-3480)*

Williamson: *(75 W. 4th Avenue, Zip: 25661. Phone: 304/235-2187)*

Regional Office

Huntington: Serves all counties except Brooke, Hancock, Marshall, and Ohio, which are served by the regional office in Pittsburgh, Pennsylvania. *(640 4th Avenue, Zip: 25701. Phone: 800/827-1000)*

Vet Centers

Beckley: *(1000 Johnstown Road, Zip: 25801. Phone: 304/252-8220)*

Charleston: *(521 Central Avenue, Zip: 25302. Phone: 304/343-3825)*

Huntington: *(3135 16th Street, Zip: 25701. Phone: 304/523-8387)*

Martinsburg: *(900 Winchester Avenue, Zip: 25401. Phone: 304/263-6776)*

Morgantown: *(1083 Greenbag Road, Zip: 26508. Phone: 304/291-4303)*

Princeton: *(905 Mercer Street, Zip: 24740. Phone: 304/425-5653)*

Wheeling: *(1058 Bethlehem Road, Zip: 26003. Phone: 304/232-0587)*

National Cemeteries

Grafton: *(431 Walnut Street, Zip: 26354. Phone: 304/265-2044)*

West Virginia: *(Route 2, Grafton, Zip: 26354. Phone: 304/265-2044)*

WISCONSIN
Medical Centers

Madison: Nearly 100 beds. Medicine, surgery, psychiatry. Cardiac catheterization, epilepsy center, hemodialysis, open-heart surgery, sleep lab. *(2500 Overlook Terrace, Zip: 53705. Phone: 608/256-1901)*

Milwaukee: More than 600 beds, including nursing unit and domiciliary. General medicine, surgery, mental health. Aging, spinal cord injury, female veterans, open-heart surgery, pain clinic, dysphagia program. *(5000 W. National Avenue, Zip: 53295. Phone: 414/384-2000)*

Tomah: More than 250 beds, including nursing unit and domiciliary. General medicine, surgery, mental health. Post-traumatic stress, drug and alcohol treatment, long-term care, hospice. *(500 E. Veterans Street, Zip: 54660. Phone: 608/372-3971)*

Clinics

Appleton: *(10 Tri-Park Way, Zip: 54914. Phone: 920/831-0070)*

Baraboo: *(626 14th Street, Zip: 53913. Phone: 608/356-9318)*

Beaver Dam: *(215 Corporate Drive, Zip: 53916. Phone: 920/356-9415)*

Chippewa Falls: *(2503 County Road 1, Zip: 54729. Phone: 715/720-3780)*

Cleveland: *(1205 North Avenue, Zip: 53015. Phone: 920/693-5600)*

Green Bay: *(141 Siegler Avenue, Zip: 54303. Phone: 920/497-3126)*

Hayward: *(15748 Couty Road B, Zip: 54843. Phone: 715/934-5454)*

Janesville: *(111 N. Main Street, Zip: 53545. Phone: 608/758-9300)*

Kenosha: *(800 55th Street, Zip: 53140, 262/653-9286)*

La Crosse: *(2600 State Road, Zip: 54601. Phone: 608/784-3886)*

Loyal: *(141 N. Main Street, Zip: 54446. Phone: 715/255-9799)*

Rhinelander: *(639 West Kemp Street, Zip: 54501. Phone: 715/362-4080)*

Rice Lake: *(2700-A College Drive, Zip: 54843. Phone: 715/236-3355)*

Superior: *(3520 Tower Avenue, Zip: 54880. Phone: 715/392-9711)*

Union Grove: *(21425 Spring Street, Zip: 53182. Phone: 262/878-7000)*

Wausau: *(515 South 32nd Street, Zip: 54401. Phone: 715/842-2834)*

Wisconsin Rapids: *(710 East Grand Avenue, Zip: 54494. Phone: 715/424-3844)*

Regional Office

Milwaukee: *(5000 W. National Avenue, Bldg. 6, Zip: 53295. Phone: 800/827-1000)*

Vet Centers

Madison: *(706 Williamson Street, Zip: 53703. Phone: 608/264-5342)*

Green Bay: *(1600 E. Ashland Avenue, Zip: 54304. Phone: 920/435-5650)*

Milwaukee: *(5401 N. 76th Street, Zip: 53218. Phone: 414/536-1301)*

National Cemetery

Wood: *(5000 W. National Avenue, Bldg. 1301, Milwaukee, Zip: 53295. Phone: 414/382-5300)*

WYOMING

Medical Centers

Cheyenne: More than 70 beds, including nursing unit and domiciliary. Medicine, surgery, mental health. Long-term care, dentistry, audiology. rehabilitation. *(2360 E. Pershing Boulevard, Zip: 82001. Phone: 307/778-7550)*

Sheridan: More than 200 beds, including nursing unit and domiciliary, Psychiatric, alcohol abuse, and nursing care. Geriatric evaluation, post-traumatic stress. *(1898 Fort Road, Zip: 82801. Phone: 307/672-3473)*

Clinics

Afton:*(125 S. Washington, Zip: 83110. Phone: 307/886-5266)*

Casper: *(4140 S. Poplar Street, Zip: 82601. Phone: 307/235-4143)*

Gillette: *(604 Express Drive, Zip: 82718. Phone: 307/685-0676)*

Newcastle: *(1124 Washington Boulevard, Zip: 82701. Phone: 605/745-2000)*

Powell: *(777 Avenue H, Zip: 82435. Phone: 307/754-7257)*

Riverton: *(2300 Rose Lane, Zip: 82501. Phone: 307/857-1211)*

Rock Springs: *(1401 Gateway Boulevard, Zip: 82901. Phone: 307/362-6641)*

Regional Office

Cheyenne: *(2360 E. Pershing Boulevard, Zip: 82001. Phone: 800/827-1000)*

Vet Centers

Casper: *(1030 North Poplar, Zip: 82601. Phone: 307/261-5355)*

Cheyenne: *(3219 E. Pershing Boulevard, Zip: 82001. Phone: 307/778-7370)*

STATE VETERANS FACILITIES

The following state-supported facilities are devoted primarily to the care of military veterans. They operate under rules set down by the U.S. Department of Veterans Affairs, which periodically inspects the facilities.

Unlike VA nursing homes and domiciliaries, they charge a fee for their services. Typically, those fees are smaller than those at comparable private-sector facilities because of VA financial support.

Nursing homes are for patients who require assistance in daily living. Domiciliaries are for veterans who can take care of many basic needs.

ALABAMA

Alexander City: 150-bed nursing home. *(Bill Nichols State Veterans Home, 1801 Elkahatchee Road, Zip: 35010. Phone: 205/329-0868)*

Bay Minette: 150-bed nursing home. *(William F. Green State Veterans Home, 300 Faulkner Drive, Zip: 36507. Phone: 251/937-9881)*

Huntsville: 150-bed nursing home. *(Floyd E. "Tut" Fann State Veterans Home, 2701 Meridian Street, Zip: 35811. Phone: 256/851-2807)*

ALASKA

Palmer: 80-bed domiciliary. *(Alaska State Veterans and Pioneers Home, 250 East Fireweed, Zip: 99645. Phone: 907/745-4241)*

ARIZONA

Phoenix: 200-bed nursing home. (Arizona State Veterans Home, 4141 North S. Herrera Way, Phoenix, Zip: 85012. Phone: 602/248-1550)

Tuscon: 120-bed nursing facility. (Scheduled for opening after Oct. 2011. Information at 602/234-8409)

ARKANSAS

Fayetteville: 108 beds for skilled care. *(Arkansas Veterans Home, 1125 North College Avenue, Zip: 72703. Phone: 479/444-7001)*

Little Rock: 55-bed domiciliary, 60-bed nursing home. *(Arkansas Veterans Home, 4701 West 20th Street, Zip: 72204. Phone: 501/324-9454)*

CALIFORNIA

Barstow: 100 nursing beds, 220-bed domiciliary. *(Veterans Home of California - Barstow, 100 E. Veterans Parkway, Zip: 92311. Phone: 760/252-6285)*

Chula Vista: 180 nursing beds, 165-bed domiciliary. *(Veterans Home of California - Chula Vista, 700 East Naples Court, Zip: 91911. Phone: 619/482-6010)*

Yountville: 820-bed domiciliary, 570-bed nursing home, 50-bed hospital. *(Veterans Home of California - Yountville, Zip: 94599. Phone: 707/944-4500)*

COLORADO

Aurora: 180 beds, skilled nursing care. *(Colorado State Veterans Nursing Home-Fitzsimons, 1919 Quentin Street, Zip: 80010. Phone: 720/857-6400)*

Florence: 120-bed nursing home. *(Colorado State Veterans Nursing Home, Moore Drive, Zip: 81226. Phone: 719/784-6331)*

Homelake: 130-bed domiciliary, 90-bed nursing home. *(Colorado State Veterans Center, P.O. Box 97, Zip: 81135. Phone: 719/852-5118)*

Rifle: 100-bed nursing home. *(Colorado State Veterans Home, 851 East 5th Street, P.O. Box 1420, Zip: 81650. Phone: 303/625-0842)*

Walsenburg: 120 skilled nursing beds. *(Colorado State Veterans Nursing Home, 23500 US Highway 160, Zip: 81089. Phone: 719/738-5133)*

CONNECTICUT

Rocky Hill: 650-bed domiciliary, 350-bed hospital. *(Connecticut Veterans Home & Hospital, 287 West Street, Zip: 06067. hone: 203/529-2571)*

DELAWARE

Milford: 120 beds for long-term care, 30 for dementia. *(Delaware Veterans Home, 100 Delaware Veterans Boulevard, Zip: 19963. Phone: 302/424-6000)*

FLORIDA

Daytona Beach: 120-bed nursing home. *(Emory Bennett Memorial Veterans Home, 1920 Mason Avenue, Zip: 32117. Phone: 386/274-3460)*

Lake City: 150-bed domiciliary. *(Veterans Home of Florida, 1300 Sycamore Lane, Zip: 32055. Phone: 904/758-0600)*

Land-O-Lakes: 12-bed nursing home. *(Baldomero Lopez Veterans Nursing Home, 6919 Parkway Boulevard, Zip: 34639. Phone: 813/558-5000)*

Pembroke Pines: 60 beds for skilled nursing, 60 beds for dementia. *(Alexander "Sandy" Nininger State Veterans Nursing Home, 8401 W. Cypress Drive, Zip: 33025. Phone: 954/985-4824)*

Port Charlotte: 60 beds for skilled nursing, 60 beds for dementia. *(Douglas Jacobson State Veterans Nursing Home, 21281 Grayton Terrace, Zip: 33954. Phone: 941/613-0919)*

Springfield: 60 beds for skilled nursing, 60 beds for demential. *(Clifford Chester Sims State Veterans Nursing Home, 4419 Tram Road, Zip: 32404. Phone: 850/747-5401)*

St. Augustine: 60 beds for skilled nursing, 60 beds for dementia. *(Clyde E. Lassen State Veterans Home, 4659 State Road 16, Zip: 32092. Phone: 727/518-3202)*

GEORGIA
Augusta: 190-bed nursing home. *(Georgia War Veterans Nursing Home, 1101 - 15th Street, Zip: 30910. Phone: 706/721-2351)*
Milledgeville: 290-bed domiciliary, 390-bed nursing home. *(Georgia State War Veterans Home, Vinson Highway, Zip: 30162. Phone: 912/453-4219)*

HAWAII
Hilo: 95 beds. *(Yukio Okutsu Veterans Home, 1180 Waianuenue Avenue, Zip: 96720. Phone: 808/961-1500)*

IDAHO
Boise: 50-bed domiciliary, 140-bed nursing home. *(Idaho State Veterans Home, 320 Collins Road, Zip: 83707. Phone: 208/334-5000)*
Lewiston: 66-bed nursing unit. *(Idaho State Veterans Home, 821 21st Avenue, Zip: 83501. Phone: 208/799-3422)*
Pocatello: 70-bed nursing home. *(Idaho State Veterans Home, 1957 Alvin Ricken Drive, Zip: 83201. Phone: 208/233-6699)*

ILLINOIS
Anna: 50 beds for skilled nursing, 12-bed domiciliary. *(Illinois Veterans Home, 792 N. Main, Zip: 62906. Phone: 618/833-6302)*
LaSalle: 120-bed nursing home. *(Illinois Veterans Home, 1015 O'Conor Avenue, Zip: 61301. Phone: 815/223-0303)*
Manteno: 10-bed domiciliary, 300-bed nursing home. *(Illinois Veterans Home, One Veterans Drive, Zip: 60950. Phone: 815/468-6581)*
Quincy: 150-bed domiciliary, 630-bed nursing home. *(Illinois Veterans Home, 1707 North Twelfth Street, Zip: 62301. Phone: 217/222-8641)*

INDIANA
West Lafayette: 190-bed domiciliary, 610-bed nursing home. *(Indiana Veterans Home, 3851 North River Road, Zip: 47906. Phone: 317/463-1502)*

IOWA
Marshalltown: 110-bed domiciliary, 690-bed nursing home, 25-bed hospital. *(Iowa Veterans Home, 1301 Summit Street, Zip: 50158. Phone: 515/752-1501)*

KANSAS
Fort Dodge: 230-bed domiciliary, 90-bed nursing home. *(Kansas Soldiers Home, Zip: 67843. Phone: 316/227-2121)*
Winfield: 107 beds for long-term care, 48-bed domiciliary. *(Kansas Veterans Home, 1220 World War II Memorial Drive, Zip: 67156. Phone: 620/221-9479)*

KENTUCKY
Hanson: 120-bed skilled nursing home. *(Western Kentucky Veterans Center, 926 Veterans Drive, Zip: 42413. Phone: 270/322-9087)*
Hazard: 120-bed nursing home. *(Eastern Kentucky Veterans Center, 200 Veterans Drive, Zip: 41701. Phone: 608/435-6196)*
Wilmore: 300-bed nursing home. *(Kentucky Veterans Center, 100 Veterans Drive, Zip: 40390. Phone: 606/858-2814)*

LOUISIANA
Bossier City: 156 intermediate care beds. *(N.W. Louisiana War Veterans Home, 3130 Arthur Ray Teague Parkway, Zip: 71112. Phone: 318/741-2763)*
Jackson: 100-bed domiciliary, 140-bed nursing home. *(Louisiana War Vet-*

erans Home, P.O. Box 748, Zip:
70748. Phone: 504/634-5265)
Jennings: 132 nursing beds, 55 de-
mentia and skilled nursing beds.
(S.W. Louisiana War Veterans
Home, 1610 Evangeline Road, Zip:
70546. Phone: 337/824-2829)
Monroe: 156 nursing beds. (N.E.
Louisiana War Veterans Home,
6700 Highway 165 N., Zip: 71211.
Phone: 318/362-4206)
Reserve: 136 nursing beds, 20 skilled
nursing beds. (S.E. Louisiana War
Veterans Home, 4080 W. Airline
Highway, Zip: 70084. Phone:
985/479-4080)

MAINE

Augusta: 120-bed nursing home.
(Maine Veterans Home, Conry
Road, RFD 2, Zip: 04330. Phone:
207/622-2454)
Bangor: 120-bed nursing home. (Main
Veterans Home, 44 Hogan Road,
Zip: 04401. Phone: 207/942-2333)
Caribou: 40-bed nursing home.
(Maine Veterans Home, 39 Van
Buren Road, Zip: 04736. Phone:
207/498-6074)
Machias: 30 nursing beds. (Maine Vet-
erans Home, 1 Veterans Way, Zip:
04854. Phone: 207/255-0162)
Scarborough: 120-bed nursing home.
(Maine Veterans Home, 290 U.S.
Route One, Zip: 04074. Phone:
207/883-7184)
South Paris: 62 beds for skilled nurs-
ing care, 28 beds for residential
care. (Maine Veterans Home, 477
High Street, Zip: 04281. Phone:
207/743-6300)

MARYLAND

Charlotte Hall: 100-bed domiciliary,
150-bed nursing home. (Charlotte
Hall Veterans Home, Route 2, Box
5, Zip: 20622. Phone: 301/884-
8171)

MASSACHUSETTS

Chelsea: 300-bed domiciliary, 60-bed
nursing home, 170-bed hospital.
(Soldiers Home in Massachusetts,
91 Crest Avenue, Zip: 02150.
Phone: 617/884-5660)
Holyoke: 50-bed domiciliary, 260-bed
nursing home, 30-bed hospital.
(Soldiers Home in Massachusetts,
110 Cherry Street, Zip: 01040.
Phone: 413/532-9475)

MICHIGAN

Grand Rapids: 140-bed domiciliary,
620-bed nursing home. (Michigan
Veterans Facility, 3000 Monroe,
Northwest, Zip: 49505. Phone:
616/364-5300)
Marquette: 60-bed domiciliary, 180-
bed nursing home. (D.J. Jacobetti
Home for Veterans, 425 Fisher
Street, Zip: 49855. Phone:
906/226-3576)

MINNESOTA

Fergus Falls: 85 beds for skilled nursing. (Minnesota Veterans Home,
1821 North Park Street, Zip:
56537. Phone: 218/736-0400)
Hastings: 200-bed domiciliary. (Minnesota Veterans Home, 1200 East
18th Street, Zip: 55033. Phone:
612/438-8500)
Luverne: 85 beds for nursing care.
(Minnesota Veterans Home, 1800
N. Kriss, Zip: 56156. Phone:
507/283-1100)
Minneapolis: 80-bed domiciliary, 350-
bed nursing home. (Minnesota Veterans Home, 5101 Minnehaha Avenue, South, Zip: 55417. Phone:
612/721-0600)
Silver Bay: 90-bed nursing home.
(Minnesota Veterans Home, 45
Banks Boulevard, Zip: 55614.
Phone: 218/226-3350)

MISSISSIPPI

Collins: 150 beds for skilled nursing. *(Mississippi Veterans Home, 3261 Highway 49, Zip: 39428. Phone: 601/765-0403)*

Jackson: 150-bed nursing home. *(Mississippi Veterans Home, 4607 Lindberg Street, Zip: 39209. Phone: 601/354-7205)*

Kosciusko: 150 beds for skilled nursing. *(Mississippi Veterans Home, 310 Autumn Ridge Drive, Zip: 39090. Phone: 662/289-7809)*

Oxford: 150 beds for skilled nursing. *(Mississippi Veterans Home, 120 Veterans Boulevard, Zip: 38655. Phone: 662-236-7641)*

MISSOURI

Cameron: 200 beds for skilled nursing. *(Missouri Veterans Home, 1111 Euclid, Zip: 64429. Phone: 816/632-6010)*

Cape Girardeau: 150-bed nursing home. *(Missouri Veterans Home, Route 2, Box 495, Zip: 63701. Phone: 314/290-5870)*

Mexico: 150-bed nursing home. *(Missouri Veterans Home, 920 Mars Street, P.O. Box 473, Zip: 65265. Phone: 314/581-1088)*

Mt. Vernon: 100-bed nursing home. *(Missouri Veterans Home, 600 North Main, Zip: 65712. Phone: 417/466-7103)*

St. James: 150-bed nursing home. *(Missouri Veterans Home, Zip: 65559. Phone: 314/265-3271)*

St. Louis: 300 beds for skilled nursing. *(Missouri Veterans Home, 10600 Lewis & Clark Boulevard, Zip: 63136. Phone: 314/340-6389)*

Warrensburg: 200 beds for skilled nursing. *(Missouri Veterans Home, 1300 Veterans Road, Zip: 64093. Phone: 660/543-5064)*

MONTANA

Columbia Falls: 60-bed domiciliary, 90-bed nursing home. *(Montana Veterans Home, P.O. Box 250, Zip: 59912. Phone: 406/892-3256)*

Glendive: 64 beds for nursing care, 16 beds for dementia. *(Eastern Montana Veterans Home, 2000 Montana Avenue, Zip: 59330. Phone: 406/345-8855)*

NEBRASKA

Grand Island: 35-bed domiciliary, 410-bed nursing home. *(Nebraska Veterans Home, Burkett Station, Zip: 68803. Phone: 308/382-9420)*

Norfolk: 30-bed domiciliary, 130-bed nursing home. *(Nebraska Veterans Home, P.O. Box 409, Zip: 68702. Phone: 402/370-3177)*

Omaha: 30-bed domiciliary, 160-bed nursing home. *(Thomas Fitzgerald Veterans Home, 156 W. Maple Road, Zip: 68116. Phone: 402/595-2180)*

Scottsbluff: 90-bed domiciliary, 50-bed nursing home. *(Western Nebraska Veterans Home, 1102 West Forty-Second Street, Zip: 69361. Phone: 308/632-3381)*

NEVADA

Boulder City: 180 skilled nursing beds. *(Nevada State Veterans Home, 100 Veterans Memorial Drive, Zip: 89005. Phone: 702/332-6864)*

NEW HAMPSHIRE

Tilton: 150-bed nursing home. *(New Hampshire Veterans Home, Winter Street, Zip: 03276. Phone: 603/286-4412)*

NEW JERSEY

Edison/Menlo Park: 40-bed domiciliary, 350-bed nursing home. *(New Jersey Veterans Memorial Home,*

Edison, Zip: 08818. Phone: 908/603-3013)

Paramus: 260-bed nursing home. (New Jersey Veterans Memorial Home, P.O. Box 608, One Veterans Drive, Zip: 07653. Phone: 201/967-7676)

Vineland: 300-bed nursing home. (New Jersey Memorial Home, 524 Northwest Boulevard, Zip: 08360. Phone: 609/696-6400)

NEW MEXICO

Fort Bayard: 40-bed nursing home. (New Mexico State Veterans Home, P.O. Box 36210, Zip: 36219. Phone: 505/537-3302)

Truth or Consequences: 20-bed domiciliary, 160-bed nursing home. (New Mexico Veterans Center, P.O. Box 927, Zip: 37901. Phone: 505/894-9081)

NEW YORK

Batavia: 126-bed nursing home. (New York State Veterans Home, 220 Richmond Avenue, Zip: 14020. Phone: 716/345-2000)

Jamaica: 215 beds for skilled nursing, 35 beds for dementia. (New York State Veterans Home, 178-50 Linden Boulevard, Zip: 11434. Phone: 718/481-6268)

Oxford: 240-bed nursing home. (New York State Veterans Home, Zip: 13830. Phone: 607/843-6991)

Montrose: 252-bed nursing home. (New York State Veterans Home, 2090 Albany Post Road, Zip: 10548. Phone: 914/788-6003)

Stoneybrook: 350-bed nursing home. (Long Island State Veterans Home, State University of New York, 100 Patriots Road, Zip: 11790. Phone: 516/444-8500)

NORTH CAROLINA

Fayetteville: 150 nursing beds. (State Veterans Nursing Home, 214 Cochran Avenue, Zip: 28301. Phone: 910/482-4131)

Salisbury: 99 nursing beds. (State Veterans Nursing Home, Zip: 28145. Phone: 704/638-4200)

NORTH DAKOTA

Lisbon: 110-bed domiciliary, 30-bed nursing home. (North Dakota Veterans Home, Lock Box 673, Zip: 58054. Phone: 701/683-4125)

OHIO

Georgetown: 168 nursing beds. (Ohio Veterans Home, Georgetown, 2003 Veterans Boulevard, Zip: 45121. Phone: 937/378-2900)

Sandusky: 200-bed domiciliary, 350-bed nursing home. (Ohio Veterans Home, S. Columbus Avenue, Zip: 44870. Phone: 419/625-2454)

OKLAHOMA

Ardmore: 35-bed domiciliary, 140-bed nursing home. (Oklahoma Veterans Center, P.O. Box 489, Zip: 73402. Phone: 405/223-2266)

Claremore: 350-bed nursing home. (Oklahoma Veterans Center, P.O. Box 988, Zip: 74018. Phone: 918/342-5432)

Clinton: 30-bed domiciliary, 145-bed nursing home. (Oklahoma Veterans Center, P.O. Box 1209, Zip: 73601. Phone: 405/323-5540)

Lawton: 200 beds for skilled nursing and dementia. (Lawton-Ft. Sill Veterans Center, 501 SE Flowermound Road, Zip: 73501. Phone: 580/351-6511)

Norman: 190-bed nursing home. (Oklahoma Veterans Cetner, P.O. Box 1668, Zip: 73070. Phone: 405/360-5600)

Sulphur: 30-bed domiciliary, 140-bed nursing home. *(Oklahoma Veterans Center, 200 E. Fairlane, Zip: 73086. Phone: 405/622-2144)*
Talihina: 210-bed nursing home. *(Oklahoma Veterans Center, P.O. Box 1168, Zip: 74571. Phone: 918/567-2251)*

OREGON

Dalles: 126 nursing beds, 25 Alzheimer's beds. *(Oregon State Veterans Home, 700 Veterans Drive, Zip: 97058. Phone: 541/296-7190)*

PENNSYLVANIA

Erie: 100-bed domiciliary, 75-bed nursing home. *(Pennsylvania Soldiers & Sailors Home, P.O. Box 6239, Zip: 16512. Phone: 814/871-4531)*
Hollidaysburg: 170-bed domiciliary, 350-bed nursing home. *(Hollidaysburg Veterans Home, P.O. Box 319, Zip: 16648. Phone: 814/696-5356)*
Philadelphia: 100 beds for nursing care, 30 beds for dementia. *(Delaware Valley Veterans Home, 2701 Southampton Road, Zip: 19154. Phone: 215/965-5900)*
Pittsburgh: 160 beds for nursing care, 44 beds for dementia. *(Southwestern Veterans Center, 7060 Highland Drive, Zip: 15206. Phone: 412/665-6706)*
Scranton: 176 beds in nursing unit. *(Gino J. Merli Veterans Center, 401 Penn Avenue, Zip: 18503. Phone: 570/961-4304)*
Spring City: 150-bed domiciliary. *(Southeastern Pennsylvania Veterans Center, Veterans Drive, Zip: 19475. Phone: 215/948-2400)*

PUERTO RICO

Juana Diaz: 120 nursing beds, 120-bed domiciliary. *(Casa del Veterano, 115 Bo. Amuelas, Zip: 00795. Phone: 787/837-6674)*

RHODE ISLAND

Bristol: 80-bed domiciliary, 260-bed nursing home. *(Rhode Island Veterans Home, Metacom Avenue, Zip: 02809. Phone: 401/253-8000)*

SOUTH CAROLINA

Anderson: 220-bed nursing home. *(Richard M. Campbell Veterans Nursing Home, 4605 Belton Highway, Zip: 29621. Phone: 803/261-5350)*
Columbia: 150-bed nursing home. *(South Carolina Veterans Pavilion, 2200 Harden Street, Zip: 29203. hone: 803/737-5302)*
Walterboro: 168 nursing beds, 52 dementia beds. *(Veterans Victory House Nursing Home, 2461 Sidneys Road, Zip: 29488. Phone: 843/538-3000)*

SOUTH DAKOTA

Hot Springs: 275-bed domiciliary, 50-bed nursing home. *(South Dakota State Veterans Home, 2500 Minnekahta Avenue, Zip: 57747. Phone: 605/745-5127)*

TENNESSEE

Humboldt: 120 nursing beds. *(Tennessee State Veterans Home, 2865 Main Street, Zip: 38343. Phone: 731/784-8405)*
Knoxville: 120 nursing beds, 20 skilled nursing beds. *(Tennessee State Veterans Home, 9910 Coward Mill Road, Zip: 37931. Phone: 865/862-8100)*
Murfreesboro: 120-bed nursing home. *(Tennessee Veterans Home, 345 Compton Road, Zip: 37130. Phone: 615/895-8850)*

TEXAS

Amarillo: 120 nursing beds. *(Usserv-Roan Texas State Veterans Home, 1020 Tascosa Road, Zip: 79124. Phone: 806/322-8387)*

Big Spring: 160 nursing beds. *(Lamun-Lusk-Sanchez Texas State Veterans Home, 1809 North Highway 87, Zip: 79720. Phone: 432/268-8387)*

Bonham: 160 nursing beds. *(Clyde W. Cosper Texas State Veterans Home, 1300 Seven Oaks Road, Zip: 75418. Phone: 903/640-8387)*

El Paso: 160 beds. *(Ambrosio Guillen Texas State Veterans Home, 9650 Kenworthy Street, Zip: 79924. Phone: 915/751-0967)*

Floresville: 160 nursing beds. *(Frank M. Tejeda Texas State Veterans Home, 200 Veterans Drive, Zip: 78114. Phone: 830/216-9456)*

McAllen: 160 beds. *(Alfredo Gonzalez Texas State Veterans Home, 301 East Yuma Avenue, Zip: 78503. Phone: 956/682-4224)*

Temple: 32-bed Alzheimer's unit. *(William R. Courtney Texas State Veterans Home, 1424 Martin Luther King Lane, Zip: 76504. Phone: 254/791-8280)*

UTAH

Salt Lake City: 81 nursing beds. *(Utah State Veterans Nursing Home, 700 Foothill Boulevard, Zip: 84113. Phone: 801/584-1900)*

VERMONT

Bennington: 20-bed domiciliary, 185-bed nursing home. *(Vermont Veterans Home, 325 North Street, Zip: 05201. Phone: 802/422-6353)*

VIRGINIA

Richmond: 120 nursing beds, 40 dementia beds. *(Sitter and Barfoot Veterans Care Center, 1601 Broad Rock Boulevard, Zip: 23224. Phone: 804/371-8000)*

Roanoke: 60-bed domiciliary, 180-bed nursing home. *(Virginia Veterans Care Center, 4550 Shenandoah Avenue, N.W., Zip: 24017. Phone: 703/982-2860)*

WASHINGTON

Orting: 50-bed domiciliary, 150-bed nursing home. *(Washington Soldiers Home, P.O. Box 500, Zip: 98360. Phone: 206/893-2156)*

Retsil: 145-bed domiciliary, 270-bed nursing home. *(Washington Veterans Home, P.O. Box 698, Zip: 98378. Phone: 206/895-4700)*

Spokane: 100 beds for skilled nursing care. *(Spokane Veterans Home, 222 East 5th Avenue, Zip: 99202. Phone: 509/344-5770)*

WEST VIRGINIA

Barboursville: 200-bed domiciliary. *(Barboursville Veterans Home, 512 Water Street, Zip: 25504. Phone: 304/736-1027)*

Clarksburg: 120 beds. *(West Virginia State Veterans Nursing Facility, 1 Freedoms Way, Zip: 26301. Phone: 304/626-1600*

WISCONSIN

King: 145-bed domiciliary, 590-bed nursing home. *(Wisconsin Veterans Home, Zip: 54946. Phone: 715/258-5586)*

Union Grove: 120-bed nursing home, 115-bed domiciliary. *(Wisconsin Veterans Home, 21425 G Spring Street, Zip: 53182. Phone: 262/878-6752)*

WYOMING

Buffalo: 120-bed domiciliary. *(Veterans Home of Wyoming, 700 Veterans Lane, Zip: 82834. Phone: 307/684-5511)*

VETERANS HELPING VETERANS

By the time most people are ready to leave active duty, they're convinced they've heard a large percentage of the world's total collection of acronyms. They may be right.

There's one acronym, however, that isn't heard much on active duty, but that is very important to veterans. It's "VSO," or veteran-speak for "Veterans Service Organization." These are groups that have special authority under federal law to represent veterans and their survivors in cases before the Department of Veterans Affairs or any VA body.

VSO service officers are professionals. That's what they do for a living. They have been specially trained by their organizations to represent veterans. They understand the law and the administrative processes.

VSOs must offer their services, without charge, to any veteran. You don't have to be a member of that organization.

VA rules even have provision that enable veterans and their survivors to appoint an entire VSO, not just one service officer from a VSO, as their representative. That permits veterans to draw upon the full resources of an organization, especially the VSO offices in Washington.

Not every VSO is equally effective. Not all of their representatives, or service officers, are equally skilled. Here are the VSOs that are legally entitled to represent veterans and their survivors before the VA:

African American Post Traumatic Stress Disorder Association
9129 Veterans Dr., SW
Lakewood, WA 98498
(253) 589-0766

Air Force Sergeants Association
5211 Auth Rd.
Suitland, MD 29746
(301) 899-3500

American Defenders of Bataan
1963 Silverlee Circle
Carlsbad, CA 92009
(703) 527-6983

American Ex-Prisoners of War
3201 East Pioneer Pkway
Suite 40
Arlington, TX 76010
(817) 649-2979

American GI Forum
2879 N. Speer Blvd.
Suite 102
Denver, CO 80211
(303) 458-1700

American Gold Star Mothers
2128 LeRoy Place, NW
Washington, DC 20008
(202) 265-0991

American Legion
P. O. Box 1055
Indianapolis, IN 46206
(317) 630-1200

American Red Cross
2025 E. St., NW
Washington, DC 20006
(202) 303-5834
17th & "D" St., N.W.

American War Mothers
5415 Connecticut Ave., NW
Suite L-30
Washington, DC 20015

AMVETS
4647 Forbes Blvd.
Lanham, MD 20706
(301) 459-9600

Armed Forces Services Corp.
2800 Shirlington Rd.
Suite 350
Arlington, VA 22206
(703) 379-9311

Army and Navy Union
604 Robbins Ave.
Niles, OH 44446
(330) 349-4724

Associates of Vietnam Veterans of America
8719 Colesville Rd.
Silver Spring, MD 20910
(304) 248-7316

Blinded Veterans Association
477 "H" St., N.W.
Washington, DC 20001
(202) 371-8880

Blue Star Mothers of America
718 Daniel Dr.
Grand Junction, CO 81506
(970) 242-3845

Catholic War Veterans
419 North Lee St.
Alexandria, VA 22314
(703) 549-3622

Congressional Medal of Honor Society
40 Patriots Point Rd.
Mt. Pleasant, SC 29464
(843) 884-8862

Disabled American Veterans
3724 Alexandria Dr.
Cold Spring, KY 41076
(859) 441-7300

Fleet Reserve Assn.
125 N. West Street
Alexandria, VA 22314
(800) 372-1924

Gold Star Wives
P. O. Box 361986
Birmingham, AL 35236
(205) 823-1778

Iraq and Afghanistan Veterans of America
292 Madison Ave.
10th Floor
New York, NY 10017
(212) 982-9699

Italian-American War Veterans
122 Mather St.
Syracuse, NY 13203
(508) 624-9735

Jewish War Veteran
1811 "R" St., N.W.
Washington, DC 20009
(202) 265-6280

Korean War Veterans
8452 Marys Creek Dr.
Benbrook, TX 76116
(817) 244-0706

Legion of Valor
4706 Calle Reina
Santa Barbara, CA 93110

Marine Corps League
8550 Lee Highway
Suite 201
Fairfax, VA 22031
(703) 207-9588

Military Chaplains Assn.
P.O. Box 7056
Arlington, VA 22207
(703) 533-5890

Military Order of Purple Heart
5413-B Backlick Rd.
Springfield, VA 22151
(703) 354-2140

Military Order of the World Wars
435 N. Lee St.
Alexandria, VA 22314
(703) 683-4911

National Amputation Foundation
40 Church St.
Malverne, NY 11565
(516) 887-3800

National Association for Black Veterans
P.O. Box 11432
Milwaukee, WI 53211
(800) 842-4597

National Assn. of County Veterans Service Officers
2200 Wilson Blvd.
Suite 102-530
Arlington, VA 22301
(910) 592-2862

National Association of State Directors of Veterans Affairs
30 W. Mifflin St.
Madison, WI 53703
(608) 266-1311

National Veterans Legal Services Program
1600 K St., NW
Suite 500
Washington, DC 20006
(202) 265-8305

National Veterans Organization of America
P. O. Box 2510
Victoria, TX 79902
(210) 200-8756

Navy Club of the United States
4627 Innsbruck
Fort Wayne, IN 46835
(260) 432-3188

Navy Mutual Aid Assn.
Arlington Annex
Room G-070
Washington, DC 20370
(703) 614-1638

Non Commissioned Officers Assn.
9330 Corporate Dr.
Suite 701
Selma, TX 78154
(210) 653-6161

Paralyzed Veterans of America
801 - 18th St., N.W.
Washington, DC 20006
(202) 872-1300

Pearl Harbor Survivors Assn.
P.O. Box 1816
Carlsbad, CA 92016
(760) 727-9027

Polish Legion of American Veterans
P. O. Box 42024
Washington, DC 20015
(202) 630-2677

Retired Enlisted Assn.
1111 S. Abilene Ct.
Aurora, CO 80012
(303) 338-9337

Swords to Plowshares
1600 Howard St.
San Francisco, CA 94103
(415) 252-4788

United Spinal Assn.
75-20 Astoria Blvd.
Jackson Heights, NY 11370
(718) 803-3782

United States Submarine Veterans
P.O. Box 3870
Silverdale, WA 98353
(877) 542-3483

Veterans Assistance Foundation
P.O. Box 109
Newburg, WI 53060
(608) 372-1282

Veterans of Foreign Wars
406 West 34th St.
Kansas City, MO 64111
(816) 756-3390

Veterans of the Vietnam War
805 South Township Blvd.
Pittston, PA 18640
(570) 603-9740

Vietnam Veterans of America
8605 Cameron St.
Suite 400
Silver Spring, MD 20910
(301) 585-4000

Women's Army Corps Veterans Assn.
P.O. Box 5577
Ft. McClellan, AL 36205
(256) 820-6824

Wounded Warrior Project
7020 AC Skinner Pkwy.
Suite 100
Jacksonville, FL 32256
(904) 296-7350

NONMILITARY VETERANS

Not everyone who is officially a veteran actually wore the uniform of one of the U.S. armed forces. The federal government has extended special "veterans status" to select groups of people who rendered service to the U.S. military without having ever been on active duty themselves. This "veterans status" makes members of these groups eligible for many VA programs, including medical treatment.

To begin receiving benefits, these people must first receive an official set of discharge papers from the Department of Defense. A local VA benefits office can help veterans through the application process.

Following are the groups that have earned many VA benefits by their service to the United States. Although this list is subject to change, it's unlikely that any groups will lose their veterans status. To be put on the list, they have had their wartime records carefully screened by a Department of Defense panel over a period of several years. It is very likely, however, that additional groups that performed wartime service to the U.S. military may be added to the list in the coming years.

- Women's Air Forces service pilots.
- Signal Corps female telephone operators unit of World War I.
- Engineer field clerks.

- Women's Army Auxiliary Corps.
- Quartermaster Corps female clerical employees with American Expeditionary Forces during World War I.
- Civilian employees of Pacific naval air bases at Wake Island who participated in defense during World War II.
- Reconstruction aides and dietitians in World War I.
- Male civilian ferry pilots.
- Wake Island defenders from Guam.
- Civilians assigned to the Secret Intelligence element of the Office of Strategic Services.
- Guam Combat Patrol.
- Quartermaster Corps vessel Keswick crew on Corregidor during World War II.
- U.S. civilian volunteers in defense of Bataan.
- U.S. merchant seamen who served on blockships in support of Operation Mulberry during World War II.
- U.S. merchant seamen in oceangoing service from December 7, 1941, to August 15, 1945.
- Civilian Navy IFF technicians who served in combat areas of the Pacific from December 7, 1941, to August 15, 1945.
- U.S. civilians with the American Field Service overseas from August 31, 1917, to January 1, 1918.
- U.S. civilians of the American Field Service who served overseas under U.S. armies and U.S. army groups between December 7, 1941, and May 8, 1945.
- U.S. civilian employees of American Airlines overseas under a contract with the Air Transport Command from December 14, 1941, to August 14, 1945.
- Civilian crewmen of U.S. Coast and Geodetic Survey vessels in areas of immediate military hazard during operations with U.S. armed forces between December 7, 1941, and August 15, 1945.
- Members of the "Flying Tigers" who served between December 7, 1941, and July 18, 1942.

- U.S. civilian flight crews and aviation ground support employees of United Airlines overseas under a contract with the Air Transport Command from December 14, 1941, to August 14, 1945.
- U.S. civilian flight crew and aviation ground support employees of Transcontinental and Western Air, Inc., overseas under a contract with the Air Transport Command between December 14, 1941, and August 14, 1945.
- U.S. civilian flight crew and aviation ground support employees of Consolidated Vultee Aircraft Corporation overseas under a contract with the Air Transport Command between December 14, 1941, and August 14, 1945.
- U.S. civilian flight crew and aviation ground support employees of Pan American World Airways and its subsidiaries and affiliates, overseas under a contract with the Air Transport Command and Naval Air Transport Service from December 14, 1941, to August 14, 1945.
- Honorably discharged members of the American Volunteer Guard, Eritrea Service Command, between June 21, 1942, and March 31, 1943.
- U.S. civilian flight crew and ground support employees of Northwest Airlines who served overseas under a contract with Air Transport Command from December 14, 1941, through August 14, 1945.
- U.S. civilian female employees of Army Nurse Corps who served in defense of Bataan and Corregidor in 1942.
- U.S. civilian flight crews and aviation ground support employees of Northeast Airlines overseas under a contract with the Air Transport Command between December 7, 1941, and August 14, 1945.
- U.S. civilian flight crews and aviation ground support personnel of Braniff Airways who served overseas in the North Atlantic or under a contract with the Air Transport Command between February 26, 1945, and August 14, 1945.

- Chamorro and Carolina former native police who received military training in the Donnal area of central Saipan and were placed under command of Lt. Casino of the 6th Provisional Military Police Battalion to accompany U.S. Marines on active combat patrol from August 19, 1945 to September 2, 1945.
- The Operational Analysis Group of the Office of Scientific Research and Development, Office of Emergency Management, which served overseas with the U.S. Army Air Corps from December 7, 1941, through August 15, 1945.
- Service as a member of the Alaskan Territorial Guard during World War II of any individual who was honorably discharged under Section 8147 of the Defense Department Appropriations Act of 2001.

OFFICIAL WARTIME PERIODS

Some veterans benefits are restricted to people who served on active duty during times of war. For example, wartime service is needed to qualify for a VA pension, and it's sometimes a factor in determining priority for the so-called "veterans preference" in civil service.

When wartime service is needed to qualify for a benefit, veterans should pay attention to the fine print. Sometimes the rules for a benefit require a specific length of wartime service.

Reservists and National Guardsmen during periods of wartime can usually qualify as "wartime vets" if they spent at least one day on active duty for training.

It's important to note that for the Gulf War, the Vietnam War, the Korean War, and World War II, you need not have served in a combat region to qualify as a wartime vet. Service in the states or anywhere in the world is sufficient to establish you as a wartime veteran, as long as you were in the military during the prescribed period.

Some World War I veterans could qualify as wartime veterans if they were stationed in Russia after the normal wartime period.

And Mexican War veterans must have served in Mexico, along the border, or in adjacent waters during the period of war to qualify as wartime veterans. People who were on active duty during that time but who weren't stationed near the war zone could not qualify as wartime veterans of the Mexican Border War.

The official periods of wartime are set by federal law. Not all official wars had a declaration of war from Congress. For those that did, the federally-recognized wartime period may begin before the declaration.

Here is some of the fine print for wars of the twentieth and twenty-first centuries:

Mexican Border War: From May 9, 1916, through April 5, 1917. Service must have been in Mexico, on the Mexican border, or in adjacent waters.

World War I: From April 6, 1917, through November 11, 1918. For people who served in Russia, the period is April 6, 1917, through April 1, 1920. In order to help World War I veterans qualify for benefits that required a certain number of days in uniform during wartime, Congress extended the official wartime period to July 2, 1921, for veterans who had already spent at least one day in the military between April 6, 1917, and November 11, 1918.

World War II: From December 7, 1941, through December 31, 1946. To help World War II veterans meet the minimum time-in-service-during-wartime requirements for loan guaranty, vocational rehabilitation, and educational programs, Congress extended the official wartime period to run from September 16, 1940, through July 25, 1947. That extension applies only to veterans with at least one day in the military between December 7, 1941, and December 31, 1946, who apply for one of the three programs mentioned above.

Korean Conflict: From June 27, 1950, through January 31, 1955.

Vietnam Era: From February 28, 1961, through May 7, 1975.

Persian Gulf War: From August 2, 1990. The end date for the official wartime period hadn't been set when *Veteran's Guide* went to press in 2010.

Note: Also as this book went to press, Congress had not passed a law establishing an official definition for wartime service in Iraq and Afghanistan. That's because the Persian Gulf War was still officially underway. Veterans of Iraq and Afghanistan qualify for federal benefits as veterans of the Persian Gulf War.

Two Centuries of Veterans: Some Statistics

American Revolution (1717–1784)
Participants 217,000
Deaths in service 4,435
Last veteran died, April 5, 1869 .... Age 109
Last dependent died, April 25, 1911 .... Age 90

War of 1812 (1812–1815)
Participants 287,000
Deaths in service 2,260
Last veteran died, May 13, 1905 .... Age 105
Last dependent died, March 12, 1946 .... Age 89

Indian Wars (Approx. 1817–1898)
Participants 106,000
Battle deaths 1,000
Last veteran died, June 18, 1973 .... Age 101

Mexican War (1846–1848)
Participants 79,000
Battle deaths 1,733
Other deaths.. 11,550
Last veteran died, Sept. 3, 1929 .... Age 98
Last dependent died, Nov. 1, 1962........................... Age 94

Civil War—Confederate (1861–1865)
Participants 1,050,000
Battle deaths... 74,524
Other deaths 59,297
Last veteran died, March 16, 1958 .... Age 112

Civil War—Union (1861–1865)

Participants 2,213,000
Battle deaths 140,414
Other deaths 224,097
Last veteran died, Aug. 2, 1956 .... Age 109
Last widow died, Jan. 17, 2005 .... Age 93

Civil War—Dependents, both sides

Children (drawing VA pension) 2

Spanish-American War (1898–1902)

Participants 306,700
Battle deaths 385
Other deaths 2,061
Last veteran died, Sept. 10, 1992 .... Age 106
Spouses (drawing VA pension) 82
Children (drawing VA pension). 69

World War I (1971–1918)

Participants 4,735,000
Battle deaths 53,402
Other deaths. 63,114
Last veteran died, Feb. 27, 2011 .... Age 110
Spouses (drawing VA pension) 2,885
Children (drawing VA pension) 3,986

World War II (1940–1947)

Participants 16,112,600
Battle deaths 291,557
Other deaths. 113,842
Living veterans 2,079,000
Parents (drawing VA pension) 82
Spouses (drawing VA pension) 216,028
Children (drawing VA pension) 13,883

Korean Conflict (1950–1955)

Participants 5,720,000
Battle deaths 33,739
Other deaths. 20,500
Living veterans 2,507,000
Parents (drawing VA pension) 188
Spouses (drawing VA pension). 60,121
Children (drawing VA pension) 3,087

Vietnam Era (1964–1975)

Participants	8,744,000
Battle deaths	47,434
Other deaths	42,786
Living veterans	7,569,000
Parents (drawing VA pension)	2,660
Spouses (drawing VA pension)	168,085
Children (drawing VA pension)	8,346

Persian Gulf War / War on Terror (Aug. 2, 1990–Undated)

Latest DoD statistics at http://siadapp.dmdc.osd.mil/personnel/
MMIDHOME.HTM

Two Centuries of Veterans

Veterans	41,892,128
Battle deaths	651,031
Other deaths in theater	308,800
Other deaths in service	230,254
Living war veterans	16,962,000
Living veterans	22,795,000
Parents (drawing VA pension)	5,021
Spouses (drawing VA pension)	495,867
Children (drawing VA pension)	44,013
Veterans (drawing VA pension, disability)	3,383,898

As of May 2010
Compiled by Department of Veterans Affairs

INDEX

STACKPOLE BOOKS

Military Professional Reference Library

Air Force Officer's Guide
Airman's Guide
Armed Forces Guide to Personal Financial Planning
Army Dictionary and Desk Reference
Army Officer's Guide
Career Progression Guide for Soldiers
Combat Leader's Field Guide
Combat Service Support Guide
Enlisted Soldier's Guide
Guide to Effective Military Writing
Guide to Military Operations Other Than War
Job Search: Marketing Your Military Experience
Military Money Guide
NCO Guide
Servicemember's Guide to a College Degree
Servicemember's Legal Guide
Soldier's Study Guide
Today's Military Wife
Veteran's Guide to Benefits

Professional Reading Library

Beyond Baghdad
Beyond Terror
Endless War
Fighting for the Future
Lines of Fire
Looking for Trouble
Never Quit the Fight
Wars of Blood and Faith
by Ralph Peters

Roots of Strategy, Books 1, 2, 3, and 4

---

*Stackpole Books are available at your Exchange Bookstore or
Military Clothing Sales Store or from Stackpole at*
1-800-732-3669 *or* **www.stackpolebooks.com**